D1479227

THE JAPANESE AND
SUKARNO'S INDONESIA

Monographs of the Center for Southeast Asian Studies, Kyoto University

English Series

1. Takashi SATO, *Field Crops in Thailand*, 1966
2. Tadayo WATABE, *Glutinous Rice in Northern Thailand*, 1967
3. Kiyoshi TAKIMOTO (ed.), *Geology and Mineral Resources in Thailand and Malaya*, 1969
4. Keizaburo KAWAGUCHI & Kazutake KYUMA, *Lowland Rice Soils in Thailand*, 1969
5. Keizaburo KAWAGUCHI & Kazutake KYUMA, *Lowland Rice Soils in Malaya*, 1969
6. Kiyoshige MAEDA, *Alor Janggus: A Chinese Community in Malaya*, 1967
7. Shinichi ICHIMURA (ed.), *The Economic Development of East and Southeast Asia*, 1975
8. Masashi NISHIHARA, *The Japanese and Sukarno's Indonesia*, 1976

Japanese Series:

1. Joji TANASE, *Primitive Form of the Idea of the Other World*, 1966
2. Toru YANO, *Modern Political History of Thailand and Burma*, 1968
3. Takeshi MOTOOKA, *Agricultural Development of Southeast Asia*, 1968
4. Yoshihiro & Reiko TSUBOUCHI, *Divorce*, 1970
5. Shigeru IIJIMA, *Social and Cultural Change of Karens*, 1971
6. H. STORZ (trans. by H. NOGAMI), *Burma: Land, History and Economy*, 1974
7. Shinichi ICHIMURA (ed.), *Southeast Asia: Nature, Society and Economy*, 1974
8. Yoneo ISHII (ed.), *Thailand: A Rice-Growing Society*, 1975
9. Yoneo ISHII, *Political Sociology of Theravada Buddhism*, 1975
10. Shinichi ICHIMURA (ed.), *The Economic Development of East and Southeast Asia*, 1975
11. Takeshi MOTOOKA, *Rice in Indonesia*, 1975
12. KUCHIBA, TSUBOUCHI & MAEDA, *The Structure and Change of Malayan Villages*, 1976
13. Masashi NISHIHARA (ed.), *Political Corruption in Southeast Asia*, 1976
14. A. ECKSTEIN (trans. by S. ICHIMURA, *et al.*), *Economic Trends in Communist China* (forthcoming)

The Japanese and Sukarno's Indonesia

Tokyo-Jakarta Relations, 1951–1966

MASASHI NISHIHARA

*Monographs of the Center
for Southeast Asian Studies
Kyoto University*

AN EAST-WEST CENTER BOOK
THE UNIVERSITY PRESS OF HAWAII
Honolulu

Monographs of the Center for Southeast Asian Studies, Kyoto
University, are published and distributed as *East-West Center Books*
under joint arrangements with The University Press of Hawaii to
foster international understanding and cooperation through the
dissemination of knowledge.

Nishihara, Masashi.
    The Japanese and Sukarno's Indonesia.

(Monographs of the Center for Southeast Asian Studies,
Kyoto University)
    "An East-West Center book."
    Bibliography: p.
    Includes index.
    1. Japan—Foreign relations—Indonesia. 2. Indonesia—Foreign
relations—Japan. 3. Japan—Foreign economic relations—
Indonesia. 4. Indonesia—Foreign economic relations—Japan.
I. Title. II. Series: Kyōto Daigaku. Tōnan Ajia Kenkyū Sentā.
Monographs of the Center for Southeast Asian Studies, Kyoto
University.

DS849.155N57   1975   327.52′0598   75-35765

ISBN 0-8248-0379-5

Filmset in Hong Kong by Asco Trade Typesetting Limited
Printed in Hong Kong

Contents

Tables

Preface

This book treats the relationship between Japan and Indonesia, between an industrialized nation with sparse natural resources and a developing nation with rich natural resources, over the period from 1951 to 1966—from the time when the two nations began negotiating the terms of Japanese war reparations with Indonesia to the time when President Sukarno lost power after the 1965 abortive coup. First examined is the nature of their interdependency between 1950 and 1970, comparing their national interests, foreign policies, volumes of trade, flow of people, and frequency of mutual visits by high-ranking officials. Then, focusing on contacts between specific individuals and their roles as lobbyists during the fifteen-year period, the study covers the following issues: (1) formal negotiations on war reparations and the Peace Lobby (1951–1958); (2) the reparations funds of $223 million and the reparations lobbies (1958–1965); (3) Japan's role in the Indonesian-Malaysian conflict (1963–1966) and the Kawashima Lobby (1964–1965); (4) pro-Sukarnoist groups in Tokyo, their role in the West Irian problem of 1960–1962, and the impact of the 1965 coup upon them; (5) the anti-Sukarnoist lobby and its role in the Sumatra Rebellion of 1958 and in the post-1965 preeminence of the military; and (6) the Japanese government's reaction to the 1965 coup.

The research for this thesis is based primarily upon Indonesian and Japanese sources, including government reports, newspapers, popular magazines, biographies and memoirs, as well as academic works. It also draws heavily upon interviews conducted in Tokyo and Jakarta with diplomats, government officials, wartime officers, correspondents, and businessmen.

Among the major findings are: (1) the settlement of the prolonged negotiations over war reparations owes much to the Peace Lobby; (2) the reparations funds functioned as an important source of foreign aid to Indonesia while also serving to promote Japanese exports to Indonesia; (3) while the Kishi government used the funds to prop up the Sukarno regime, the latter used them to build "prestige projects" and to promote Sukarnoism; (4) the reparations lobbies, which allegedly involved top leaders in the two countries and through which Ratna Sari Dewi was introduced to Sukarno, functioned to tie the two countries together at a time when they were pursuing different ideologies;

(5) both Prime Minister Ikeda Hayato and the ruling party's Vice-president Kawashima Shōjirō failed in their attempts to mediate the Indonesian-Malaysian disputes, but subsequent personal ties between former diplomat Shirahata Tomoyoshi and Foreign Minister Adam Malik and between Ambassador to Malaysia Kai Fumihiko and Prime Minister Abdul Rahman contributed to the beginning of the post-1965 peace negotiations between Indonesia and Malaysia; (6) the 1965 coup shattered the Sukarnoist group in Tokyo after it had earlier been successful in 1960–1962 in the West Irian incident; (7) the post-coup political upheaval also ended the political career of Dewi, who from 1964 to 1965 had acted as a link between Japanese and Indonesian interests and had competed with Subandrio in an attempt to keep Sukarno on her side and have him reach a reconciliation with the military; (8) the Japan Communist party believed in 1966 that the ultimate responsibility for the 1965 coup lay with Peking and subsequently broke its ties with that country partially for this reason; and (9) right-wing nationalists and former wartime officers supported the Sumatra Rebellion of 1958 and remained in contact with anticommunist and anti-Sukarnoist military leaders, providing the basis for the Japanese government's swift shift of support to the Suharto regime in March 1966.

Acknowledgments

This monograph is the product of research and observations in three countries, the United States, Indonesia, and Japan from late 1969 to mid-1972. After months of research in the libraries of the University of Michigan, Jakarta proved to be a rich and exciting, if often frustrating, site for research conducted from May 1970 through March 1972. This was followed by a short but very useful period of research in Tokyo from April to August 1972. During this period many people in all three countries helped me.

I wish to express my deepest appreciation to the members of my dissertation committee at the University of Michigan: Professors Robert E. Ward, Russell H. Fifield, Richard L. Park, and Gayl D. Ness for their encouragement of my research and reading of my manuscript. I would like especially to thank Professors Ward and Fifield for their advice on my general graduate training and on this thesis. My appreciation also goes to Professor Ichimura Shin'ichi, director, Center for Southeast Asian Studies of Kyoto University, Japan, who awarded me a grant to do research in Indonesia, and to the Indonesian Institute of Sciences (LIPI) which granted its approval for my research topic. For access to written materials my thanks go also to the Central Museum Library, the National Scientific Documentation Center (PDIN), the National Institute of Economic and Social Research (LEKNAS), the Social and Political History Library, and the Foreign Ministry Library in Indonesia, and in Japan to the National Diet Library, the Library of the Bureau of Statistics of the Prime Minister's Office, and the Library of the Institute of Developing Economies. I also consulted the Indonesian materials at the Institute of Southeast Asian Studies of Singapore during short visits there in 1971. Almost everyone in Indonesia, including the government officials, journalists, students, shopkeepers, and *becak* drivers, with whom I had contact, helped to form my views of Indonesia. My particular thanks go to those who responded to my lengthy and often sensitive questions. Special appreciation goes to Mr. Nishijima Shigetada of the North Sumatra Oil Development Cooperation Company for giving me access to his materials of historical significance and introducing me to other key figures in Japanese-Indonesian relations.

For conscientious editorial assistance, credit should go to Mrs. Margaret Yamashita, who struggled with my English and greatly improved its clarity and organization. While saluting these individuals, I cannot resist bowing in all humbleness to the Oriental virtue of sustained endurance demonstrated by my wife Suzuko and our daughter Aya, so fittingly born in "that crossroads of the seas, Singapore," who both cheerfully joined me in this rewarding adventure in transcontinental mobility and intercultural adjustments.

Portions of the earlier draft were read by Gotō Ken'ichi, Dr. Lee Tek-tjeng, Zulkifli Lubis, Adam Malik, Nishijima Shigetada, Ali Sastroamidjojo, Shirahata Tomoyoshi, and Dr. Ahmad Subardjo for whose comments and corrections my hearty thanks should be expressed. But all views and interpretations presented here are solely my own; they should not be attributed in any way to the institutions with which I have been associated.

Introduction

The Japanese and the Indonesians are Asiatic, oceanic peoples, inhabiting regions north and south of the equator, who have shared a long tradition of cultural and commercial intercourse. In contemporary history they were brought even closer from March 1942, during Japan's military occupation of Indonesia. It lasted for three-and-a-half years and ended with Japan's surrender to the Allied powers, which included the Netherlands, Indonesia's former colonial master. The occupation, however, had such a significant impact on all phases of Indonesian life that post-1945 Japanese-Indonesian relations can hardly be discussed without referring to its influence.

Sukarno became Indonesia's first president with the help of the Japanese military administration with which he collaborated, thus earning its recognition of him as a central figure of the independence movement. Had he not been given moral and material support from the Japanese Navy Liaison Office in Jakarta, Indonesia's proclamation of independence in August 1945 would have faced even greater difficulties. Sukarno's successor, Suharto, was trained by the Japanese military and served as a platoon commander of the Indonesian volunteer army (PETA), also created by the Japanese. With little exaggeration, one can say that Suharto owes much to the occupation for his achievements in the years since 1945.

Despite the occupation the Japanese capitulation abruptly reversed wartime relations, and a series of subsequent events granted the victor's status to the Indonesians, who gained their national independence from the Dutch in late 1949. These new circumstances established a basic pattern for the postwar issues between Japan and Indonesia: Indonesia's peace settlement with Japan and with it, the Japanese payment of war reparations. Negotiations of the terms of the reparations dominated their relationship after 1951, when the question was first taken up officially by the two governments at the San Francisco Peace Conference. In January 1958 the issue finally was settled and led to the establishment of formal diplomatic relations in April of that year.

The peace settlement was then followed by the new problem of using the reparations funds, some $223 million to be paid over a period of twelve years, beginning in 1958. This allowed for keen competition among the Japanese and the Indonesians who wished to have a share of the funds, and this competition overshadowed the first six or seven years of payment. The abortive coup of September 30, 1965, known as the "Gestapu affair*," marked the beginning of the fall of Sukarno's supremacy and made a considerable impact upon Japanese-Indonesian relations, insofar as Japan's "Sukarno supporters" began to be replaced by "Suharto supporters." Nevertheless, Japanese economic support of Jakarta's new regime grew stronger than that of the old regime. A considerable portion of this new Japanese aid went to complete half-finished reparations projects. Thus, two-and-a-half decades after the end of the Pacific War, the former Japanese presence in Indonesia as its military occupants still maintained its influence over their binational relations.

A trace of the Japanese occupation can be seen in the presence of certain former occupation officials, both military and civil, who returned to Japan after the war but later reemerged as "Indonesia experts," offering their assistance in the reparations negotiations and as intermediaries between the two sides. Along with these "experts" were the so-called right-wing nationalists, who, in a similar vein, offered their help in solving problems between the two countries. These nationalists were not a direct product of the occupation, but their prewar convictions of Pan-Asianism, culminating in the governmental concept of the Greater East Asia Co-prosperity Sphere, had justified the Japanese occupation of Southeast Asia (then called the "southern region"). Some of them managed to establish direct and indirect contacts with high-ranking postwar government and business leaders in both countries. Through this connection, other nationalists attempted to profit from the reparations funds and other types of government aid to Indonesia. Their functions varied according to personal capability, connections, and convictions as well as general conditions in the postwar period; they acted as advisors, brokers, assistants, negotiators, unofficial diplomats, or simple contact men—in general, as lobbyists.

The lobbyists' respective roles were highly complex, as were their connections with party leaders and business firms. Sometimes they appeared to act with the genuine purpose of improving relations between Japan and Indonesia but seldom without the assurance of personal profit from their services. It is not surprising, therefore, that what is popularly termed the "Indonesia Lobby" in Tokyo and the "Japan Lobby" in Jakarta were not actually integrated lobby groups. This is instead a collective reference to the complicated lines of personal connections crisscrossing those individuals and organizations having varied interests in each other's countries.

*An acronym for *Gerakan Tigapuluh September*, the September 30th movement.

Despite the loosely structured lobbies, the study of postwar Japanese-Indonesian interaction suggests that the active presence of the lobbyists and the continued contacts with their Indonesian friends (including President Sukarno himself) centered on these binational relations. Particularly during the period from 1958 to 1965, when Sukarno's power reached its climax, the relationship between Tokyo and Jakarta was referred to as "special"—a term which recognized their close affinity in spite of the differing ideologies behind their foreign policies.

Because Japan's position in Asia today draws close public attention, it is useful to study the nature of its policies and actions in reference to Indonesia, the most populous country in Southeast Asia. This book deals with Japanese-Indonesian relations from 1951 through 1966, which is the period from the first official contact between the two governments at the San Francisco Peace Conference of September 1951 to the March 11, 1966 affair in which General Suharto virtually took over the presidency from Sukarno.

This fifteen-year period may also be seen as three subperiods in Japanese-Indonesian relations. The first of these is from September 1951 through April 15, 1958 when Japan and Indonesia officially established diplomatic relations. The second subperiod runs from 1958 through the Gestapu affair of September 30, 1965. This period saw the allocation of the reparations funds become a dominant concern of the two governments as well as those interested in profits from the funds. This second subperiod roughly coincides with Indonesia's Guided Democracy period during which Sukarno was in power, ruling over the competing nationalist, Communist, religious, and military forces which shaped domestic politics. The Gestapu affair in which the Communists allegedly staged a coup d'etat against the so-called Council of Generals, which was accused of existing within the army. The incident, however, destroyed the balance of power among the competing forces, and the Communists soon were crushed while Sukarno himself began to be suspected of complicity with the coup attempt. The third subperiod, from October 1965 to March 11, 1966, saw a bitter struggle between the Sukarno forces and the Nasution-Suharto supporters, with the eventual victory of the latter. This was also a time of transition for the participants in the Japan and Indonesia lobbies in their respective capitals.

In this work, greater emphasis will be placed on the first and second subperiods, partly because more data on these are available to the public at this time, and largely because the first and second subperiods seem to provide more important material for the study of Japanese relations with other Asian countries. As mentioned earlier, the two countries maintained friendly relations during these periods, particularly the second subperiod, despite their ideological differences. In seeking to explain this unusual arrangement, general characteristics of other inter-Asian relationships may be revealed. The last subperiod, intriguing as it is, is still too recent to produce a balanced analysis.

The study of Japanese-Indonesian relations may also provide some insight into the relative position of a major and a minor power in Asia. What diplomatic means does a minor power tend to employ toward a major one? Or, conversely, what methods does a major power use toward a minor one? If influence is seen in terms of moral, remunerative, or coercive means, to which of these are major and minor powers inclined to resort? Do they discriminate among these means, depending on the diplomatic issues involved? These questions may find answers in the research presented here.

While the 1951–1966 period of Japanese-Indonesian relations may be divided into three subperiods, this thesis is not meant to describe the postwar interactions of the two countries historically, although a sense of history is a major concern of the writer. Rather, this is a study of international politics. It strives to identify the character of the relations between Japan and Indonesia by selecting several major issues and subjects of concern for the two countries. For instance, the Indonesian confrontation with Malaysia which lasted from 1963 through 1966, overlaps the second and third subperiods in Japanese-Indonesian relations. Similarly, some of the ties between the Japanese nationalists and the Indonesian military also overlap the second and third subperiods. The study of the reparations funds extends over all three subperiods.

The first chapter attempts to present an overview of both the Japanese and Indonesian policies toward Asia, within which framework their binational relations may be given a better perspective. This chapter also indicates the general scale of contact between the two countries by looking at their foreign policy aims, trade volume, flow of ordinary citizens, and visits of leading figures. Chapter 2 treats the formal phase of the reparations negotiations from 1951 through 1958, whereas chapter 3 analyzes the informal phase of the negotiations, the role of the lobbyists, Japanese and Indonesian, in settling the reparations negotiations. These lobbyists are termed here the "Peace Lobby." Chapter 4 traces the distribution of the funds, evaluating the projects involved and the economic effects of the funds on both Japan and Indonesia. Chapter 5 describes the general nature of the reparations lobbies, from 1958 to 1965, and identifies the lobbyists and their personal ties with prominent figures. Chapter 6 discusses Japan's role as mediator in the Indonesian confrontation with Malaysia, again including the parts played by both the formal and informal participants. The subject of Japanese mediation is doubly significant in that this was the first explicitly political role that the Japanese government played in post-1945 Asia. The informal participants in Japan's mediation were represented by Kawashima Shōjiro, vice-president of the ruling party, and are referred to here as the "Kawashima Lobby." Chapter 7 focuses on the role of the "Sukarnoist groups" in Japanese-Indonesian relations during the Guided Democracy period and studies the impact of the abortive coup of 1965 on these groups. Chapter 8 explains the sources of Japanese support for the new Suharto regime. This support originated with private assistance for the anti-Sukarno movements that began in about 1955. This chapter also treats the Satō government's reaction to the Suharto regime.

Special attention has been given to the unofficial participants in the formal relations between Japan and Indonesia. This informal diplomacy is observable in almost all binational negotiations and in this sense is not unique to Japanese-Indonesian affairs. The active participation of those outside the government in governmental decisions may be attributed to that aspect of Asian political culture which places greater emphasis on personal favoritism than on public accountability. The possible connection between what this writer calls "political culture" and "informal diplomacy" will be explored in the concluding chapter of this monograph. The informal diplomacy discussed earlier involves the diplomatic activities conducted by those not holding official government positions, for the purpose of influencing their government's relations with and policy toward another government.

The relative lack of data on the Indonesian side makes unavoidable a Japanese bias in this study—a bias which hopefully can be corrected in the future. Much of the information in this thesis was collected in interviews but in those cases in which the person interviewed asked not to be identified, the sources are cited in only general terms. Much of the data concerning the personal ties of members of the reparations lobbies is dependent upon popular magazines rather than upon more academic materials. However, these are the only written materials available to date. Hopefully these data can be documented more widely in the future.

Individual names appear here in the order that they are used in their respective countries. For example, in the case of Japanese, Chinese, and Indonesian names, surnames precede given names (Prime Minister Kishi Nobusuke, Premier Chou En-lai, Prime Minister Mohammed Natsir, etc.). Many Indonesian names are expressed customarily by either surname or given name only.

Chapter 1
Japanese-Indonesian Interdependency and the Intensity of Their Contacts

JAPANESE INTERESTS IN SOUTHEAST ASIA

Japan's postwar policy toward Southeast Asia was at first restrained. During the seven years of the American-dominated Allied Occupation from September 1945 through April 1952 practically all of Japan's diplomatic activities had been suspended, though they resumed under the aegis of the San Francisco Peace Treaty of September 1951.[1] The preparatory process for the San Francisco conference and the resulting treaty were carefully tailored to American interests in the Pacific, exchanging Tokyo's cooperation with Washington's cold-war policy toward the Soviet Union and Communist China for Washington's commitment to defend Japan. The peace settlement also obliged Japan to pay war reparations to the Southeast Asian claimant countries.

By recognizing Nationalist China, Japan differed from some Asian nations, including Indonesia, which chose to recognize the Peking regime as early as April 1950. The obligation imposed upon Japan by the treaty to negotiate war reparations with the claimant Asian countries also precluded the immediate establishment of diplomatic relations with those countries. Those involved were Burma, the Philippines, Indonesia, South Vietnam, Laos, and Cambodia.[2]

Despite such obstacles in its Asian program, Japan's interests in the region formed a major undercurrent of concern in its overall foreign policy together with a pro-American current. This link between Asia and America is clearly reflected in Japan's trade patterns. Table 1 shows its trade performance from 1951 to 1970, indicating that in 1951, 52 percent of Japan's exports went to Asia and 16 percent to North America, whereas 29 percent of Japan's imports came from Asia and 46 percent from North America. The large exports to Asia and imports from the

TABLE 1

REGIONAL COMPOSITION OF JAPANESE TRADE IN PERCENT, 1951–1970

YEAR	TOTAL AMOUNT (in millions of dollars)	EXPORT (in percent)						TOTAL[a] (in percent)
		Asia	Europe	North America	South America	Africa	Oceania	
1951	1,355	52	11	16	6	8	8	101
1952	1,273	52	14	21	3	7	3	100
1953	1,275	52	9	24	5	10	1	101
1954	1,629	49	9	22	10	8	3	101
1955	2,011	42	10	27	7	10	3	99
1956	2,501	41	10	26	5	16	2	100
1957	2,858	40	12	26	3	17	2	100
1958	2,877	37	12	30	4	14	3	100
1959	3,456	33	11	36	4	12	3	99
1960	4,055	36	13	33	4	9	4	99
1961	4,236	37	14	31	6	9	3	100
1962	4,916	34	17	34	5	7	4	101
1963	5,452	34	16	33	4	9	4	100
1964	6,673	33	16	34	3	9	5	100
1965	8,451	33	16	35	3	10	5	102
1966	9,776	34	16	36	3	7	4	100
1967	10,441	34	16	35	3	8	5	101
1968	12,971	34	15	37	3	7	4	100
1969	15,990	31[b]	13[b]	34	6	7	4	95
1970	19,318	28[b]	15[b]	34	6	7	4	94

IMPORT

Year	Value							Total
1951	2,047	29	8	46	5	4	8	100
1952	2,027	31	7	50	2	3	8	101
1953	2,410	33	8	43	5	2	8	99
1954	2,399	31	8	46	7	2	6	100
1955	2,471	37	7	41	4	3	8	100
1956	3,230	32	7	44	4	3	9	99
1957	4,284	29	9	46	3	2	10	99
1958	3,033	32	9	45	3	3	9	101
1959	3,599	32	11	41	3	4	9	100
1960	4,491	30	11	42	3	4	9	99
1961	5,810	26	12	45	4	3	9	99
1962	5,637	29	13	41	4	4	9	100
1963	6,736	31	13	40	4	4	9	101
1964	7,938	30	13	38	4	5	9	99
1965	8,169	33	12	37	5	4	8	99
1966	9,523	33	13	36	5	4	9	100
1967	11,663	31	15	36	5	6	8	101
1968	12,987	31	14	35	5	6	9	100
1969	15,024	29ᵇ	10ᵇ	32	8	7	10	96
1970	18,881	28ᵇ	10ᵇ	34	7	6	10	95

ᵃ Total does not always amount to 100 percent because numbers have been rounded off.

ᵇ Does not include figures for trade with the Communist bloc.

Sources: Quoted from *Japan Statistical Yearbook 1963*, pp. 255–259 for 1951–1954; *Japan Statistical Yearbook 1969*, pp. 291–294 for 1955–1968; *Asahi nenkan 1971*, p. 372; and *Tsūshō hakusho 1971*, II, p. 346.

United States were influenced significantly by the Korean War, as Japan received large procurement orders from the United States. Postwar Japanese economic recovery was initially accomplished in substantial part as a result of the Korean War. Although these figures changed after the truce in 1953, there is a general pattern over the next two decades of one-third of Japan's trade being with Asia, another third with North America, and the remaining third with the rest of the world.

This postwar pattern should be compared to the prewar trade pattern.[3] In 1930, 48 percent of Japan's exports went to Asia and 36 percent to North America. But in 1940, 68 percent of Japan's exports went to Asia and 17 percent to North America. This sharp increase in Japanese exports to Asia and a similarly sharp decrease in exports to North America, within a period of ten years, signaled Japan's military advances in Asia and the mounting tensions between Tokyo and Washington. Japan's prewar import pattern is not as illustrative of its political relations with Asia and North America as is the export pattern, although Japan remained heavily dependent upon Asia and North America for imported materials and goods. In 1930, 41 percent of Japan's imports came from Asia and 32 percent from North America. In 1940, these figures were 43 percent from Asia and 38 percent from North America.

The comparison between prewar and postwar trade patterns demonstrates that Japan depended more heavily on Asia in the prewar period (some 48 to 68 percent of its exports and 41 to 43 percent of its imports) than in the postwar period (28 to 52 percent of its export market and the source of 26 to 37 percent of Japan's imports). This in turn suggests that defeat in the Pacific War forced Japan further into the American camp: during the 1950s Japan relied less on Asia than on North America for imports. This considerable economic dependence upon the United States restricted Japan's political and economic relations with the rest of Asia, as in the case of Japan's recognition of Nationalist China instead of the People's Republic of China.

Among the Asian countries Indonesia has particularly attracted Japan by its rich natural resources and geopolitically important location since before the Pacific War. It should be remembered that Japan's southward advance in the late 1930s was motivated primarily by Indonesia's—then the Dutch East Indies'—oil. One of the main items in the Japanese-Dutch trade negotiations in 1940–1941 was Japan's demand for an increased oil quota. When this and other demands were not fully met, Japan broke off negotiations with the Dutch and began to work out plans to take military control of the resources in the Dutch East Indies. The Outline of Administrative Plans for Southern Occupied

Areas was formulated on November 20, 1941 and stipulated "three principles" of Japanese military occupation, one of which was to secure the essential resources for the defense of Japan.[4] Three weeks later the Pacific War broke out.

Generated by geographical proximity and justified by ethnic affinity, Japan's concept of Pan-Asianism reinforced its efforts to "liberate its Asian brothers" from white colonial rule in the 1930s and the first half of the 1940s and helped to establish Japan's *Lebensraum*. Indonesia was counted on as an essential member of this Asian economic bloc. Overlooking the Indian Ocean and the South China Sea and sharing the Strait of Malacca with the Malayan peninsula, the Dutch East Indies presented a geopolitical, defense line for Japan. This explains why during the Pacific War the Japanese Imperial Army administered the Malay Peninsula, Singapore, and Sumatra under the Twenty-fifth Army's control rather than placing them under separate military administrations.

Japan's interest in Indonesia's natural resources and geopolitical location continued into the postwar period. As early as 1951 the Japanese government began discussing measures to develop Indonesian industries and to import Indonesian resources.[5] Japan held its first reparations talks with the Indonesian mission in Tokyo in December 1951. Also in regard to the reparations issue, Foreign Minister Okazaki visited Jakarta in 1953. Kubota Yutaka, who had built the huge Suihō hydroelectric power station in the Amur River, was interested in developing a similar water power system in the Asahan Valley of northern Sumatra and, at the same time, building an aluminum refinery in that vicinity, using Asahan's water and electricity and bauxite from the neighboring island of Bintan.[6] In 1956 Prime Minister Kishi sent a prominent businessman, Kobayashi Ataru, as a special advisor to observe the economic conditions of various Asian countries. Upon his return Kobayashi recommended to Kishi that Japan's Asian policy be geared toward close ties with Indonesia because of its rich natural resources and with India because of its political potential.[7] That same year, Yamashita Tarō, another prominent businessman, went to Jakarta to obtain oil concessions.[8] Ayukawa Gisuke, who in the 1930s had developed Manchurian agricultural and iron mining resources, went to Indonesia in 1956 in connection with reparations problems but also showed a strong interest in the Japanese development of Sumatran oil.[9]

Indonesia's oil was not able to be imported immediately to Japan because of three principal obstacles. First, there remained ill feelings among the Indonesians over Japan's wartime conduct; second, there existed both political instability and antiforeign sentiment in Indonesia, hindering foreign investment; and third, Japan's businesses lacked sufficient capital for foreign investment.

To minimize Indonesia's—as well as the whole Asian region's—hostility toward them, the Japanese made their approaches cautiously, retaining neutrality on political issues and striving to expand trade activity in the area. An example is Japan's behavior at the Asia-Africa Bandung Conference in 1955 during which Chief Delegate Takasaki Tatsunosuke, then director of the National Economic Planning Agency, took extreme care not to take sides in any ideological arguments. Instead he apologized for Japan's wartime conduct in Asia and encouraged economic and cultural cooperation among Asians.[10]

Japan's geopolitical interest in Indonesia as a defense line against the Allies naturally disappeared in 1945, but in the postwar period Japan hoped that Indonesia would remain noncommunist. The Maoist regime established in mainland China in 1949 had increased the communist threat to the whole Southeast Asian region, where local subversives, aided by China as well as the Soviet Union, were very active. Japan would have had difficulty conducting trade with a communist regime in Indonesia which would have preferred business relations with Peking or Moscow. As the largest country in Southeast Asia, Indonesia also might have conceivably impeded Japan's trade with the rest of the region.

A noncommunist Indonesia as well as a noncommunist Asia also would insure the security of the Japanese oil route from the Middle East via the Strait of Malacca and the South China Sea. Postwar Japanese dependence on Middle Eastern oil increased from 76 percent in 1955 to 91 percent in 1967.[11] Thus Japan's importation of oil through the Strait of Malacca added a new dimension to its interests in Indonesia: the safety of the strait became more vital to Japan than Indonesian oil, which even in 1969 still constituted less than 10 percent of Japan's total oil imports. This consideration in turn reinforced Japan's desire for a friendly Indonesia and partially explains its offer to mediate between Jakarta and Kuala Lumpur from 1963 to 1966, when the two capitals broke diplomatic relations.

JAPANESE POLICY TOWARD SOUTHEAST ASIA

Japan's cautious, postwar diplomacy toward Asia, with its emphasis away from politics and toward economic and cultural cooperation, was actually designed to achieve Japan's political goals in the area, to wit, an economically viable and politically stable noncommunist Asia. The term "economic cooperation" was used by the Japanese government to designate the private capital investment and commercial loans assisting trade expansion. By attaching "economic cooperation agreements" to all war reparations agreements, Japan advantageously used its payments to expand its trade. Thus the war reparations which originally were meant to redeem Japan's wartime conduct, were actually utilized to promote its exports. With such countries as Laos and Cambodia that renounced reparations, and with Thailand, Malaya, and Singapore which were not able to claim them, Japan made other "economic cooperation" arrangements.[12]

A noncommunist Asia would help to protect Japan's trade from possible competition with the People's Republic of China, which wished to market its own goods in Southeast Asia. Too, a noncommunist Asia would protect the security of the aforementioned Japanese oil route from the Middle East. Finally, strengthening Asia against communism was consonant with Japan's policy of cooperation with Washington.

Kishi Nobusuke's emergence as foreign minister in the short-lived Ishibashi Cabinet (December 1956–February 1957) and as prime minister in February 1957 marked the advent of a more positive posture by Japan toward Asian problems. Kishi became the first Japanese prime minister to visit Southeast Asia. He also formulated the "three principles" of Japan's foreign policy: cooperation with the Free World, support of the United Nations as a peacekeeping organization, and protection of Asian interests.[13] Stressing the theme "Japan is a member of the Asian community," Kishi advocated Japan as a spokesman for Asia and as a promoter of Asian concerns.[14] In his trips to the area in 1957, he carried with him a proposal for a Southeast Asia Development Fund which was aimed at the economic development of the region with Japanese and, if possible, American support. This plan never materialized because most of the other Asian countries suspected that the fund might be used to facilitate Japanese economic control over the region. Nevertheless, the fact that in November 1957 Kishi settled the long-standing issue of reparations with Southeast Asia's largest nation, Indonesia, marked a step forward in Japan's relations with the rest of Asia.

It should not be forgotten that Kishi's two predecessors, Yoshida Shigeru (May 1946–May 1947, October 1948–December 1954) and Hatoyama Ichirō (December 1954–December 1956), had paved the way for this positive diplomacy toward noncommunist Asia. In December 1951, soon after the San Francisco Peace Conference and half a year before Japan regained its sovereignty, Yoshida set up an Asian Affairs Bureau within the Foreign Ministry, and Foreign Minister Okazaki Katsuo visited Southeast Asia in 1953. Upon his appointment as foreign minister in December 1954, Shigemitsu Mamoru promoted Japan's top-ranking envoys in Asia to ambassador, thereby demonstrating the seriousness of Japan's concern for Asia. In addition, reparations talks were concluded successfully with Burma in 1954 and with the Philippines in 1956. Japan established diplomatic relations with the Soviet Union in October 1956 and with Soviet consent became a member of the United Nations in December of that year. These diplomatic activities undoubtedly assisted Kishi's endeavors in Southeast Asia.

Kishi's successor, Ikeda Hayato (July 1960–November 1964), opened another era of Japanese diplomacy toward Southeast Asia. In 1963 when tensions grew between Indonesia and Malaya over Indonesia's opposition to Malaya's plan to form the Federation of Malaysia by joining the former British colonies of Sabah (North Borneo), Sarawak, and Singapore, Prime Minister Ikeda offered to mediate. This was Japan's first political role in Asia since the war. Ikeda felt that Japan was responsible for keeping Indonesia from communism, a belief borne out by the Indonesian Communist party's (PKI) strong support for Indonesia's "Crush Malaysia" policy and by the party's increased influence in Indonesia's foreign affairs. Japan's intervention was accepted by the disputing parties, although in the end mediation was unnecessary.

Japan's offer of such political diplomacy (as contrasted with "economic" diplomacy) can be traced in part to Japan's increased self-confidence through its economic growth. Another important element was undoubtedly Japan's concern for the security of the Strait of Malacca, and still another factor was the completion of reparations negotiations with the last claimant, Burma, in March 1963.[15] Finally, eighteen years after the end of the Pacific War, Japan was freed from the burden of war indemnification.

After 1963 Japan became involved in Indonesian matters to a greater extent than before. When Indonesian foreign policy moved closer to the Communist camp, the Japanese government extended yen credits equivalent to $49 million from 1963 to 1965 to prevent Indonesia's leaning even farther to the left.[16] After Indonesia's abortive coup in 1965, Japan under Prime Minister Satō Eisaku (November 1964–July 1972) took stronger measures to prop up the country with economic aid and to bring about stability. This expressed Japan's deepest concern for any Southeast Asian country since 1945. Japan initiated the organization of an international consortium for Indonesia in 1966 and, at the same time, in April sponsored the Southeast Asian Ministerial Conference on Economic Development.

Since 1966 Japan has shown a more positive approach toward Asian affairs. In that year Japan decided to join the Asia and Pacific Council, a meeting-ground for the region's foreign ministers to discuss political, economic, and cultural issues. Also that year, Japan's contribution to the Asian Development Bank Fund was one-third of the total. In 1968 the Satō Cabinet stated its willingness to participate in an international conference on the settlement of the Vietnam War and proposed an international fund for postwar Vietnamese development. Foreign Minister Miki Takeo then advanced the idea of an Asian and Pacific economic community. In November 1969 Satō went so far as to remark that Japan would play "a leading role" (*shuyaku*) in Asia.[17] In May 1970 Japan participated in an Asian conference on Cambodia and even agreed to be one of three mediating member nations. In October of that year the Satō government expressed its intention to participate in a Vietnam armistice control team, if one should be formed.[18]

Japan's postwar involvement in Asia began with economic diplomacy centered on reparations negotiations and economic cooperation. Since 1963, Japan gradually has been widening its role as a leader in political as well as economic spheres. It is suggested that Japan's policies in Southeast Asia evolved first from its interests in Indonesia's natural resources, potential export market, and geopolitical location. It is noteworthy also that these postwar policies were formulated and carried out under a simple political aegis, the Liberal Democratic party.

INDONESIA'S EXTERNAL BEHAVIOR: AN OVERVIEW

After 1945 while Japan was protected politically and economically under the American security umbrella, Indonesia experienced repeated domestic upheavals and foreign interventions. From 1945 to 1949 the Indonesians fought with the returned Dutch and other former Allied forces. In December 1949 independence finally was gained, but Indonesia's territorial claim to West New Guinea, or what it called West Irian, was not recognized. Left unresolved, West Irian remained one of Indonesia's largest national issues until it was settled in 1962.

Indonesia was pressed by Washington to participate in the 1951 San Francisco Peace Conference. Indonesia went partly from a sense of obligation to the United States for helping Indonesia gain independence from the Netherlands through United Nations mediation. However, after 1945, during the bitter struggles against the returned Dutch forces, Indonesia's nationalism became synonymous with anticolonialism, antiimperialism, and an anti-Western attitude. The desire to be freed (*merdeka*) from foreign dominance has greatly influenced Indonesia's foreign policy positions.

This desire engendered Indonesia's main principle of foreign policy, active independence (*bebas aktif*). This theme, formulated in 1948–1952, led Jakarta to recognize the Peking regime in April 1950, while participating in the American-controlled San Francisco meeting the following year.[19] However Indonesia's internal political condition after the conference favored the growth of political forces opposed to ties with the West. Under the Wilopo Cabinet (April 1952–July 1953), Indonesia refused to ratify the peace treaty with Japan and instead dispatched an ambassador to Peking.

At first Indonesia took little interest in Japan's foreign policies. The Indonesians resented the Japanese because of the war and as a result first demanded $17.5 billion in war reparations. Japan's attendance at the Asia-Africa Bandung Conference of 1955 helped to moderate Indonesia's ill-feeling, although during the conference no reference was made to Japan in any public speeches by Indonesia's (the host country) government leaders.[20] This illustrated Indonesia's support of the newly independent nations of Asia and Africa and its lack of interest in Japan's political posture.

Indonesia's economy was exhausted by the secessionist movements that occurred in the Outer Islands during the 1950s, as well as by the nationalistic and irredentist fervor of the campaign to recover West Irian, which led to the nationalization of Dutch properties in Indonesia. Nevertheless Sukarno gave priority to political rather than economic considerations. The anti-Sukarno rebellion in Sumatra and Sulawesi became active in 1957, protesting Sukarno's lack of interest in the economic welfare of his people and his lenient attitude toward the Communist party (PKI).

Against this background Sukarno received Prime Minister Kishi in November 1957, and between them they settled the long-standing reparations issues. For Sukarno this was a way to save his nation's deteriorating economy and to strengthen his political position. However the Sumatra and Sulawesi rebels, with the secret backing of the United States, officially declared, in February 1958, their opposition to his leadership.

Angered by America's encouragement of the rebels, Sukarno moved closer to Moscow and obtained military aid of some $1 billion, which Indonesia used first to quell the rebels and then to claim West Irian. Because the United States had no choice but to support the Netherlands, a NATO ally, West Irian thus became an issue between the two superpowers. Indonesia still claimed adherence to its policy of active independence, but opened its irredentist campaign with strong internal support from the PKI and the patronage of Moscow and Peking. As a result, the United States was forced to persuade the Dutch to retreat in the hope that Indonesia might remain open to American influence.

When the West Irian issue was settled to Indonesia's advantage, it was expected that Sukarno would concentrate upon internal economic development. He, however, took up still another international issue. Upon condemning the formation of Malaysia in September 1963 as a British neocolonialist attempt to contain Indonesia, he received strong encouragement from Peking. After a secret meeting in Shanghai with Chou En-lai in October 1964, Sukarno in turn responded more positively toward Peking's ideological leanings, forming an anticolonialist Asian axis which eventually included North Korea, North Vietnam, and Cambodia.

With respect to the Indonesia-Malaysia question, Prime Minister Ikeda Hayato and the ruling party's vice-president, Kawashima Shōjirō, attempted to mediate between Jakarta and Kuala Lumpur. By 1963 Japan's payment of reparations was under way and had generated active competition among those Japanese and Indonesians who saw profit in participating in the reparations programs. These individuals seem to have built up close connections with important figures in both countries, including Sukarno and Kawashima. Both Ikeda and Kawashima tried to use these Tokyo-Jakarta ties as a means of persuading Sukarno to take peaceful steps toward settling the Malaysian issue. Sukarno, having lost the support of Washington as well as of Moscow because of his closer ties with Peking, apparently thought it advantageous to maintain contact with Tokyo. His Japanese wife, Dewi, was a contributing factor in the continuing close relationship between the two Asian countries despite their opposing foreign policies.

The September 30, 1965 movement was an international as well as an internal affair because Communist China had allegedly supported a people's army equipped with Chinese armaments smuggled into Jakarta under the guise of construction materials for the Conference of New Emerging Forces (CONEFO) building. Turning away from its former policy of neutralism, Indonesia's new regime which emerged after the Gestapu affair, advocated a return to close relations with Washington and in 1967 broke relations with Peking.

Surveying Indonesia's external behavior during the two decades of the 1950s and 1960s, it can be seen that Indonesia at no time really maintained its purported neutralism. This position functioned only to disguise its pro-Western or procommunist leanings. It was a developing nation's way of asserting nationalist sentiment and independence.

Indonesia's fluctuating external politics is also reflected in its trade performance. Table 2 shows Indonesian trade in selected countries from

TABLE 2

COMPOSITION OF INDONESIAN TRADE WITH SELECTED COUNTRIES, 1952–1970

YEAR	TOTAL AMOUNT*	EXPORT (in percent)								TOTAL (in percent)
		Japan	USA	USSR	China	UK	Holland	Malaysia	Singapore	
1952	10,652	3	25	†	††	3	21	3	25	80
1953	9,344	5	21	†	††	2	23	3	22	76
1954	9,759	6	17	†	††	5	19	4	22	73
1955	10,618	7	18	†	1	10	16	3	20	75
1956	10,054	8	16	†	1	9	19	3	21	77
1957	11,052	4	15	†	3	7	17	3	27	76
1958	8,612	4	17	†	6	13	4	4	25	73
1959	8,158	4	16	†	6	22	1	3	23	75
1960	841	4	23	3	††	11	††	7	23	71
1961	784	7	24	4	5	6	††	7	21	74
1962	682	6	14	5	5	16	††	9	21	76
1963	696	10	12	4	6	17	1	4	15	69
1964	724	17	24	3	7	3	10	††	††	64
1965	708	16	22	4	6	1	13	††	††	67
1966	679	18	20	4	1	2	14	††	3	62
1967	665	29	15	2	††	4	6	††	10	66
1968	751	23	15	2	††	1	6	4	15	66
1969	831	29	13	1	††	1	4	3	16	67
1970	1,009	29	11	2	††	1	4	2	15	64

IMPORT

Year	Total									
1952	10,806	14	17	†	††	7	13	†	2	53
1953	8,584	17	18	†	††	7	12	†	1	55
1954	7,172	22	14	†	1	5	10	†	1	53
1955	6,888	14	16	†	2	6	12	†	2	52
1956	9,799	16	16	†	4	6	11	†	1	54
1957	9,158	15	17	†	3	6	10	†	2	53
1958	5,860	14	16	†	8	5	6	†	2	51
1959	5,229	15	16	†	13	7	4	†	2	57
1960	577	16	15	1	10	8	3	†	2	54
1961	794	18	17	1	5	6	1	††	2	50
1962	647	21	18	3	7	9	††	††	2	58
1963	521	17	11	2	8	8	††	††	1	48
1964	680	21	2	2	9	7	1	††	††	42
1965	695	23	9	1	14	4	3	††	††	55
1966	527	27	9	1	8	3	5	††	††	53
1967	649	28	8	1	8	3	7	††	3	58
1968	716	22	16	1	5	3	7	1	4	59
1969	697	29	19	1	6	3	5	††	5	68
1970	893	30	18	1	3	3	5	1	5	65

* 1952–1959 in millions of rps., and 1960–1970 in millions of $.

† Data not available.

†† Negligible.

Sources: 1952–1955, Bank of Indonesia, *Report for the Years 1955–1956*, p. 107; 1956–1959, Bank of Indonesia, *Report for the Years 1959–1960*, p. 119; 1960, Bank of Indonesia, *Report for the Years 1960–1965*, p. 100; 1961–1969, Bank of Indonesia, *Indonesian Financial Statistics, December 1970*, pp. 100 and 116; 1970, Bank of Indonesia, *Indonesian Financial Statistics, August 1972*, pp. 112–113, 130–131.

1952–1970. With few exceptions the table mirrors Jakarta's political relations over the past two decades with the United States, the Soviet Union, China, the United Kingdom, the Netherlands, Malaysia, and Singapore as well as with Japan.

It should be indicated first that both the exports from and the imports to Indonesia generally did not increase in terms of value during this period. This was typical of Sukarno's policy of attaching greater importance to politics than to economics. Trade with the Netherlands, which sharply decreased between 1958 and 1964, reflects the nationalization of Dutch properties by Indonesia in December 1957 and the subsequent tensions over West Irian. A marked decrease in Indonesian trade with Great Britain, Malaysia, and Singapore for a few years after 1963 was caused by the prevailing "Crush Malaysia" policy. Increased trade with China and the Soviet Union during Sukarno's Guided Democracy period of 1957–1965 bears witness to their contemporary political relations. The relatively larger trade with China also testifies to Jakarta's closer ties with Peking than with Moscow, in addition to the advantages that Peking enjoyed from overseas Chinese traders in and around Indonesia. Trade figures with the United States do not necessarily reflect political relations between Indonesia and the United States, save that the sharp decrease in imports after 1964 was caused by the American attempt to freeze the flow of goods into Indonesia where anti-Americanism had increased.

Indonesia's trade with Japan was carried out with exceptional steadiness, particularly after 1957 and demonstrated the gradually growing economic bond with Tokyo. Even during the Guided Democracy period when Indonesia was turning against the Western bloc, trade with Japan steadily increased. This is an economic indication of the "special" relationship maintained between Jakarta and Tokyo, a relationship which will be explored further in following sections of this chapter.

Table 2 reveals a striking aspect of Indonesia's trade performance. While Sukarno advocated both procommunist and pro-Afro-Asian policies, these were not substantiated by economic ties with these regions. Indonesia's trade with the Soviet Union in the 1960s was surprisingly low—no more than five percent of its total exports or imports. Only a sudden increase in imports from China in 1965 suggests economic confirmation of the Jakarta-Peking axis. Until the West Irian question grew to be a military issue, Indonesia surprisingly maintained relatively close relations with its old political enemy, the Netherlands. This also applies, to a still greater extent, to its economic relations with the United States.

JAPANESE-INDONESIAN ECONOMIC INTERDEPENDENCY

Table 3 lists the changing monetary values from 1947 to 1970 of trade between Japan and Indonesia, the ratios of Japanese exports to Indonesia to total Japanese exports and to total Indonesian imports, and, similarly, the ratios of Japanese imports from Indonesia in terms of total Japanese imports and total Indonesian exports. These ratios, taken over a period of twenty years, provide a useful index of the degree of mutual dependency between the two countries.

Various conclusions may be drawn from this table. First, until 1962 the trade balance favored Japan except in 1955 and 1956 but after 1963 the balance favored Indonesia except in 1965, indicating that from the middle of Sukarno's Guided Democracy period Japan imported more from Indonesia than it exported to it. This was because from that time Japan bought more of Indonesia's natural resources. Second, the increase in Japan's exports to Indonesia, in spite of the latter's decreasing foreign exchange holdings, was due to the "political" yen credit extended to Sukarno by Prime Minister Ikeda and the ruling party's vice-president, Kawashima. When Indonesia's anti-Western stance became more apparent, the majority of the Western nations withdrew their credits, Japan alone continuing to supply yen credit to Sukarno. A high-ranking official of the Ministry of International Trade and Industry (MITI) reasons that Japan's perseverence during Indonesia's most turbulent and unstable years was responsible for the easy and fast-growing volume of trade between the two countries in the post-1965 years.[21] This leads to the third conclusion drawn from Table 3; that Japan's trade with Indonesia was more important to Indonesia than to Japan. The percentage of Japan's exports to Indonesia out of its total exports had been decreasing since the 1950s; during the Guided Democracy period it averaged only two percent and after 1966 this had shrunk to less than 1.4 percent. That Japan's exports to Indonesia in 1948 had consisted of 22 percent of its total exports is rather amazing, as it discloses that Japan was far more dependent upon Indonesia at that date than it is at the present. Likewise, Japan's imports from Indonesia now occupy a very small portion of its total imports, whereas the same imports occupy a far greater portion of Indonesia's total exports, particularly since 1963. Beginning in 1967 both Japan's exports to and imports from Indonesia have comprised nearly 30 percent of Indonesia's total trade.

The overall conclusion is that Indonesia has been more dependent upon Japan than vice versa, and that this trend became conspicuous from the middle of the Sukarno phase of Japanese-Indonesian relations. This in itself justifies an analysis of the binational relations of that period.

TABLE 3
TRADE INTERDEPENDENCY BETWEEN JAPAN AND INDONESIA, 1947–1970

YEAR	JAPANESE EXPORTS TO INDONESIA			JAPANESE IMPORTS FROM INDONESIA			(7) Trade balance (1) − (4)
	(1) (in thousands of $)	(2) Jap. exp. (in percent)	(3) Indon. imp. (in percent)	(4) (in thousands of $)	(5) Jap. imp. (in percent)	(6) Indon. exp. (in percent)	
1947	23,457	13.5	—	1,304	0.2	—	22,153
1948	56,764	22.0	16.4	11,941	1.7	2.4	44,823
1949	15,279	3.0	—	15,328	1.6	—	−49
1950	46,281	5.6	—	13,303	1.3	—	32,978
1951	128,390	9.4	18.7	104,557	5.2	3.2	23,833
1952	59,842	4.6	14.3	27,495	1.3	2.6	32,347
1953	105,436	8.2	16.8	48,848	2.0	4.5	56,588
1954	119,715	7.3	21.7	60,385	2.5	5.8	59,330
1955	64,715	3.2	13.7	81,156	3.2	7.4	−16,441
1956	76,031	3.0	15.6	91,180	2.8	8.3	−15,449
1957	67,095	2.5	15.0	65,109	1.5	3.6	1,986
1958	49,056	1.7	13.6	37,004	1.2	3.6	12,052
1959	73,019	2.1	14.9	56,588	1.5	3.8	16,431
1960	110,821	2.7	16.0	71,286	1.5	4.0	39,535
1961	154,774	3.6	17.9	86,687	1.4	7.1	68,087
1962	116,305	2.3	20.8	92,876	1.6	6.0	23,429
1963	99,068	1.8	16.7	104,808	1.5	9.7	−5,740
1964	122,089	1.8	21.0	130,740	1.6	16.8	−8,651
1965	207,192	2.4	22.9	149,282	1.8	15.9	57,910

1966	118,615	1.2	26.8	175,505	1.8	17.8	−56,890
1967	155,149	1.4	28.0	195,009	1.6	29.2	−39,860
1968	146,595	1.1	21.7	251,829	1.9	22.9	−105,234
1969	235,811	1.4	29.4	397,319	2.6	29.3	−161,508
1970	315,780	1.6	35.3	636,553	3.3	63.5*	−320,773

* This figure is too high owing to statistical discrepancies.

— Indicates the total is negligible.

Sources: Figures in (1), (2), (4), (5), and (7) are based on Japanese statistics: 1947–1956, Tsūsho Sangyō Chōsakai, *Sengo Nihon no boeki nijunenshi*, pp. 290–291; 1967–1969, *Asahi nenkan 1969*, p. 346; and *Asahi nenkan 1971*, p. 372; 1970, *Tsūshō hakusho 1971*, II, pp. 341–345.

Figures in (3) and (6) are based on Indonesian statistics: 1948–1951, United Nations, *Yearbook of International Trade Statistics 1953*, p. 229; 1952–1955, Bank of Indonesia, *Report for the Years 1955–1956*, p. 107; 1956–1959, Bank of Indonesia, *Report for the Years 1959–1960*, p. 119; 1960, Bank of Indonesia, *Report for the Years 1960–1965*, p. 100; 1961–1969, Bank of Indonesia, *Indonesian Financial Statistics, December 1970*, p. 116; 1970, Bank of Indonesia, *Indonesian Financial Statistics, August 1972*, pp. 112–130.

Japan buys primary goods from Indonesia and sells industrial products. This pattern of trade is evidenced by Table 4, which gives a commodity-based picture of trade between the two countries from 1956 to 1970. This pattern applies also to Japan's trade with most of the other developing nations. One of the most important Indonesian items that Japan imports is oil, and as Table 5 shows, its importation of Indonesian crude oil has increased every year since 1956. Between 1956 and 1970 the value of oil imported from Indonesia increased 17.5 times. Japan depended upon foreign sources for over 97 percent of its oil needs during this fifteen-year period, and over 99 percent since 1965. Annual oil imports from Indonesia averaged 8.5 percent of Japan's total crude oil imports between 1956 and 1970. This is much lower than the prewar figure: in 1936, 35 percent of Japan's oil imports came from the Dutch East Indies.[22] Since the war the major source of oil for Japan has been the Middle East, constituting some 76 percent of its total oil import in 1955, 88 percent in 1965, 91 percent in 1967,[23] and 85 percent in 1970.[24] The low-sulphur oil of Indonesia now has a special attraction for Japan. Industries and automobiles, the major causes of air pollution in the metropolitan and industrial areas of Japan, use mainly high-sulphur Middle Eastern oil.

While Indonesia's oil is important to Japan, it is much more important to Indonesia. Between 1960 and 1970 at least 46 percent of Indonesia's crude oil exports went to Japan and by 1962 this figure reached 87 percent. The percentage of oil in Indonesia's total exports to Japan has not fallen below 49 percent. It can be inferred that if Japan did not buy any Indonesian oil it would affect at least half of Indonesia's oil exports to the world and a similar proportion of Indonesia's total exports to Japan.[25] A suspension of Japan's oil imports from Indonesia would also affect severely Indonesia's total exports—by 5.8 percent in 1960, 11.8 percent in 1965, and 17.4 percent in 1970[26]—demonstrating the rapid growth of Japan's influence over Indonesia's economy.

Table 6 selects four major Indonesian goods imported by Japan— bauxite, nickel, rubber, and lumber—and shows their relative import-ance to both Japan and Indonesia. Between 1956 and 1970 all but rubber increased in import value. Japanese imports of nickel and lumber in particular rose between 1964 and 1970, although the percentage of Indonesian nickel in Japan's total imports from Indonesia did not increase over two percent. Lumber constituted only two percent of Japan's imports from Indonesia in 1964 but 28 percent in 1970. Japan has no bauxite and depends upon foreign sources for its entire supply.[27] Between 1956 and 1970 an average of 29.5 percent of Japan's total bauxite imports came from Indonesia, although they averaged less than

TABLE 4

Composition of Commodities in Japanese Trade with Indonesia, in Percent, 1956–1970

Year	Export					
	Foodstuffs	Crude fuels	Light Manuf. goods	Heavy Manuf. goods	Others	Total
1956	1	0	72	21	3	97
1957	0	0	68	26	4	98
1958	0	0	48	41	9	98
1959	0	0	39	53	7	99
1960	0	0	63	29	7	99
1961	0	0	34	57	9	100
1962	0	0	31	69	0	100
1963	0	0	29	71	0	100
1964	1	0	37	61	0	99
1965	1	1	39	60	0	100
1966	1	0	50	50	0	101
1967	1	1	44	53	0	100
1968	4	2	31	62	1	100
1969	1	2	22	73	1	99
1970	7	2	21	69	0	99

Import

	Foodstuffs	Raw Materials	Mineral Fuels	Others	Total
1956	20	57	20	—	97
1957	8	52	33	—	93
1958	5	39	52	—	97
1959	2	27	63	—	92
1960	3	23	70	—	96
1961	4	18	73	1	95
1962	4	15	77	0	96
1963	5	15	80	0	100
1964	4	27	69	1	101
1965	4	39	57	1	101
1966	7	42	50	1	100
1967	8	36	55	2	101
1968	4	32	62	2	100
1969	4	33	61	2	100
1970	3	38	58	1	100

— Indicates the number is negligible.

Sources: 1956–1958, *Tsūshō hakusho 1959*, II, pp. 240–241; 1959–1961, *Tsūshō hakusho 1962*, II, pp. 272–273; 1962–1964, *Tsūshō hakusho 1965*, II, pp. 311–312; 1965–1967, *Tsūshō hakusho 1968*, II, pp. 320–322; 1968–1970, *Tsūshō hakusho 1971*, II, pp. 341–345.

TABLE 5

IMPORTANCE OF INDONESIAN OIL TO JAPAN AND INDONESIA, 1956–1970

YEAR	(1) JAP. IMP. OF INDON. OIL (crude petroleum) (in thousands of $)	(2) TOTAL JAP. CRUDE OIL IMP. (in percent)	(3) TOTAL INDON. CRUDE OIL EXP. (in percent)	(4) TOTAL INDON. EXP. TO JAPAN (in percent)	(5) JAP. DEPENDENCE ON OIL IMP. (in percent)
1956	18,089	5.7	*	19.7	97
1957	16,846	4.0	*	25.9	98
1958	18,262	4.4	*	49.3	98
1959	34,528	6.9	*	61.0	98
1960	49,263	10.5	57.0	69.1	98
1961	61,245	11.3	45.5	70.6	98
1962	67,255	10.8	87.0	72.3	98
1963	78,822	9.9	54.9	75.2	98
1964	87,956	9.4	44.0	67.2	99
1965	84,139	8.0	48.0	56.3	99
1966	87,418	7.2	60.4	49.3	99
1967	95,413	6.5	49.6	48.9	99
1968	132,167	7.8	51.1	52.4	99
1969	207,374	10.8	53.3	52.1	99.5
1970	318,091	14.2	75.2	49.9	99.5

* Data not available.

Sources: (1), 1956–1958, *Tsūshō hakusho 1959*, II, p. 241; 1959–1961, *Tsūshō hakusho 1962*, II, p. 273; 1962–1967, *Keizai yōran 1969*, pp. 256–257; 1968–1970, *Tsūshō hakusho 1971*, II, p. 346.
(2), Calculated from the sources for column (1).
(3), 1960–1968, Bank of Indonesia, *Indonesian Financial Statistics, December 1970*, p. 98; 1969–1970, Japan-Indonesia Association, *Gekkan Indonesia*, no. 283 (June 1971), p. 23.

TABLE 6

IMPORTANCE OF SELECTED INDONESIAN EXPORTS TO JAPAN
AND INDONESIA, 1956–1970

GOODS AND YEARS	JAP. IMP. FROM INDON. (in thousands of $)	TOTAL JAP. IMP. FROM INDON. (in percent)	TOTAL JAP. IMP. OF GIVEN GOODS (in percent)
Bauxite			
1956	2,489	2.7	40.8
1960	3,095	4.3	24.5
1964	5,599	4.2	30.6
1968	6,796	2.7	26.4
1970	9,249	1.5	25.2
(Average)	(5,445.6)	(3.08)	(29.50)
Nickel			
1956	*	*	*
1960	357	0.5	1.9
1964	679	0.5	1.9
1968	3,774	1.5	6.5
1970	12,091	1.9	6.9
(Average)	(4,225.3)	(0.88)	(4.60)
Natural Rubber			
1956	26,683	29.1	36.3
1960	*	*	*
1964	14,308	10.9	15.1
1968	15,700	6.2	18.8
1970	13,100	2.1	11.3
(Average)	(17,447.8)	(12.08)	(20.37)
Lumber			
1956	495	0.5	0.6
1960	452	0.6	0.3
1964	2,699	2.1	0.6
1968	30,645	12.1	2.6
1970	176,411	27.7	11.2
(Average)	(42,140.4)	(8.60)	(3.06)

* Figures not provided in official sources.
Sources: 1956, *Tsūshō hakusho 1959*, II, pp. 168, 194, 199; 1960, *Tsūshō hakusho 1962*, II, pp. 169, 208, 209; 1964, *Tsūshō hakusho 1965*, II, pp. 198, 199, 214, 216; 1968, *Tsūshō hakusho 1970*, II, pp. 209, 223, 224; 1970, *Tsūshō hakusho 1971*, II, pp. 227, 242, 243.

three percent of Japan's total imports from Indonesia. Natural rubber and petroleum once were Japan's two major items imported from the Dutch East Indies. As synthetic rubber production increased, however, the relative importance of natural rubber was reduced and accordingly, as this table indicates, Japan's imports of Indonesian natural rubber plummeted during the fifteen-year period from 29 percent of Japan's imports from Indonesia in 1956 to two percent in 1970.

Except for natural rubber, therefore, bauxite, nickel, lumber, and oil are all essential to Japan. While their relative importance has varied, the basic pattern of Japan's importation of mineral resources in exchange for manufactured goods has remained unchanged. Indonesia's need for manufactured goods in connection with Japan's payment of reparations will be discussed in chapter 4.

THE FLOW OF NATIONALS BETWEEN JAPAN AND INDONESIA

Another indication of the closeness of Japanese-Indonesian contacts is the mobility of their nationals between the two countries. The steady flow of tourists and businessmen into a country often reflects the political stability of the country while a sudden outflow is likely to signify political instability. Both Japanese and Indonesian statistics on the interchange of foreign nationals are deficient, owing to the difficulty of obtaining such figures and also to a lack of interest by either government. Nevertheless a general picture can be obtained.

Table 7 is an attempt to identify the changing number of Japanese nationals in Indonesia through residents, size of embassy and consulate staffs, and short-term visits. The number of Japanese residents in Indonesia increased sevenfold from about 200 in 1958 to about 1,500 in 1970. Both figures appear to be underestimated, for Japanese consulates in Jakarta, Surabaya, and Medan apparently registered only those Japanese nationals who voluntarily reported their residency. Many Japanese businessmen came on short-visit visas but then extended their stays to do further business. Some Japanese, even if they registered with the Indonesian authorities in order to obtain work permits, often did not register with the Japanese consulates. For instance in December 1970 the consulate in Jakarta informed me that as of October 1, 1970 there were 1,528 Japanese nationals residing in Indonesia, whereas the Indonesian authorities had reported the number of work permits issued to Japanese as 2,136. This latter count too might be an understatement. This also applies to the 1968 figure of Japanese residents in Indonesia; while Japanese statistics list 712, an Indonesian record lists 1,277 persons.

Discrepancies between the different sources of Indonesian statistics on the number of Japanese visitors to Indonesia are unavoidable, since not every Japanese who obtained an Indonesian visa actually traveled there, nor did every Japanese who came through Indonesian Im-

TABLE 7

JAPANESE IN INDONESIA, 1958–1970

| YEAR | NO. OF RESIDENTS | SIZE OF EMBASSY STAFF[a] | NO. OF JAP. VISITORS TO INDON. | | |
| | | | By Indon. immigration | Foreign visitors (in percent) | By visas issued by Indon. emb. in Tokyo[b] |
	(1)	(2)	(3)	(4)	(5)
1958	c.200	6+4	*	*	*
1959	*	10+2	*	*	*
1960	503	11+2	394	11	655
1961	*	15+2	555	5	1,213
1962	*	15+3	1,366	10	1,846
1963	c.692	12+6	1,131	10	1,873
1964	*	16+5	*	*	*
1965	c.900	17+6	2,676	14	2,985
1966	*	18+8	1,809	12	1,841
1967	*	22+8	1,558	7	*
1968	712[c]	24+8	4,523	10	3,785
1969	1,345	24+5	*	*	6,689
1970	1,485	27+8	8,416	7	9,552

* Data not available.

Note: These figures are often underestimated as many people do not report to the authorities, who have limited means of locating their nationals.

[a] Right-hand figures are numbers of embassy staff and left-hand ones are numbers of consular staff. Both refer to "home staff" only, and not locally hired staff.

[b] Does not include number of visas issued by the consulate in Kobe.

[c] 1,277 according to an Indonesian source. *Statistical Pocketbook of Indonesia 1968–1969*, p. 39. According to an Indonesian source, there were 2,136 Japanese who obtained work permits from the Indonesian government in 1970. See *Merdeka*, May 8, 1971.

Sources: (1), 1958, Japan, Foreign Ministry, *Indoneshia Kyōwakoku benran* (1960), p. 97; 1960, *Japan Statistical Yearbook 1961*, p. 43; 1963, Japan, Foreign Ministry, *Indoneshia Kyōwakoku benran* (1964), p. 170; 1965, *Asahi Shinbun*, October 2, 1965; 1968–1969, *Asahi nenkan 1971*, p. 227; 1970, Japan, Foreign Ministry, *Waga gaikō no kinkyō*, no. 15, (1971), p. 496.

(2), 1958–1970, Japan, Finance Ministry Printing Office, *Nihon shokuinroku*, 1958–1970.

(3), 1960–1968, Indonesia, Central Bureau of Statistics, *Almanak Indonesia 1968*, I, pp. 511–519.

(4), 1970, *The Indonesian Letter*, no. 23 (September 1971). Same as sources for (3).

(5), 1960–1961, Indonesian Embassy, Tokyo, *Laporan Tahunan 1961*, p. 196; 1962–1963, *Laporan Tahunan 1963*, sec. V, p. 8; 1965–1966, *Laporan Tahunan 1966*, p. 101; 1968–1969, *Laporan Tahunan 1969*, p. 359; 1970, Japan-Indonesia Association, *Gekkan Indoneshia*, no. 292 (March 1972), p. 19.

migration obtain a visa from the Indonesian consulates in Tokyo and Kobe. In either case, columns (3) and (5) of Table 7 display corres-

ponding trends between the two official figures. The sudden drop in
Japanese visitors from 1965 to 1966 probably reflects the hesitation at
entering Indonesia after it had been thrown into confusion by the
abortive coup of September 1965. In contrast, the greater number of
visitors after 1968 indicates the restored order in Indonesia. The larger
number of entering Japanese parallels the sharply increased monetary
value of binational trade in the same period, as seen in Table 3.

Japanese government statistics revealed the occupational composition of the 2,345 Japanese visitors to Indonesia in 1965 and in 1968,
as consisting primarily of clerical workers (1,194), private company
managers (227), transportation and communication workers (216), and
engineers (202).[28] The last two groups were large probably because of
reparations projects, many of which involved construction of bridges,
dams, and communications facilities. The combined number of these
two groups dropped noticeably from 418 in 1965 to 165 in 1968. In
contrast, the number of traders rose from only 11 in 1965 to 240 in 1968.
The 2,803 Japanese visitors in 1968 were mainly clerical workers (1,232),
private company managers (509), traders (240), industrial construction
workers (96), and housewives (96). The entry of more than twice as
many private company managers and 96 housewives in 1968 reflects
Indonesia's improved climate for international trade as well as greater
internal security.

Table 7 also indicates that the size of Japanese embassy and consulate staffs has grown steadily since the establishment of the consulates
in 1952. The "home staff" grew from 6 in 1958 to 18 in 1966, and to 27
in 1970. This again can be said to represent Japan's closer diplomatic
involvement in Indonesian affairs.

The trends observed in the flow of Japanese nationals into Indonesia generally match those of Indonesians coming to Japan, as seen
in Table 8. According to Japanese statistics, the number of Indonesian
residents rose from 205 in 1952, the year the two governments established consular relations, to 260 in 1958, when full diplomatic relations
were established, and to 1,026 in 1965, decreasing to 834 in 1968. These
figures differ from Indonesian government statistics, although the dis-
crepancy is not great. Data on the sizes of the Indonesian embassy and
consulate "home staffs" are far from complete but at least suggest
gradual increases. A numerical comparison between the visitors in 1958
and those in the late 1960s suggests a phenomenal growth in the number
of Indonesians coming to Japan during this decade. The occupational
composition of Indonesian residents in Japan given in Indonesian
embassy reports shows an interesting contrast to the occupational
composition of Japanese residents in Indonesia. From 1959 to 1965 there

TABLE 8

INDONESIANS IN JAPAN, 1958–1970[a]

YEAR	NOS. OF RESIDENTS			SIZE OF EMBASSY STAFF	VISITORS TO JAPAN	TOTAL VISITORS (in percent)
	By Jap. sources	By total foreign residents (in percent)	By Indon. sources			
	(1)	(2)	(3)	(4)	(5)	(6)
1958	260	0.0	286	*	1,311	0.7
1959	297	0.0	257	*	1,267	0.6
1960	420	0.0	515	*	1,694	0.6
1961	760	0.1	782	18	2,510	0.7
1962	912	0.1	857	19	2,421	0.7
1963	897	0.1	965[b]	25	2,626	0.6
1964	976	0.1	*	*	4,498	0.8
1965	1,026	0.1	1,138	*	4,656	0.8
1966	920	0.1	1,145	28	3,699	0.5
1967	1,017	0.1	*	27	4,814	0.6
1968	834	0.1	1,250	*	4,134	0.4
1969	953	0.1	1,048	27	4,936	0.3
1970	1,036	0.1	*	*	8,692	0.5

* Data not available.

[a] More often than not, these figures are underestimated, as many people do not report to the authorities, who have limited means of locating nationals.

[b] Another Indonesian source gives 851. Quoted in Japan, Foreign Ministry, *Indoneshia Kyōwakoku benran* (1964), p. 171.

Sources: (1) and (2), 1958–1959, *Japan Statistical Yearbook 1960*, p. 21; 1960–1970, *Japan Statistical Yearbook 1970*, p. 44.

(3) and (4), 1958, Japan, Foreign Ministry, *Indoneshia Kyōwakoku benran* (1959), p. 72; 1959, Japan, Foreign Ministry, *Indoneshia Kyōwakoku benran* (1960), p. 94; 1960–1961, Indonesian Embassy, Tokyo, *Laporan Tahunan 1961*, p. 207; 1962–1963, *Laporan Tahunan 1963*, sec. V, p. 19; 1965–1966, *Laporan Tahunan 1966*, p. 112; 1968–1969, *Laporan Tahunan 1969*, p. 369.

(5) and (6), 1958–1959, Japan, Justice Ministry, *Shutsunyūgoku kanri tōkei nenpō 1964*, pp. 2–5; 1960–1969, *Japan Statistical Yearbook 1970*, pp. 44–45; 1970, *Japan Statistical Yearbook 1971*, p. 47.

were no more than 20 Indonesian businessmen registered in Japan, and even after 1968 they did not amount to more than 53 persons. [29] While a great majority of the Japanese residents in Indonesia were related to private companies, over 50 percent of the Indonesian residents in Japan were students and trainees sent under the reparations programs.

In short, these figures on Japanese and Indonesian visitors and residents suggest that the annual rate of increase did not differ greatly in any one year, although there were comparatively more Japanese in

Indonesia. Consequently, the Japanese visitors were more conspicuous in Indonesia than were the Indonesian visitors in Japan, as the former constituted 5 to 14 percent of Indonesia's total foreign visitors, while the latter constituted less than one-half of one percent of Japan's total foreign visitors. In 1960 and 1962 the Japanese were the third largest foreign group in Indonesia and in 1965 and 1968 the second largest group after the Americans.[30]

As binational trade relations also show, the Japanese trade presence is more noticeable in Indonesia than is the Indonesian presence in Japan. The Japanese visitors to Indonesia have made themselves conspicuous not only by their numbers but by their generous spending as well, thereby contributing to Indonesia's critical view of the Japanese as "rich Asians."

It may be noted parenthetically that Japan's obvious presence in Indonesia is not merely a post-1960 development. Extensive Japanese contacts with the Indonesians can be traced back to at least 1920, when the presence of 4,100 Japanese residents, mostly traders, was recorded.[31] In 1939, when the Dutch East Indies authorities made their last population survey, 6,469 Japanese were counted.[32] During the Pacific War, 90,000 Japanese occupation troops were stationed in Indonesia and 10,000 Japanese citizens were associated with 180 business establishments operating in Java and the Outer Islands.[33] During the "Sukarno period" of Japanese-Indonesian relations there were 50 to 60 Japanese firms maintaining liaison offices in Jakarta.[34] When the number of Japanese business representatives in Jakarta in the early 1960s is compared to those during the war or during the late 1930s, the postwar Japanese presence is much less remarkable. What seems to make this postwar presence more apparent is partly that before the war more Japanese lived in Surabaya than in Jakarta (then called Batavia), while after the war most Japanese have lived in Jakarta, the republic's capital.[35] The more noticeable Japanese activity in the postwar period also may be attributed to the highly visible and large-scale operations of major businesses such as the Mitsui and Mitsubishi trading companies, the Taisei and Obayashi construction companies, and Japan Air Lines.

EXCHANGE VISITS OF JAPANESE AND INDONESIAN LEADERS

Just as the flow of citizens between two nations is a fairly reliable index to their friendly relations, so may be the exchange of visits by their respective leaders. An exchange at the summit level sometimes is undertaken to solve mutual problems and to ease tensions. But generally it is the frequency of these reciprocal visits which measures the amicability between the nations concerned. Unbalanced exchanges reflect uneven relations: the leaders of subordinate nations tend to visit dominant nations more often then the reverse. These assumptions also are true for the Sukarno period of Japanese-Indonesian relations.

Every Japanese prime minister since Kishi Nobusuke and every foreign minister since Okazaki (with the exceptions of Shigemitsu, Kosaka, and Miki) has visited Indonesia officially at least once during his tenure. The first postwar foreign minister to visit Indonesia was Okazaki in 1953 and the first prime minister to visit Indonesia was Kishi in 1957. The crown prince and crown princess made a visit in 1962.

Japanese leaders seem to visit foreign countries in the order of their commercial and political importance. Until Kishi's visit to Indonesia in 1957, the United States, Canada, and Western Europe were more important to Japan than was Asia. After 1957 Japan became more concerned with its relations in Asia, and, accordingly, Japanese leaders began to visit. In 1963 and 1967 respectively, Prime Ministers Ikeda and Satō extended their Indonesian trips to Australia and New Zealand whose commercial and political importance as Pacific partners to Japan had increased.

Visits by Japanese leaders to foreign countries including Indonesia are short, rigidly scheduled, and usually capped by joint communiques carefully worded in advance by foreign ministry officials. In contrast, Indonesian leaders consider Japan a site favorable for both official and unofficial visits, as Tokyo is conveniently located as a stopover en route to the United States, the United Nations, Western Europe via the North Pole, and even to North Korea. This habitual practice has prevailed under both the Suharto and, particularly, the Sukarno presidencies. Table 9 shows the visits between 1957 and 1970 to Tokyo by Indonesian presidents and foreign ministers in contrast to their Japanese counterparts visiting Jakarta. From 1945 to 1968 President Sukarno made a total of fifteen foreign trips during his term of office.[36] His first was to the Philippines in 1951 and his fifteenth and last was to Cairo and Paris in 1965. Of these fifteen visits, ten involved Japan though only one, in 1958, was official. The rest were either unofficial or involved meetings with Malaysian and Philippine leaders in regard to the Indonesian-Malaysian disputes. These ten visits were made between January 1958 and November 1964: therefore in certain years, Sukarno visited Japan more than once, in 1960 and 1961 he went to Tokyo twice each year and in 1964, three times.

Similarly, Suharto has been to Japan twice (in 1968 and 1970) since he became president in 1968. In addition, Foreign Ministers Subandrio under Sukarno and Adam Malik under Suharto have made frequent

TABLE 9

VISITS OF JAPANESE PRIME MINISTERS AND FOREIGN MINISTERS IN
INDONESIA AND INDONESIAN PRESIDENTS AND FOREIGN MINISTERS
IN JAPAN, 1957–1970

NAME OF OFFICIAL	TERM OF OFFICE	DATES OF VISIT	DURATION OF VISIT (days)	SIZE OF PARTY (no. of persons)
Japanese Prime Ministers				
Kishi	1957–1960	Nov. 26–28, 1957	3	13
Ikeda	1960–1964	Sept. 26–28, 1963	3	14
Satō	1964–1972	Oct. 8–11, 1967	4	11
Japanese Foreign Ministers				
Fujiyama	1957–1960	Nov. 26–28, 1957	3	*
		Jan. 19–23, 1958	5	*
Kosaka	1960–1962	no visit		
Ōhira	1962–1964	Sept. 26–28, 1963	3	*
Shiina	1964–1966	Oct. 25–28, 1966	4	*
Miki	1966–1968	no visit		
Aichi	1968–1971	May 15–18, 1970	4	*
		May 21–25, 1970	5	*
Indonesian Presidents				
Sukarno	1945–1968	Jan. 29–Feb. 15, 1958	18	13
		June 6–19, 1959	14	29
		May 24–June 3, 1960	11	33
		Sept. 26–28, 1960	3	35
		June 23–July 2, 1961	10	44
		Sept. 18–21, 1961	4	50
		Nov. 4–21, 1962	18	40
		May 23–June 2, 1963	11	30
		Jan. 15–20, 1964	6	61
		June 7–21, 1964	15	30
		Oct. 26–Nov. 1, 1964	7	44
Suharto	1968 to date	March 28–April 1, 1968	5	45
		June 3, 1970	1	*
Indonesian Foreign Ministers				
Subandrio	1957–1966	Sept. 18–20, 1957	3	*
		April 15–18, 1958	4	*
		Oct. 13–17, 1959	5	*
		Nov. 14–21, 1960	8	*
		June 24–July 2, 1961	9	*
		Oct. 2–3, 1961	2	*

TABLE 9 (Cont.)

		Dec. 1–3, 1961	3	*
		March 13, 1962	1	*
		Aug. 10–11, 1962	2	*
		Aug. 19, 1962	1	*
		Nov. 17–21, 1962	5	*
		May 23–June 2, 1963	11	*
		June 13–15, 1963	3	*
		Sept. 20, 1963	1	*
		Sept. 26, 1963	1	*
		Jan. 15–20, 1964	6	*
		June 7–21, 1964	15	*
		Oct. 26–Nov. 1, 1964	7	*
		Nov. 26–29, 1964	4	*
		Feb. 11–14, 1965	4	*
		May 19–25, 1965	7	*
Malik	1966 to date	Oct. 7–12, 1966	6	*
		April 1–9, 1967	9	*
		Oct. 3–4, 1967	2	*
		March 28–April 1, 1968	5	*
		Oct. 11–13, 1968	3	*
		Oct. 26–27, 1969	2	*
		Nov. 23–27, 1969	5	*
		June 3, 1970	1	*
		Oct. 17–19, 1970	3	*
		Dec. 11–14, 1970	4	*

* Data not available.

visits to Tokyo. Between 1957 and 1965 Subandrio came to Japan twenty-one times, and between 1966 and 1970 Adam Malik came ten times, though only once officially with President Suharto in March 1968.

Another conspicuous feature of the trips abroad by Indonesian leaders is the huge size of their entourages. Sukarno's traveling parties to Tokyo were usually quite large, ranging from 29 persons in 1959 to 61 persons in 1964.[37] Most of these parties included cabinet ministers such as Subandrio, Leimena, the Sultan, Chairul Saleh, Yani, and Nasution—six of the ministers in 1960 and seven in September 1961. In contrast, Kishi's party to Indonesia in 1957 consisted of only 13 persons. The reasons for these large retinues remain unclear, but they appear to be the outcome of Sukarno's promises of political rewards and of expanding his overseas popularity. Sukarno himself was reported to have been satisfied with his attendants' pride in their great welcome in Moscow and Peking in 1956—presumably in recognition of Indonesia's and Sukarno's importance.[38] Former Japanese ambassador to Indonesia, Ōda Takio, wrote that Sukarno had wanted as many Indonesian leaders as possible to travel abroad with him, because he had felt that Indonesia had suffered earlier an indescribable loss by not being privy to world affairs.[39] A deeper look into Sukarno's personality reveals that he felt comfortable and self-assured only in the presence of many familiar faces and felt lonely without them. In either case, there is a correspondence between the style of his foreign trips and of his "100 Minister Cabinet," formed in August 1964 under the name of the Dwikora Cabinet.[40]

Most of President Sukarno's trips were long, often lasting for two months and covering more than a dozen countries in a single tour. Sukarno's 1959 trip lasted from April 23 through June 29 and covered sixteen nations scattered around the world.[41] In 1961 he visited twenty-one countries during his first trip from April 16 through July 2, and four during his second trip between August 28 and September 21.[42]

Many of Sukarno's trips were termed "rest abroad," but in reality they often included serious discussions with the leaders of the host countries, appealing Indonesia's case in the West Irian campaign and advocating its foreign policy of "active independence" in addition to the usual ceremonial occasions. Sukarno's frequent visits to Tokyo often constituted the last stop of a long "rest abroad." Here, while he enjoyed Japanese food, drink, and women, Sukarno also conducted business with government leaders and businessmen with concerns in Indonesia and had audiences with the emperor and reunions with his wartime friends. Sukarno spent altogether 117 days in Japan between 1957 and 1964. This contrasts with the total of 6 days that Prime Ministers Kishi and Ikeda spent in Indonesia during the same period. Doubtlessly, Japan was the only country which Sukarno visited so often and in which he stayed so long with such a large retinue.

There are several reasons for this contrast between the length of visits made by Japanese and Indonesian leaders. As mentioned earlier, the location of Tokyo as a convenient stopover between Jakarta and other major world sites must count as a factor in Sukarno's, Subandrio's, and their successors' visits. Compared to Tokyo, Jakarta is not as accessible, but were it situated between Tokyo and Washington, the Japanese leaders might have "stopped over" more often, though it is still doubtful that these occasions would have been as numerous as the Indonesian leaders' visits to Tokyo.

Another important cause was Sukarno's personal attraction to Japan. His fondness for Tokyo's night life has been reported widely and does not need to be documented here, save to note that his third official wife, Dewi, was a former nightclub hostess in Tokyo. A third factor was Indonesia's economic dependence upon Japan. As calculated from Table 3, Japan's exports to Indonesia from 1958 to 1965 averaged 2.1 percent of its total exports, but the comparable figure for Indonesia was 18.9 percent of its total imports. Likewise Japan's imports from Indonesia during the same period averaged 1.5 percent of its total imports but 8.9 percent of Indonesia's total exports.

In Western and Oriental history, subordinate countries frequently visit dominant powers. Every Japanese prime minister in the post-1952 period has had to begin his term of office by going to Washington as soon as possible to formulate his foreign and even his domestic policies. While more Japanese leaders visit Washington than the reverse, more American citizens travel to Japan than Japanese citizens to America.[43] This is true of Japanese-Indonesian relations too: more Indonesian leaders come to Tokyo than Japanese to Jakarta, whereas more ordinary Japanese visit Jakarta than Indonesians to Tokyo. Sukarno's trips to Japan thus were symbolic of the dependent relationship between Indonesia and Japan. Accordingly, it was the Indonesians who came to Tokyo to request greater Japanese "economic cooperation." Taking advantage of this, the Japanese government and business firms invited them to their country and plied them with Japanese entertainment to seek ways to ease political and economic problems.

It is not surprising then that Tokyo became a center for Indonesia's diplomatic and intelligence activities. During the Gestapu affair in 1965, the Indonesian embassy in Tokyo played a special role by passing information of its country's political developments to the Indonesian embassies in other major capitals of the world which lacked telecommunications facilities.[44] Also in the early 1960s the Indonesian ambassador to Tokyo occupied the fifth-ranking position in Indonesia's foreign service, after Washington, Moscow, London, and Amsterdam. Since about 1966, however, the ambassadorship to Tokyo ranks after Washington, thus reflecting Tokyo's large share of governmental aid to Indonesia and its purchase of one-third of Indonesia's export goods.

Both pro-Sukarno and anti-Sukarno groups initiated their political activities in Tokyo. In early 1958 a few anti-Sukarno military leaders of the Sumatra-Sulawesi Rebellion gathered secretly in Tokyo, reportedly to plot the assassination of President Sukarno. In the first half of the 1960s, Tokyo's Indonesian Students Association (PPI) was supposedly one of the strongest Indonesian student organizations overseas, serving to promote Sukarno's West Irian and anti-Malaysia campaigns. There was also a sporadic Free Papuan Movement conducted by West Irian (Papuan) students and supported by Japanese businessmen with interests in West Irian and New Guinea.

A brief review of the volume and frequency of Japanese-Indonesian contacts in the areas of trade, flow of people, and visits of leaders reveals, in short, Indonesia's growing dependence upon Japan, beginning with the emergence of Kishi Nobusuke in Tokyo and Sukarno in Jakarta. It appears that the two leaders paved the way for further interdependence after about 1958. In this respect the political developments during the Sukarno period of binational relations merit close attention.

NOTES

1. The Supreme Commander for the Allied Powers (SCAP) which controlled Japan from September 2, 1945 through April 28, 1952, instructed Japan on October 25 and November 4, 1945 to suspend all diplomatic activities but after mid-1948 moved to relax these restrictions. On April 12, 1949, it permitted Japan to go to Geneva to participate in a conference on international treaties as an observer and as an advisor to the SCAP delegation. From April 19, 1950, Japan was permitted to open overseas offices in order to establish communication with foreign countries. Offices first were opened in New York, Seattle, Honolulu, and later in India, France, and so forth. After February 1951, Japan was permitted to enter into direct negotiations with foreign governments on limited subjects such as exit and reentry permits for foreign nationals. See Japan, Foreign Ministry, ed., *Gaimushō no hyakunen* (2 vols.; Tokyo: Hara Shobō, 1969), II, 796 ff. After the San Francisco Peace Conference, on September 13, 1951, Japan was given practically complete power to negotiate directly with foreign representatives in Tokyo on all subjects. See *Asahi nenkan 1952*, p. 548.

2. Thailand had no legal right to claim reparations because it retained its independence during the war and was not occupied by the Japanese. Nor were the colonies of Malaya and Singapore able to claim reparations, because Great Britain had renounced their rights. Laos and Cambodia at first claimed reparations but later, in December 1956, also renounced them.

3. Figures in this paragraph are computed from the data in Bank of Japan, *Hundred-Year Statistics of the Japanese Economy* (Tokyo: Bank of Japan, 1966), pp. 290–297.

4. Kishi Kōichi, et al., *Indoneshia ni okeru Nihon gunsei no kenkyū* (Tokyo: Kinokuniya Shoten, 1959), p. 112 ff.

5. Japan's Economic Stabilization Board, which later became the current Economic Planning Agency under the Prime Minister's Office, discussed measures to promote Indonesian industries. See its *Indoneshia sangyō shinkō taisaku* (Tokyo: Economic Stabilization Board, 1951).

6. Daiyamondo Sha, ed., *Nippon Kōei* (Tokyo: Daiyamondo Sha, 1971), p. 102.

7. David Conde, *Indoneshia no henbō* (Tokyo: Kōbundō, 1966), p. 144. See also *Asahi Shinbun*, October 19, 1957.

8. Sugimori Hisahide, *Arabiya Tarō* (Tokyo: Bungei Shunjū Sha, 1960), p. 185.

9. From Ayukawa's correspondence with Djamaluddin Malik of the Nahdlatul Ulama Party in July 1956. The letters are in the possession of Nishijima Shigetada of the North Sumatra Oil Development Cooperation Company in Tokyo.

10. *Asahi Shinbun*, April 20 and 22, 1955. See also Takasaki Tatsunosuke, "Ajia no han'ei to Nihon no unmei," *Chūō Kōron*, January 1958, pp. 105–109.

11. Japan, Ministry of International Trade and Industry (MITI), *Sōgō enerugī tōkei*

1968 (Tokyo: MITI, 1969), pp. 144–145.

12. For the economic cooperation agreements, Burma was to receive a yen credit of $50 million over 10 years beginning in 1955, the Philippines $250 million over 20 years beginning in 1956; Indonesia $400 million over 20 years beginning in 1958; and South Vietnam $7.5 million over 3 years beginning in 1963 and $9.1 million more after 1965; and Thailand $26.7 million over eight years beginning in 1962. These credits were in the form of commercial, reimbursible loans from private Japanese groups. Laos was given a nonreimbursible grant (in lieu of reparations) of $2.8 million beginning in 1959; similarly Cambodia received $4.2 million over three years beginning in 1959. Burma then also received $140 million over 12 years beginning in 1965. Singapore claimed $16 million in 1967, while Malaysia claimed and received $50 million in 1967, all in the form of nonreimbursible grants. See the Reparations Problems Study Group, *Nihon no baishō 1963* (Tokyo: Sekai Jānaru Sha, 1963), pp. 13–19; and *Gaimushō no hyakunen*, II, 1141, 1170–1171.

13. *Gaimushō no hyakunen*, II, 935.

14. See Kishi's New Year's message in *Asahi Shinbun*, January 1, 1958.

15. When the first reparations agreement was concluded with Burma in 1954, it contained a provision whereby Burma retained the right to request a later reexamination of the reparations amount. Burma requested a reexamination in 1959 and in March 1963 reached a new settlement on the basis of an additional grant of $140 million for reparations, plus $30 million for yen credit (deferred payment of imports from Japan). See *Nihon no baishō 1963*, p. 15.

16. Japan, Foreign Ministry, Economic Affairs Bureau, *Indoneshia* (Tokyo: Nihon Kokusai Mondai Kenkyūjo, 1972), p. 117.

17. *Shūkan Asahi*, November 28, 1969, p. 23.

18. *Asahi Shinbun*, October 12, 1970.

19. On September 2, 1948 to the Working Body of the then Indonesian Parliament (KNIP) the government mentioned the Indonesian "right to take an independent position." On September 21, 1950 the Natsir cabinet favored in parliament an "independent policy, not an opportunistic policy." On May 28 of the following year the Sukiman cabinet indicated that an independent policy was not one based on the principle of neutralism. "An active independent policy" became a slogan on May 22, 1952 when the Wilop cabinet stated that independent positions should connotate active attitudes. The historical development of "an active independent policy" is described in J. M. Anton Soewarso, "Politik Bebas Aktif," *Research Publikasi*, I, no. 1 (1969): 12–14.

20. The texts of their addresses appear in Indonesia, Foreign Ministry, *Asia-Africa Speaks from Bandung* (Jakarta, n.p. 1955 [?]), pp. 19–29; and pp. 31–39. Little attention likewise is given to Japan and its activities in the conference, mentioned in the classic study by George Kahin, *The Asia-African Conference, Bandung, Indonesia, April 1955* (Ithaca, N.Y.: Cornell University Press, 1956).

21. Noto Isamu, Director-General of JETRO (Japan External Trade Organization), private interview in Jakarta, December 13, 1971.

22. *Japan Statistical Yearbook 1949*, p. 518.

23. *Sōgō enerugī tōkei 1968*, pp. 144–145.

24. *Sōgō enerugī tōkei 1971*, pp. 170–171.

25. These two percentages are respectively, 57 percent and 69.1 percent in 1960, 48.0 percent and 56.3 percent in 1965, and 75.2 percent and 49.9 percent in 1970.

26. Obtained from column (1) of Table 5 (Japanese oil imports from Indonesia) divided by the first column of Table 2 (Indonesia's total exports).

27.   *Keizai yōran 1970*, p. 242.
28.   *Jiji nenkan 1968*, p. 910; and *Jiji nenkan 1971*, p. 1076.
29.   Indonesian Embassy, Tokyo, *Laporan Tahunan 1961, 1963, 1966*, and *1969*.
30.   Indonesia, Central Bureau of Statistics, *Almanak Indonesia 1968*, I, 511–519.
31.   Takeda Shigesaburō, ed., *Jagatara kanwa* (Nagasaki: By the editor, 1968), pp. 20–23. The first Japanese consulate general was established in Java in 1909, soon after the Russo-Japanese War of 1904–1905.
32.   Ibid.
33.   Ibid.
34.   "Representatives of Japanese Firms and Banks in Jakarta as of October 1, 1963" (mimeographed), prepared unofficially by the Jakarta office of the JETRO (Japan External Trade Organization), lists 48 entries. "Daftar Nama Pengusaha2 Djepang, DSB," prepared by the Indonesia-Japan Friendship Society (LPIJ) in 1964, lists 58 entries. The inaugural meeting of the Japan Club of Jakarta—a sort of mini-Japanese Chamber of Commerce and Industry in Jakarta—took place in late April 1965, when 43 firms registered with the club, according to its office record.
35.   Out of 692 Japanese living in Indonesia in 1963, 412 lived in Jakarta, 170 in Medan but only 30 in Surabaya. See Japan, Foreign Ministry, Asian Affairs Bureau, ed., *Indoneshia Kyōwakoku benran* (Tokyo: Nihon Kokusai Mondai Kenkyūjo, 1964), p. 170. In 1970, 640 out of a total of 1,485 Japanese nationals lived in Jakarta, according to information obtained from the Japanese Consulate-General, December 10, 1970.
36.   *Indoneshia Kyōwakoku benran* (1964), pp. 204–205.
37.   For 1960, 1961, 1962, 1963, and 1964, see respectively, Japan, Foreign Ministry, *Waga gaikō no kinkyō*, no. 5 (1961): 82; no. 6 (1962): 100; no. 7 (1963): 101; no. 8 (1964): 95; and no. 8 (1964): 96.
38.   Sukarno, *Sukarno, An Autobiography as Told to Cindy Adams* (Indianapolis, Indiana: The Bobbs-Merrill Co., 1965), p. 295.
39.   Ōda Takio, "Kokoro no atatakai shin no ningen—Sukaruno shi o itamu," *Nihon Keizai Shinbun*, June 22, 1970.
40.   The Dwikora Cabinet formed on August 27, 1964, had 111 cabinet posts (or 92 ministerial positions plus 19 positions of ministerial rank). The cabinet was reshuffled on March 28, 1966 and had 104 cabinet posts (87 department representatives plus 17 posts of ministerial rank). Calculated from Indonesia, Department of Information, *Susunan Kabinet 1945–1970* (Jakarta: Pradnya Paramita, 1970), pp. 32–42.
41.   The countries visited were Turkey, Poland, Sweden, Denmark, the Soviet Union, Hungary, Italy, Portugal, Senegal, Brazil, Argentina, Mexico, the United States, Japan, Cambodia, and North Vietnam, in that order. See *Indoneshia Kyōwakoku benran* (1964), p. 204.
42.   Ibid., p. 205.
43.   For instance in 1966 some 223,000 Americans visited Japan while 55,000 Japanese visited the United States. See *Asahi nenkan 1969*, p. 222.
44.   *Laporan Tahunan 1966*, p. 77.

Chapter 2
Formal Reparations Negotiations and the Kishi-Sukarno Settlement, 1951–1958

The peace treaty and the reparations agreement between Japan and Indonesia were signed on January 20, 1958 and diplomatic relations officially began on April 15. To reach this stage, the two countries had had to carry on long negotiations, which had begun nearly seven years earlier at the San Francisco Peace Conference in September 1951. For Indonesia these were the longest negotiations it had ever held, save those over the West Irian territory which lasted from 1945 through 1962. For Japan too, the negotiations stretched out into the lengthiest war reparations talks it had held with the Asian nations.[1]

An examination of the negotiations process from September 1951 to December 1957 reveals that first, despite Japan's initial commitment to pay war reparations to Indonesia, it did not consider them seriously until mid-1957; second, while prolonging the negotiations, Japan made a flexible interpretation of the San Francisco Peace Treaty, which stipulated that the reparations should be in the form of services, and decided also to pay them in capital goods; and third, Japan reduced Indonesia's original claim of $17.5 billion to $800 million (including economic aid and cancellation of Indonesia's outstanding trade debt). A survey of the negotiations also shows that Indonesia's position changed from one demanding reparations to one requesting them. Behind the scenes of the negotiations is seen the role of the lobbyists, among whom were former wartime Japanese officers, prominent industrialists, and their Indonesian friends. This phase of informal lobbying will be discussed in chapter 3.

THE EARLY NEGOTIATION TALKS, 1951–1956

The San Francisco Peace Conference, September 1951

The San Francisco Peace Conference offered Japan the opportunity to regain its position in the international community after the Allied Occupation. The conference also offered Indonesia the opportunity to terminate the prevailing state of war with Japan. Nonetheless, the conference stirred up controversy in both nations. Japan's Socialist party, the largest opposition party, advocated a neutralist foreign policy and opposed the peace conference, complaining that it would not lead to peace in the Far East unless the People's Republic of China were invited, and that the peace treaty was concerned solely with the protection of American interests in the western Pacific and its domination of Japan. Indonesia's official, newly pronounced foreign policy of "active independence" also was at odds with the American-controlled conference, and there was much debate before the country finally decided to send a delegation.[2] Indonesia's internal political climate also did not completely favor its participation in the conference and the Indonesian Nationalist party (PNI) particularly opposed it. Nevertheless, the Western-oriented Masjumi party cabinet led by Sukiman Wirjosandjojo finally decided on August 24 to send a delegation.

The United States did not want to discuss the content of the Peace Treaty at the conference but wanted only to use it as the site for signing the treaty which already had been drawn up.[3] This was to ward off opposition by the Communist bloc, which the United States and its Western allies feared might hamper the proceedings of the conference. On August 6, 1951, when Indonesia received the draft of the peace treaty from the United States, it responded with five requests, two of which were accepted.[4] The first was that the treaty include a specific clause recognizing Japan's right to sovereignty and the second, that Indonesia be entitled to Japanese reparations. The United States objected to Indonesia's request for a referendum of former Japanese territories to ascertain whether they wished to become part of Japan. This request Indonesia placed when it received by telegram such desire from the Okinawan people. The United States also objected to inviting the People's Republic of China to the conference, and lastly turned down Indonesia's request to hold debates at the conference on the text of the treaty.

Indonesia recognized the People's Republic of China in April 1950 and assumed a neutralist position similar to that of India and Burma. While Indonesia was debating whether it should go to San Francisco, India and Burma declared that they would not go but that they would sign separate bilateral peace treaties with Japan, a decision which pressured Indonesia to follow suit.

The Sukiman Cabinet, in considering the cordial relations between Indonesia and the United States, could not ignore the decisive role that the latter had played in the United Nations in bringing about the "transfer of sovereignty" from the Netherlands to Indonesia less than two years earlier. Nor could Indonesia neglect the possible advantage of again using American influence to regain the disputed West Irian areas from the Netherlands. Therefore, the Sukiman Cabinet sent a delegation but ordered it to attend only and not to sign the treaty unless later instructed. In this way Indonesia tried to avoid possibly unfavorable reactions by India and Burma and at the same time tried to satisfy the United States, which was eager for as many participants as possible.

On September 6 the executive committee of the Masjumi party, the majority party, decided in favor of signing the treaty by seventeen votes to fourteen. The following day the second strongest party, the PNI, voted unanimously against signing the treaty. Subardjo telephoned Prime Minister Sukiman from San Francisco, advising his cabinet to vote for signing the treaty. Finally, the Masjumi-controlled cabinet, also meeting that day, voted for signing, sixteen to six, with all the PNI ministers opposed. Subardjo thus was instructed to sign the treaty.

Subardjo thus signed the treaty.[5] Prior to a speech by the Indonesian delegation head, Foreign Minister Ahmad Subardjo, in which he stated Indonesia's position on the peace treaty, Indonesia asked the United States for assurance of Japan's payment of reparations. Ali Sastroamidjojo, then ambassador to the United States, spoke with Dean Rusk, then assistant secretary of state for Far Eastern affairs, who said that the decision regarding payment of reparations rested with Japan and suggested that the Indonesian delegation meet with the Japanese. The United States did not want to commit itself yet to this guarantee, for it had no data on how much damage was caused in Indonesia during the war and hoped that Japan would not have to pay much because that would mean more American aid to Japan. The Japanese delegation appeared reluctant to have a meeting, deeming that the Indonesians should come to them if they wanted to talk. The Indonesian delegation thought that it was the Japanese who should come and talk, as it was they who were in the subordinate position. However, perhaps due to Rusk's pressure, Prime Minister Yoshida Shigeru and his party went to see the Indonesians at their hotel on September 5. Yoshida did deliver a pledge from the Japanese government to pay reparations to Indonesia, but there was no discussion of the amount of the payment either in this meeting or in the conference.

On September 6 in the conference, Subardjo delivered a speech in which he stressed the importance of Japanese reparations as a prerequisite to a peace treaty with Japan.[6] He said: "... my government wishes to obtain the assurance that, subsequent to the conclusion of the Peace Treaty, it will be able to conclude an agreement with Japan which will set out in greater detail than is provided in the Peace Treaty, the terms under which Japan will pay for war damages to Indonesia, and an agreement concerning fishing and fisheries." He declared further that Japan's response "will greatly influence my government in determining its position in regard to the signing of the treaty." Subardjo then directly asked the Japanese delegation whether, immediately following the peace conference, Japan would negotiate a separate, bilateral reparations agreement with Indonesia, stipulating the amounts and specific terms of payment. Prime Minister Yoshida accepted all of Indonesia's demands.[7]

Indonesia anticipated that the United States in some way would oversee Japan's reparations payments to Indonesia. For instance, Ambassador to Great Britain Subandrio felt that the United States might help Indonesia to secure reparations from Japan in the same way it helped its World War I allies secure reparations from Germany by formulating the Dawes Plan in 1924 and the Young Plan in 1929.[8] Subandrio thus felt that Indonesia should have signed the peace treaty as that would have put the United States in a more likely position of guaranteeing Japan's reparations payments.[9]

The Djuanda Mission, December 1951–January 1952

After the San Francisco Peace Conference, Japan immediately was obliged to open reparations negotiations with Indonesia. At the conference, Foreign Minister Subardjo had stated that the damage and suffering caused by the Japanese during the war amounted to a loss of four million Indonesian lives and "billions of dollars." Later the Djuanda Mission estimated Indonesia's damages at $17.5 billion.[10]

Indonesia's first reparations mission was headed by Djuanda Kartawidjaja, minister of communications and later prime minister, and was in Tokyo from December 15, 1951 to January 18, 1952 to investigate Japan's economic conditions and to ascertain Japan's capability to pay reparations to Indonesia. While the mission was evaluating Japan's capital goods and industrial facilities, it suggested, on December 22, that the goods and use of the industrial facilities be considered part of reparations payment. It argued that Japan's capital goods could be included in the category of "services of the Japanese people" as stipulated in Article 14 of the San Francisco Peace Treaty.

The Indonesians made a general demand of $17.5 billion in reparations in capital goods and services. In reply, the Yoshida government interpreted Article 14 literally and opposed the payment of war debts through capital goods, arguing that Japan's goods and industries were indispensable to its own economic recovery. It regarded Indonesia's demand of $17.5 billion as far too high, nearly equal to Japan's 1952 gross national product of $17.39 billion. In addition, Japan that year had foreign currency reserves of only $979 million, with exports worth $1,273 million and imports worth $2,028 million.[11] In contrast, at the end of 1951 Indonesia had reserves of $511 million and in 1952, $314 million.[12] Indonesia's demand for $17.5 billion in reparations obviously was inflated. Many Japanese leaders even agreed with Wajima Eiji, director of the Asian Affairs Bureau and a principal negotiator with the Djuanda Mission, who thought that Japan should not have to pay any reparations because it never actually fought with Indonesia.[13]

The Djuanda Mission had come to a stalemate.[14] After a reminder by Wajima that Japan had made no written commitment of the exact amount of reparations, Ali Sastroamidjojo, who had flown in from Washington to assist the mission, then contacted the United States embassy in Tokyo. He met with U. Alexis Johnson, director of the Office of Northeast Asian Affairs, who said that he would refer the matter to the State Department and request a reexamination of the San Francisco Peace Conference proceedings. After learning that Japan indeed had made no written commitment about the amount but had replied affirmatively to Indonesia's demand for negotiations on fisheries as well as on war debts, Johnson suggested to the Japanese government that there be some agreement, if only to offset a complete failure by the mission. He invited both parties to his own residence for an evening, and on January 17, 1952, an interim agreement was written just before the otherwise unsuccessful Djuanda Mission left Japan. This interim agreement was only provisional, however, as Japan was waiting for the other claimant nations in Southeast Asia to submit their demands.

On April 3, 1952 Wilopo, belonging to the PNI, succeeded Prime Minister Sukiman of the Masjumi party. On May 17 Wilopo postponed indefinitely the ratification of the San Francisco Peace Treaty and postponed to endorse the interim reparations agreement. Thus the Djuanda Mission was disbanded and the first round of negotiations ended. Indonesia now supported a separate, bilateral peace treaty following India's and Burma's examples.

It should be noted that John M. Allison was ambassador to Japan from 1953 to 1956 while the reparations talks between Japan and Indonesia were in progress. From February 1957 to February 1958,

Allison was ambassador to Indonesia. This invites the speculation that Allison might have acted as mediator between the two parties although he himself denies this.[15] In 1971 an American government official in Jakarta told me that he thought that Ambassador Allison had maintained close contact with both sides.[16]

The next five years, from 1952 to 1956, saw many changes during the negotiations between Japan and Indonesia. In 1954 Japan settled on a payment of $200 million to Burma, in 1956 on a payment of $550 million to the Philippines, and in that same year Indonesia proposed a settlement of $550 million for war damages and $250 million in loans.

Japan's Reinterpretation of Article 14 after October 1952

During 1952 little progress was made in the negotiations, although the Japanese made some concessions. In October, Foreign Minister Okazaki Katsuo stated in a foreign policy speech that Japan's reparations should be established on a political level and that Japan would be flexible in its interpretation of "the services of the Japanese people."[17] After this concession was announced, Wajima Eiji was sent in November to Southeast Asia to determine these nations' reparations demands but was not successful.[18]

In October 1953 Foreign Minister Okazaki himself went to Manila, Rangoon, and Jakarta. Besides the inclusion of capital goods in the category of "services" and a payment period of ten to twenty years, he offered reparations of $250 million to the Philippines, $60 million to Burma, and $125 million to Indonesia. On October 3 while in Jakarta, Foreign Minister Okazaki talked with Prime Minister Ali Sastroami- djojo, who now claimed $17.2 billion.[19] Although an exact figure could not be reached, the two leaders agreed to draw up a bilateral peace treaty and to schedule the reparations payments over ten to twenty years. Soon after this meeting the Ali Cabinet dispatched a second fact- finding mission to Japan. Headed by Sudarsono, chief of the Asia and Pacific Bureau of the Foreign Ministry, this mission was to determine Japan's capacity to meet Indonesia's demands and to reach an interim agreement on Japan's assistance in salvaging vessels sunk in Indonesian waters. Negotiations on the salvaging of sunken ships began on November 2 and were led by Sudarsono and Ōno Katsumi, counselor in the Foreign Ministry. Two weeks later an interim agreement was made and Sudarsono went back to Indonesia on November 24. On December 10 Sudarsono returned to Japan to sign the agreement on December 16 with Okumura Katsuzō, a vice-minister in the Foreign Ministry.

On March 17, 1954 the Japanese Diet ratified the interim agree- ment on ship salvaging and awaited its cosigner's ratification. The

Indonesian government was not satisfied with the agreement, however, and never moved to ratify it.[20] It insisted that the exact amount of reparations first should be determined and clung to the original demand of $17.5 billion.

In the Ōno-Sudarsono talks in November 1953, it was agreed that a representative of the Japanese government would be sent to Jakarta to maintain closer ties with the Indonesian government. Wajima Eiji was selected and went to Jakarta on January 4, 1954 as a special envoy to negotiate future diplomatic relations between Japan and Indonesia.[21] His duty was not only to discuss the reparations issues but was also to establish diplomatic relations with Indonesia.

Wajima continued his argument that since Japan had not actually fought with Indonesia, it should not have to pay reparations, and, furthermore, Indonesia had taken possession of all the materials that the Japanese government and people had brought over during the war. His position was that Japan should provide some assistance as a gesture of regret for the mental anguish—not the physical damage—that Japan might have caused by occupying Indonesia for three-and-a-half years. This was not solely Wajima's view. Although Yoshida had promised at San Francisco that Japan would pay reparations to Indonesia, many Japanese political and business leaders disagreed over whether Japan should have to pay reparations at all. Prime Minister Yoshida felt that Japan should pay but that there was no hurry. A special envoy, Ogata Taketora, visited Southeast Asia in the spring of 1952 and upon his return urged that Japan should adopt a wait-and-see position regarding this politically unstable area, rather than quickly settling the reparations.[22]

In February 1953, urged by a member of the Diet to speed up reparations settlements with Southeast Asia, Prime Minister Yoshida answered that the damages inflicted upon Asia by several years of war with Japan could not be repaired immediately despite Japan's willingness to do so.[23] Obviously Japan had no intention of hastening the settlement. The Japanese government also felt that if reparations to Indonesia were paid at all they should be paid through commercial loans and private investments. These plus the exchange of Japanese imports for Indonesian raw materials would develop the Indonesian economy by means of Japanese technology and capital.[24] Therefore Wajima did not negotiate seriously with Indonesia except to try to persuade it to lower its claim from $17.5 billion. This, not unexpectedly, irritated Indonesia, and early in 1954 began tightening the residence requirements for Japanese nationals living in Indonesia and hinted that it would refuse to pay its $16 million trade debt to Japan.[25] On June 30 when Indonesia actually stated its refusal, Japan began considering restrictions on imports from Indonesia. In early July Indonesia proposed talks on the trade-debt issue, thereby complicating the reparations issue even further. Indonesia's political climate continued to be unstable and constructive discussion was impossible.

The Afro-Asian conference, held in Bandung in April 1955, provided a new opportunity for the two governments to discuss these issues. Takasaki Tatsunosuke, head of the Japanese delegation, held talks with Indonesia's Foreign Minister Sunario, also a leader of the PNI. Takasaki pressed for a more realistic reparations claim in view of Japan's economic condition. He reportedly remarked that Japan's payment to Indonesia would be somewhere between those to the Philippines and Burma. In April 1954 Burma had concluded a separate, bilateral peace treaty with Japan and had agreed to compensation of $200 million, $20 million annually for 10 years starting in April 1955. Negotiations between Japan and the Philippines at that time were approaching an agreement in which Japan would pay $550 million over 20 years.

Indonesia's Demand of $1 Billion in April 1955

The Takasaki-Sunario talks had a more positive outcome at least for Japan as Indonesia's reparations claim dropped drastically from $17.5 billion to $1 billion. But this was still too high for Japan. Indonesia became anxious without a settlement in sight, without which its economic development would be delayed, and then the Ali Cabinet fell.[26] In the meantime Japan maintained a wait-and-see attitude due to the coming general elections to be held in late September. Prime Minister Harahap stated that negotiations should be resumed without waiting for the results of the general elections on September 29 and refrained from referring to Indonesia's new claim of $1 billion.

In the fall of 1955 Foreign Minister Ide Anak Agung Gde Agung, or Anak Agung, delivered a new reparations proposal to the Harahap Cabinet. The amount should not be less than the Philippines claim and would include Indonesia's trade debt of $180 million, as well as capital goods worth $200 million, consumer goods worth $300 million, services worth $50 million, and loans of $70 million, totaling $800 million.[27] Before the Harahap Cabinet could decide on this, though, it fell on March 26, 1956.

After Japan made a reparations agreement with the Philippines in May 1956, it paid more attention to its negotiations with Indonesia.[28] In May Wajima and Sukardjo tried to discuss the terms of payment but to no avail as Indonesia insisted that Japan first state the amount of payment, which Japan would not do. In June Wajima was summoned back to Tokyo for further consultations. The Japanese government outlined a new proposal that would put the total amount somewhere between the settlements of the Philippines and Burma, that would pay the reparations in the form of capital goods and services, and that might include Indonesia's trade debt to Japan as part of the reparations talks.[29] Indonesia informally decided to demand at least as much as the Philippines payment. Upon his return to Jakarta on August 16, Wajima stated that Japan would pay $250 million in war indemnifications but that it would not cancel Indonesia's trade debt of $180 million. In the meantime, in mid-August, Japanese Foreign Minister Shigemitsu Mamoru and his Indonesian counterpart, Roeslan Abdulgani, who both had gone to London to attend the Suez Conference, held an informal meeting. According to the latter, Shigemitsu was noncommittal and not ready to change Japan's tactic to delay the negotiations.[30]

At this point, Indonesia withdrew its claim for the same amount as the Philippines had received and talked in terms of $400 to $500 million. There still were so many differences in the terms of the loans and the trade-debt settlement that Wajima's negotiations with Maramis, director of the Asia and Pacific Bureau, did not progress. In the meantime Japan's political situation became muddled as Prime Minister Hatoyama's controversial efforts to establish diplomatic relations with the Soviet Union had caused fighting within the ruling party over who should be his successor. Wajima was forced to postpone the reparations talks until a new cabinet was formed. Finally a successor to Hatoyama was chosen, Ishibashi Tanzan, and he selected a new cabinet on December 23, 1956. Because of a sudden illness, however, Foreign Minister Kishi Nobusuke succeeded Ishibashi on February 25, 1957 and with Kishi's emergence as prime minister, the prospects of the reparations talks turned brighter.

KISHI AND THE REPARATIONS AGREEMENT OF 1958

The Kishi government took a more serious attitude toward the reparations issue than the previous governments had. The importance of improving Japan's relations with Southeast Asia often had been debated in and out of government circles, but now that Japan had restored diplomatic relations with the Soviet Union and had entered the United Nations, the time seemed ripe to make peace with Indonesia.

Japan still considered its relations with the rest of Asia as of only secondary importance, regarding its relations with the United States as paramount to its defense as well as to its economy. But in order to strengthen Japan's position toward the United States, Kishi found it necessary to restore normal diplomatic relations and to enlarge Japan's presence in the other Asian countries. Indonesia's potentially large market for Japanese exports as well as its rich natural resources continued to be a great attraction to Japan. By 1956 Indonesia had accumulated a trade debt to Japan of $180 million, and it was in Japan's interest to settle this debt and to promote its exports.

In 1957 Indonesia appeared as eager as Japan was to settle the war reparations problem. Indonesia's economy deteriorated as the government intensified its anti-Dutch campaign for its territorial claim to West Irian. Its foreign currency holdings had dropped from $511 million in 1951 to $255 million in 1956.[31] By 1957 only Indonesia and South Vietnam had not agreed upon their war debt from Japan. It was not to Indonesia's advantage to prolong these negotiations and to delay the utilization of the reparations. Therefore, in 1957 talks began again although Indonesia's feeling of urgency had weakened its bargaining position.

Japan's $200 Million against Indonesia's $400 Million, and the Winoto Mission, January–July 1957

On January 16, 1957 Prime Minister Ali agreed with Wajima that formal negotiations should be held at the ministerial level. On February 5 Wajima submitted to the Indonesian government an offer of $200 million in reparations and $100 million in lieu of Indonesia's trade debt, $500 million in nongovernmental economic cooperation, plus $70 million in government loans.[32] On the following day Indonesia's Foreign Ministry revised the offer to $300 million in reparations, $110 million in lieu of the trade debt, $500 million in economic aid, and $60 million in loans.[33] On February 26 Prime Minister Ali made a proposal similar to the Foreign Ministry's, except that he lowered the economic aid allotment to $400 million.[34] Wajima did not accept the $300 million in reparations and stood by his original offer of $200 million.[35] On March 8 Prime Minister Ali amended his proposal to $250 million in reparations and $450 million in economic cooperation,[36] but on March 13 the Ali Cabinet collapsed.

A new cabinet was formed on April 9, headed by Djuanda Kartawidjaja with Subandrio as the foreign minister. The Djuanda Cabinet, which first met on May 3, 1957, endorsed the proposal submitted by the previous cabinet on March 8. Because this endorsement had encountered much opposition outside the cabinet, however, the Djuanda Cabinet later decided to reexamine the proposal and summoned back from Tokyo its consul general, Iskandar Ishak. On July 2 still another proposal was issued: this one requested $400 million in reparations and $400 million in economic aid which would include

Indonesia's trade debt to Japan.[37] This represented an increase of $100 million over the previous proposal. Ishak returned to Tokyo on July 8 and on July 13 delivered the Djuanda proposal to Prime Minister Kishi.

The selection of the Djuanda Cabinet had not involved the participation of Indonesia's political parties, which on previous occasions had submitted a list of nominees for cabinet posts. This time the ministers in the Djuanda Cabinet had been chosen by President Sukarno himself in a drive to consolidate his power. Although Prime Minister Djuanda had wide knowledge of and experience in economic planning, President Sukarno decided to handle the reparations issue himself. He presented the issue to the National Council (Dewan Nasional), which had been formed on July 12, 1957 as a policy advisory board to the cabinet.[38] But with Sukarno as its chairman, the council became more powerful than the cabinet. Sukarno studied both the Japanese and the Indonesian terms and them drew up a proposal of his own which he asked Roeslan Abdulgani, the vice-chairman and others to discuss with party leaders. After the council endorsed his proposal, it was sent to the cabinet.[39]

Wajima Eiji's position as the chief negotiator of the reparations issue was taken over in late July by Takagi Hiroichi, the new consul general to Indonesia. Previously Takagi had served from 1955 to 1957, as chief of the Reparations Division of the Asian Affairs Bureau in the Foreign Ministry and had handled the reparations payments to Burma and the Philippines. Upon his arrival in Jakarta, Takagi began negotiations in a rather aloof fashion, knowing that there still was no consensus among Japanese leaders as to whether or not their country should pay reparations to Indonesia.[40] He told me that he even told the Indonesian government that Japan did not want to pay reparations to a country in which the Communists were gaining power.[41] Despite the cold reception given to him by the newspapers, Takagi perceived among the Indonesians an attitude favorable to the Japanese, concluded that a swift settlement of the reparations issue would be advantageous to Japan's future economic activities in Indonesia, and urged his government to hasten its decision.[42]

Six years after the San Francisco Peace Conference in which Yoshida had committed Japan to paying reparations to Indonesia, Japan still had not decided whether or not it would pay them. This uncertain, prolonged solution of the reparations issue worried President Sukarno, who was apprehensive of the growing anti-Japanese feeling, which would make the negotiation process harder. He searched for some compromising formula with the Japanese and quietly sent to Tokyo his special envoys, who were Winoto Danuasmoro, his secretary, Elkana Tobing, then legal advisor to the Indonesian Nationalist party, and Adam Malik, then president of Antara News Agency. They were instructed to discuss some formula or terms of payment with prominent Japanese leaders in the government, business, and industrial circles. The contacts made by the presidential envoys successfully convinced the Japanese of the importance of a swift solution, and the envoys reported to the president that the Japanese were willing to pay reparations in accordance with their economic strength. With Takagi's added urging and pressure from other sources (which will be discussed in the following chapter), Japan began to move toward a settlement. In this respect, the crucial role played by the three envoys in the history of the binational reparations negotiation should be given due regard. On September 18, 1957 Foreign Minister Subandrio stopped in Tokyo en route to the United Nations General Assembly in New York and talked with Prime Minister Kishi, emphasizing the psychological effect of Japan's reparations on the Indonesians and mentioning their growing interest in Japan's advanced industrial technology. Kishi in reply suggested a top-level meeting to discuss the issue and requested that Sukarno visit Japan.

The Kobayashi Proposal and Hatta's Visit to Tokyo, September–October 1957

After Subandrio's visit to Tokyo, the Foreign Ministry asked Kobayashi Ataru, a prominent businessman, to go to Southeast Asia as Prime Minister Kishi's personal envoy to evaluate the area's economic and political conditions.[43] Before the Kobayashi party arrived, Shirahata Tomoyoshi, counselor in the Asian Affairs Bureau and a former consul in Surabaya and Jakarta during 1952–1953, went secretly to Jakarta to work out, with Takagi, ways to draw Kobayashi into the problem of reparations to Indonesia.[44]

Shirahata appears to have had enough political good sense to rise above bureaucracy, perhaps in part owing to his experience as the prime minister's secretary from 1953 to 1955. In any case, he should be credited with making Kishi's visit and Kobayashi's work worthwhile. It also was Shirahata who first thought of selecting Kobayashi to handle the reparations issue.[45] Instead of speaking directly with Kobayashi, Shirahata discussed the idea with another influential businessman, Ishihara Hiroichirō, who in turn consulted a third businessman, Matsunaga Yasuzaemon. Matsunaga was regarded as a senior member of the business world, having been responsible for the swift postwar reconstruction of Japan's electrical power administration. It was he who finally suggested to Kobayashi that Kobayashi go to Southeast Asia to help formulate Japan's foreign policy toward this area. Once Kobayashi had made his decision, Shirahata flew ahead to Indonesia to arrange ways in which to involve him in the reparations negotiations.

On September 22 Kobayashi arrived in Jakarta not expecting to negotiate the reparations issue.[46] Takagi and Shirahata took Kobayashi immediately to the Japanese consul general's summer house south of Jakarta, where they tried to persuade him that his mission could not be accomplished without discussing the reparations problem. The United States ambassador, John Allison, also was invited on this side trip and he too stressed the importance of Japan's payment of reparations to Indonesia.[47] According to Takagi, Allison pointed out that the Communist forces did not occupy as significant a position in Indonesia's politics as it might appear from their victories in the recent local elections. Allison also remarked that the United States and Japan should coordinate their efforts in helping Indonesia's economic development, although he added that this should not be revealed to Indonesia.

Convinced, Kobayashi hurriedly drew up a proposal for Indonesia's $177 million trade debt to Japan. His proposal included the collection of these debts in dollars over a twenty-year period with an annual interest of 3 percent, a plan that seemed to satisfy both Jakarta and Tokyo. Kobayashi also proposed that $200 million be paid in reparations in the first ten years and $400 million be extended as economic cooperation by private Japanese groups for ten years after the reparations payment was completed. Prime Minister Djuanda considered Kobayashi's proposal "wise and practical,"[48] as extending Indonesia's payments over twenty years would ease the burden on Japan. Japan's Finance Ministry had strongly opposed the idea of canceling the trade debt through the reparations and had stressed the need to collect it. By collecting the debt in dollars as Kobayashi proposed, Japan's foreign currency holdings would be increased while the 3 percent interest would bring in at least $30 million beyond the debt itself.

Kobayashi, Takagi, and Shirahata thought that a reparations agreement soon would be concluded on the basis of Kobayashi's proposal. When Kobayashi returned to Tokyo on October 11, he reported to Foreign Minister Fujiyama Aiichirō that Indonesia was ready for serious negotiations. Japan was informed that Mohammed Hatta, a still influential former vice-president, would visit Tokyo in mid-October, and the Japanese government prepared for the conclusion of a reparations agreement.

Hatta's visit to Japan, which lasted from October 16 to 29, was made in a private capacity as he had resigned his governmental position as vice-president of the republic in December 1956. Responsible for Hatta's resignation were the great differences between him and his old coworker for independence, President Sukarno. There had been several attempts at reconcilliation, and in September 1957 when the National Conference on Development (Musyawarah Nasional Pembangunan) convened, Hatta and Sukarno seemed to be in agreement. At the end of the conference they signed a joint statement praising the "Indonesian Revolution," but it was only a sham. Sukarno was determined not to give Hatta any real political power, and Hatta finally succumbed to "letting Sukarno try to run things his way."[49] Before a nine-member committee, appointed by the conference, was able to create a working relationship between the two leaders, Hatta had made a trip to Peking and then had come to Tokyo.

On October 12, 1957, just before Hatta's arrival, Sudjono, director of the Asia and Pacific Bureau, and Djanamar Adjam, the senior officer in charge of reparations in the Foreign Ministry, also were sent to Tokyo by Prime Minister Djuanda.[50] When Prime Minister Kishi, Foreign Minister Fujiyama, and Director Itagaki of the Asian Affairs Bureau talked with Hatta, he agreed with the basic forms of Kobayashi's proposal. But it did not seem that Hatta could be working in accord with Sudjono and Adjam who had expressed dissatisfaction with the proposal. Dismayed, Hatta left Japan and shortly afterwards Sudjono and Adjam departed, also achieving nothing. It was rumored in Japan that this was because Sukarno did not want Hatta to be credited with the long-sought reparations agreement and thus sent Sudjono and Adjam to stifle the negotiations. This would be one of the few instances that the conflict between Sukarno and Hatta was revealed in diplomatic matters.

Kishi's Visit, November 1957

Not being able to fathom Indonesia's position, Prime Minister Kishi wanted to try the Kobayashi proposal again and sent Kobayashi back to Jakarta. Kishi selected him on the basis that he, Kishi, could not afford to have his major political opponent, Ikeda Hayato, blame him for the mishandling of the issue. It was known that Kobayashi favored Ikeda, and Kishi found it expedient to have his opponent share (albeit indirectly) any repercussions that might ensue. Kobayashi decided to go on the understanding that he personally would not be held responsible for the possible failure of the negotiations.[51] He was accompanied to Indonesia by his secretary Mizuno Sōhei, and Nishijima Shigetada, a wartime political analyst in the navy, and was assisted by Shirahata Tomoyoshi and Tsurumi Kiyohiko, the Japanese consul already in Jakarta. The Kobayashi party was to arrive in Indonesia on November 25, the day before Prime Minister Kishi planned to visit, in order to pave the way for Kishi's top-level discussions with Indonesian leaders.

On November 17, a meeting was held among Kishi, Kobayashi, and Ichimada Hisato, Japan's finance minister. They agreed that Japan's policy would follow the Kobayashi proposal of $200 million in reparations, $200 million in long-term loans (the collection of Indonesia's trade debt) and $400 million in economic aid. Ichimada previously had opposed cancellation of the trade debt but now favored it, because he thought that collecting the debt from a country already deficient in foreign currency holdings would only create new problems and complicate the issue. Kishi, though, opposed cancellation by saying that Japan should not change its position at this stage.[52] Before Kishi left for Indonesia, Kawashima Shōjirō, the ruling party's secretary, announced on November 18 that the Kishi government did not have to settle the reparations issue "at any cost" during Kishi's upcoming visit,[53] adding, however, that Kishi had been granted the authority to draw up an agreement with Indonesia if one should arise.[54] This statement was intended to strengthen Kishi's and Kobayashi's bargaining positions before the talks commenced.

Besides Kobayashi's official mission to work on the reparations issue, he and Nishijima wanted to evaluate Indonesia's internal affairs. En route to Jakarta on the November trip, they stopped in Singapore where they met secretly with E. S. Pohan, a leader of the Sumatran group, to explain that Japan's reparations were to be used for all of Indonesia and were not earmarked especially for the Sukarno group or for the Sumatran group, as suspected.[55] Since late 1956, military and political forces outside Java had become openly critical of Sukarno's government and his lack of interest in their regions. They disapproved of Sukarno's leftist leanings and in December 1956, these forces organized the autonomous Buffalo Council (Dewan Banteng).[56] The council gradually mobilized support locally and abroad, their foreign contacts often made in Singapore through Pohan.

Upon arriving in Jakarta on November 22, 1957, a few days before Kobayashi and Kishi, it was from an acquaintance made while consul in Surabaya and Jakarta that Shirahata learned confidentially of the anti-Kishi movements in Jakarta. Members of the radical Murba party whom Shirahata had known were planning to stage anti-Kishi demonstrations, but Shirahata managed to have them stop overt anti-Kishi campaigns.[57] Consul General Takagi naturally opposed this, but Shirahata went anyway "for a rest," and succeeded in stopping both the anti-Kishi and anti-Sukarno campaigns.

Shirahata also was told confidentially that within a week the Indonesian government might sever diplomatic relations with the Netherlands because of the West Irian issue.[58] This information, too, might have been relevant to the reparations issue, so Shirahata passed it on to Kobayashi and Kishi, who decided to limit their talks with Sukarno to a general discussion of the settlement. The tenor of the Kishi-Sukarno talks was revealed in the November 28 joint communique, as will be seen later. On December 1 as expected, Sukarno announced strong economic measures against the Dutch, including the halt of Dutch shipping operations within the area of Indonesia.

Kobayashi arrived in Indonesia on November 25 and Kishi on the following day. On November 26 the Indonesian cabinet held a meeting in which they apparently discussed Kobayashi's latest proposal. After the meeting Information Minister Sudibjo announced that the talks between Prime Ministers Djuanda and Kishi set for November 27 would be informal.[59] Both the Kishi and the Kobayashi parties met with Prime Minister Djuanda on November 27 to discuss Kobayashi's proposal. Although both parties had been scheduled to meet with Sukarno later that morning, Sukarno suddenly requested a private, closed meeting with only Kishi. Only Takagi, as his interpreter, accompanied him.[60]

In this meeting Sukarno stated that Indonesia wanted Japan to pay reparations of $400 million and $400 million in economic aid. This would total $800 million, the amount Japan paid to the Philippines ($550 million in reparations and $250 million in loans). Kishi objected, saying that Japan could not pay much more than $200 million, the amount paid to Burma. Sukarno then suggested that the nominal reparations be $400 million but that the actual amount be $400 million minus $170 million for Indonesia's trade debt. Takagi disagreed because this amount, $230 million, would exceed Japan's estimation of $200 million by $30 million. However, the formula of subtracting trade debts from the nominal reparations of $400 million proposed by Sukarno was exactly what Kishi sought. Takagi tried to point out that since $170 million in trade debts actually amounted to some $240 million including interest, the reparations should be $160 million ($400 million minus $240 million, not $400 million minus $170 million). Kishi turned down Takagi's suggestion, declaring it "trivial." The Kishi-Sukarno talks ended with Kishi's concession of $30 million more for reparations and with the cancellation of Indonesia's trade debt. Sukarno had declared earlier that he would settle the reparations issue and apparently he had.

The agenda of Kishi's visit was vague. The purpose of his visit allegedly was goodwill, but everyone knew that the reparations issue was the real purpose. To maintain the facade, President Sukarno was not present at the airport for Kishi's arrival, Kishi's later meeting with him was termed only a courtesy call, and the reparations talks were labeled as informal. The joint communique issued by Prime Ministers Djuanda and Kishi on November 28, prior to Kishi's departure, did not reveal the amounts of Japan's reparations and loans to Indonesia; it did not even disclose that a final settlement had been made. It merely stated that they "finally reached a mutual understanding on the basic principles of its settlement." Kobayashi was to remain in Jakarta to proceed with negotiations "for a speedy conclusion of the reparations agreement" and "for an early establishment of normal diplomatic relations."[61] Only a few days later did the press and the public learn that Kishi and Sukarno indeed had settled on the amount of $230 million in reparations.[62] According to an Indonesian newspaper, the Japanese government had confirmed this rumor on December 1, and, in turn, Indonesia's Deputy Foreign Minister Hardi also had confirmed it.[63] Thus the Kobayashi proposal had become worthless, making unnecessary all the hard work that Kobayashi, Shirahata, Takagi, and Nishijima had done since September.

The Kobayashi-Djuanda Memorandum, December 8, 1957

Kobayashi and his party had little choice but to help the Kishi government settle the matter. Before his departure from Tokyo, Shirahata was told by Ikeda Hayato to see that there was no mishandling of the matter lest Kobayshi's reputation—and indirectly Ikeda's—be tarnished.[64] Yet to leave Indonesia and withdraw from the negotiations would reveal the tension and disagreement between Kishi and Kobayashi, which is to say, the tension between the two competing factions of the ruling party. To bring intraparty strife into the diplomatic arena would not enhance Kobayashi's prestige at home or abroad, even if it would increase Ikeda's power over Kishi.

Kobayashi remained in Indonesia until December 8. His work centered on the establishment of a fifteen-year payment period for the reparations and on the inclusion of a "most-favored-nation" clause in the peace treaty. Japan had had a bad experience with the treaty it had signed with the Philippines because it did not contain a most-favored-nation clause. This was unsatisfactory to the opposition party and delayed ratification of both it and the reparations agreement. Apparently Indonesia did not understand the meaning of a "most-favored nation" clause, because it maintained that such treatment contradicted its policy of "active independence." Finally Japan substituted "non-discriminatory treatment" for the most-favored-nation clause, but Indonesia still was not pleased. Kobayashi was adamant and prepared to leave on December 7, but Shirahata persuaded him to delay his departure for twenty-four hours. In the early morning of December 7,

Kobayashi called in Nishijima and instructed him to try final efforts to reach agreement with the Indonesians. Nishijima and Shirahata then spoke with Adam Malik who invited two men to meet with them that evening at his residence. These two men were Elkana Tobing and Winoto Danuasumoro, who together with Malik had visited Tokyo earlier in the year as Sukarno's special mission. At the meeting they discussed the major points of the peace treaty but could not reach an agreement over the most-favored-nation clause. The Japanese noted that Kobayashi was prepared to leave Indonesia without an agreement and left Adam Malik's house. Then Tobing contacted Suwirjo, president of the PNI; Malik went to see Djuanda; and Winoto talked with Sukarno. Just before midnight Adam Malik called the Japanese party to tell them that their terms had been accepted.[65]

Indonesia and Japan still could not agree, however, on the length of the reparations payment period: Indonesia insisted on ten years and Japan clung to fifteen. On December 8, before the final session, Takagi, Shirahata, Tsurumi, and Sudjono met to work out the wording of the Kobayashi-Djuanda Memorandum. They again discussed the payment period but to no avail. Finally, as Shirahata told me in 1972, he stated that he would name a certain number somewhere between ten and fifteen, and Sudjono should clap his hands as a sign of acceptance.[66] Takagi became restless, not being sure what number Shirahata was going to choose and was about to stop him when he said, "Twelve!" Sudjono clapped his hands. Shirahata selected this number without consulting either Kobayashi or Tokyo.

The Kobayashi-Djuanda Memorandum was prepared and signed at seven o'clock in the evening of December 8. It stated that Japan's reparations would amount to $225,444,000 over twelve years; that Indonesia's trade debt of $174,556,000 would be canceled, and that a $400 million credit would be granted over twenty years for Indonesia's economic development.[67] The final terms of agreement specified that Japan would pay $20 million annually for the first eleven years and the remainder during the twelfth year. In effect, $400 million would be given as a nonreimbursible grant and another $400 million would be given in reimbursible loans and investments. The Kobayashi-Djuanda Memorandum also stated that the peace treaty would contain a "non-discriminatory-treatment" clause but as a compromise conditioned the clause by saying it "will be brought into conformity with the decisions taken at the Asia-African Conference in Bandung."

On December 9 Foreign Minister Fujiyama requested a special cabinet meeting to approve the Kobayashi-Djuanda Memorandum, and on December 10 the memorandum was approved in Jakarta. Then in late December a Japanese team of specialists directed by Takagi and Tsurumi worked in Jakarta with the Indonesian team to put the memorandum into statutory form. In two weeks, nine documents were formulated, including the reparations agreement and the peace treaty. The reparations agreement stipulated that Japan would pay $223,080,000 over a period of twelve years, would cancel Indonesia's trade debt of $176,920,000,[68] and would give $400,000,000 in economic aid. These documents were signed in Jakarta on January 20, 1958 by Foreign Ministers Fujiyama and Subandrio.

President Sukarno visited Japan from January 29 through February 15, 1958. It was said to be a goodwill visit and "rest," but actually he began to discuss the implementation of the reparations agreement. During Sukarno's visit, the Sumatra Rebellion was conducted against his central government. In the midst of such tension, on March 3, 1958, these documents were presented as bills to the Indonesian Parliament (DPR) for ratification. After some deliberation, they were passed unanimously on March 13.[69]

However, it took the Japanese Diet almost two months to ratify them. Members of the Socialist party, the opposing party, and members of the ruling party who were critical of Kishi had reservations about the documents. The Socialist party argued that $400 million in reparations to Indonesia would be unfair to Burma which got only $200 million. Fujiyama and Shirahata defended the government's position by repeating that the amount of reparations to Indonesia was not $400 million but $223 million that this would not be unfair to Burma.[70] On this issue, the Japanese government seemed to be two-sided. To Indonesia, it stated that the reparations to Indonesia would be $400 million, whereas it told the Socialist party and indirectly Burma that they would be $223 million.

The most-favored-nation clause to be inserted in the peace treaty helped appease the Socialist party and Ikeda Hayato's faction, the major rival faction to Kishi's withing the ruling party. However, the Sumatra Rebellion, which declared a Revolutionary Government of the Republic of Indonesia (PRRI) on February 15, concerned the Socialist party as well as former Prime Minister Ashida Hitoshi, now chairman of the ruling party's Foreign Affairs Committee, and his colleagues in the Diet. Pointing to the unstable political situation in Indonesia, the Socialists thought it wise to delay ratification of the documents. Ashida, being sympathetic to the anticommunist character of the rebellion, argued that ratification of the bills at that point would discourage the rebels, thus harming Japan's national interests in that region. Shirahata again made use of his continued close contact that he had had with

Nishijima, who in turn was communicating with E. S. Pohan in Singapore, who now became a local contact man for the rebels. Seeing the limited strengths of the rebels and judging Japan's national interests to be in seeking Indonesia's integrity under Sukarno's rule, Shirahata strongly suggested to Prime Minister Kishi that the Japanese government give support to Sukarno.[71] It was difficult then to support the Sukarno government when many of the Western countries were hopefully watching the future of the anticommunist rebels. Shirahata's urgings led the prime minister to pronounce Japan's continued commitment to Sukarno. The latter expressed gratitude to Japan. This in part contributed to the "special relationship" between Tokyo and Jakarta. The bills were passed by the National Diet on April 4, and the ratified documents were exchanged in Tokyo on April 15, 1958.[72] On that day, Japan and the Republic of Indonesia officially began diplomatic relations.

AN ASSESSMENT OF THE REPARATIONS NEGOTIATIONS

Chapter 2 has described the process of the official reparations negotiations. One of the most obvious reasons for the failure to reach agreement in the first six years of negotiations was Japan's indefinite position on its war reparations. When Takagi Hiroichi went to Jakarta in July 1957, succeeding Wajima Eiji, the Japanese government's position still was not certain. Japan appeared to have held simultaneously three contradictory views which, not surprisingly, led to confusion and irritation on both sides. One was that Japan should pay reparations within the limits of its economic capacity, which stemmed from the stipulation in Article 14 of the San Francisco Peace Treaty. Japan apparently had forgotten that Indonesia had refused to ratify the treaty partly because of Article 14. The second view was that Japan did not need to pay war reparations to Indonesia at all. Even Prime Minister Yoshida, who had responded affirmatively to Indonesia's demand for reparations at the San Francisco Peace Conference, was not totally opposed to this idea. The third was that the amount of reparations paid to Indonesia should be in proportion to those amounts given to other nations. This idea had been contributed by Itagaki Yoichi, professor of economics at Hitotsubashi University in Tokyo. He had suggested also that the ratio of payment to the Philippines, Indonesia, Burma, and Indochina be $4:3:2:1$.[73] Later in 1957 this ratio was changed to $4:2:1$ for the Philippines, Indonesia, and Burma. But the original reason for the ratio was merely to fit Indonesia's claim somewhere between $200 million and $550 million.

This disagreement was compounded by two other issues. One was

Indonesia's desire to cancel its trade debt to Japan by means of reparations, an issue which Japan did not feel should be made part of its payments. The other issue which discouraged the negotiations was Indonesia's continual political instability. In the period between 1951 and 1956, Japan had had only three cabinets, headed by Yoshida, Hatoyama, and Ishibashi, all of whom belonged to the same Liberal, Democratic, or later, the Liberal-Democratic party. But Indonesia had had five cabinets, headed by Sukiman, Wilopo, Ali, Harahap, and Ali again. Sukiman and Harahap belonged to the Masjumi party, Wilopo and Ali to the PNI, and conflicts between the two parties had persisted throughout this last phase of Indonesia's "liberal-democracy" period from 1949 to 1957. In addition, the Indonesian government had had other problems foreign to the Japanese government; regional secession, economic poverty, and civilian-military leadership conflicts, failure of adoption of the new constitution, and prolonged general elections, among others.

It seems that Japan took advantage of Indonesia's difficulties, for the longer the payment of reparations was delayed, the easier it would be for Japan, especially as its own economy needed time to heal. Furthermore, the attraction of Indonesia's potential resources lessened as Japan became more dependent on the United States as an export market. In 1951, 52 percent of Japan's exports went to Asia but in 1956 decreased to 41 percent. During this same period the proportion of Japan's exports going to Indonesia went from 9.4 percent to 3 percent, whereas its exports to North America increased from 16 percent to 26 percent (see also Tables 1 and 3).

Ideological differences also prolonged the negotiations. Although Japan's pro-American posture and Indonesia's neutralist posture might not have been discussed directly as an underlying cause of disagreement, it was evident to both sides that they could not be political friends— even if they did have common economic goals. For example, the Bandung conference of 1955 was dominated by the developing, neutralist countries, such as India, Burma, and Indonesia, which welcomed the emergence of the People's Republic of China. Sukarno and the Ali Cabinet wanted to use this conference to enhance Indonesia's international position but received no support for this from Japan. When the conference debated a resolution condemning colonialism, Indonesia, along with Communist China and India, joined the "peaceful coexistence" group, which equated "colonialism" with Western colonialism. Japan, on the other hand, sponsored a resolution condemning "all types of colonialism."[74] But in these political conferences Japan was virtually ignored, its image being that of a nation that had turned to anticolonialism only after defeat.[75] Even while demanding $17 billion in reparations from Japan, neither President Sukarno nor Prime Minister Ali referred to Japan in their opening addresses at the Bandung conference.[76]

The only agreements reached by Japan's political and business leaders during this six-year period were to recognize the importance of Indonesi'a natural resources and to see the construction of an economically viable and politically noncommunist Indonesia with the help of Japanese technology and capital. To these Japanese leaders, war reparations to Indonesia were acceptable only on these terms, which they called "economic cooperation." All Japanese business leaders involved in the negotiations including Matsunaga, Ayukawa, Takasaki, and Ishihara, who will be discussed in the following chapter, proposed their terms of payment within the economic cooperation programs, thus tying the future of Indonesia's economy to Japan's.

Despite these many complications, in 1957 the tenor of the negotiations improved. The new Kishi government regarded the reparations settlement with Indonesia as a major diplomatic issue, and in view of its deteriorating economy, Indonesia had softened its demands to requests.

In the settlement of the reparations issue, Japan made two large compromises. One was to pay the reparations not only in the form of "services of the Japanese people" as stipulated in the San Francisco Peace Treaty but also in the form of capital goods. The other was to cancel Indonesia's trade debt to Japan by means of the reparations. Indonesia's largest concession was to lower its estimation of Japanese reparations from $17.5 billion to $223 million. Then, to save Indonesia's face, Indonesia and Japan added $400 million in "economic cooperation" to make Japan's payment appear to be $800 million.

The final agreement, in any case, was more favorable to Japan than to Indonesia. An annual payment of $20 million in services and capital goods constituted only 0.7 percent of Japan's total exports in 1957, although it came to 30 percent of Japan's exports to Indonesia (see Table 3). Obviously Japan's payment of reparations to Indonesia did not interfere with its exports, which were mainly such industrial goods as food, textiles, and clothing, while in reality, the Reparations Agreement virtually forced Indonesia to use Japanese goods. As Table 3 shows, the proportion of Japan's exports to Indonesia's total imports gradually increased from 13.6 percent in 1958, to 20.8 percent in 1962, and to 26.8 percent in 1966.

The reparations talks, which began in 1951 with Indonesia's claims against Japan's war damages, developed after 1954 into the economic aid talks in which Indonesia argued that its trade debt should be discussed as part of the reparations problem. In early 1957, when regional secessionist movements had developed in the Outer Islands, the government also began to feel that the reparations might be used to strengthen its internal political position. The Kishi Cabinet also wished for a stable Indonesia and saw Sukarno as an acceptable leader. To enhance his prestige and increase Japan's position in Asia, Kishi therefore accepted Sukarno's proposal in November 1957. Finally, because the Sumatra Rebellion broke out when the reparations agreement bill was being deliberated in the Diet, the Kishi leadership pushed through its passage in order to use the reparations fund to prop up the Sukarno regime.

NOTES

1. India, Nationalist China, the United States, Great Britain, France, and the Netherlands renounced their rights to Japanese reparations by 1951. Japan concluded negotiations with Burma in 1954, with the Philippines in 1956, with Indonesia in 1958, and with South Vietnam in 1959. Laos and Cambodia renounced their rights in 1959. The longest negotiations took place between Japan and South Korea, which ended only in 1965.

2. "Indonesia—Political Developments since 1950," *Current Notes on International Affairs* 24 (February 1953): 49–62.

3. Ibid.

4. "Text of Indonesian Notes to U.S." (Washington, August 6, 1951), in Japan, Foreign Ministry, Public Information Division, *Collection of Official Foreign Statements on Japanese Peace Treaty* 3 (n.d.): 79.

5. This paragraph based on Ali Sastroamidjojo, private interview in Jakarta, February 28, 1972.

6. The text of Subardjo's speech appears in U.S., Department of State, Office of Public Affairs, *Conference for the Conclusion and Signature of the Treaty of Peace with Japan, San Francisco, California, September 4–8, 1951; Record of Proceedings*, Department of State Pubn. 4392 (1951), pp. 219–233. It is reprinted as "Indonesia's Contribution to World Peace," in *Indonesian Review* 1 (October-December 1951): 359–362.

7. The text of Yoshida's speech appears in *Conference for the Conclusion*, pp. 277–281. Reprinted in *Indonesian Review*, pp. 363–365.

8. From Subardjo's correspondence. When the German mark suffered sudden devaluation in 1923, Charles G. Dawes, United States vice-president, 1925–1929, and a member of the Allied Committee on German Reparations, proposed a revised German reparations plan in 1924, to meet the new conditions. Later Owen D. Young, an American businessman, proposed another revised plan in 1929, when the world depression began.

9. Subardjo, private interview in Jakarta, January 12, 1972.

10. In 1950 the Natsir Cabinet conducted a survey on Indonesian losses and damages caused by the Japanese aggression, the result of which gave an estimate of some $17.5 billion. This report, entitled "Outline of Reparations Claim of Indonesia against Japan" is classified.

11. Japan, Economic Planning Agency, *Keizai yōran 1970*, pp. 2–7.

58   *The Japanese and Sukarno's Indonesia*

12.   Japan, Foreign Ministry, Asian Affairs Bureau, ed., *Indoneshia Kyōwakoku benran* (Tokyo, Nihon Kokusai Mondai Kenkyūjo, 1964), p. 92.
13.   Wajima Eiji, private interview in Tokyo, April 25, 1972.
14.   Ali, interview and *Asahi nenkan 1953*, p. 107.
15.   John M. Allison, private conversation in Ithaca, New York, April 5, 1969.
16.   Anonymous high-ranking official in the American Embassy, private interview in Jakarta, December, 1971.
17.   *Asahi nenkan 1954*, p. 145.
18.   *Asahi nenkan 1954*, p. 145. From August 1952 the two governments agreed to exchange consul generals. Thus Japan established its consulate general in Jakarta and a consulate in Surabaya, replacing the erstwhile Overseas Offices (Zaigai Jimusho).
19.   Japan, Foreign Ministry, *Waga gaikō no kinkyō*, no. 1 (1957): 34; and *Asahi nenkan 1955*, p. 240.
20.   The agreement provided that Japan would provide $6.5 million over four years during which some sixty vessels were expected to be refloated. Indonesia felt that the overall terms of payment should be determined first. See *Waga gaikō no kinkyō*, no. 1: 34; and *Asahi nenkan 1955*, p. 242.
21.   Wajima, interview. He was often referred to as "Minister Wajima," because the position of a Minister to India, which was vacant at that time, was applied to him for salary reasons but he never went to India.
22.   Lawrence Olson, *Japan in Postwar Asia* (London: Pall Mall Press for the Council on Foreign Relations, 1970), p. 31.
23.   *Asahi Shinbun*, February 1, 1953.
24.   Kobayashi Kazuhiko, *Ajia o kakeru otoko* (Tokyo: Kokusai Kaihatsu Jānaru Sha, 1972), p. 181.
25.   *Asahi nenkan 1955*, p. 242.
26.   *Asahi nenkan 1956*, p. 242.
27.   Roeslan Abdulgani, interview in Jakarta, September 12, 1974. See also Indonesia, Foreign Ministry, *RUU Persetudjuan Perdjandjian Perdamaian dan Persetudjuan Pampasan antara Republik Indonesia dan Djepang* (December 18, 1957), p. 5. This document contains a brief history of the negotiations from 1951 to December 8, 1957.
28.   *Asahi nenkan 1957*, pp. 244–245.
29.   Ibid., p. 245.
30.   Roeslan Abdulgani, interview.
31.   Japan, Foreign Ministry, Asian Affairs Bureau, ed., *Indoneshia Kyōwakoku benran*, p. 92.
32.   Indonesia, Foreign Ministry, *RUU Persetudjuan*, p. 6.
33.   Ibid.
34.   Ibid.
35.   Ibid.
36.   Ibid.
37.   *Asahi nenkan 1958*, p. 210.
38.   The National Council, which existed from July 1957 to July 1959, was composed of forty-five members, including regional and military representatives as well as party leaders. The council was a nonpartisan advisor to the Cabinet.
39.   Roeslan Abdulgani, private interview in Jakarta, February 28, 1972. According to him, the council had a monthly, closed session, the minutes of which are still classified. Abdulgani's article "Indonesia's National Council, the First Year,"

2

Far Eastern Survey 27 (July 1958): 97–104, mentions briefly that the reparations were one of the items that the National Council discussed in its first year (p. 101).

40. Before he took up his post in Jakarta, he met with several political leaders. Former Prime Minister Ashida Hitoshi told him that Japan was not yet in an economically strong enough position to pay reparations to Indonesia. Another former prime minister, Yoshida Shigeru, remarked to him: "If Indonesia wishes to cooperate with Japan in building a new Asia, Japan is willing to add $200 to $300 million more to the net reparations fund, but if Indonesia does not wish to cooperate, Japan should not pay a single penny into the reparations fund." Takasaki Tatsunosuke, chief Japanese delegate to the Afro-Asian conference of Bandung in 1955, suggested using the reparations programs as part of a broader Japanese economic cooperation policy toward Indonesia. See Takagi Hiroichi, "Indoneshia to Nihon no keizai kyōryoku," *Kokusai Jihyō*, no. 79 (November 1971): 48–49.

41. Takagi Hiroichi, private interview in Tokyo, April 21, 1972.

42. Takagi, interview, and his article, p. 50.

43. Kobayashi Ataru first became involved in Indonesia at a meeting with Subardjo in July 1957. However, it was as early as 1951 that he first participated in the Japanese government's study on reparations. That year, at the request of Prime Minister Yoshida, Foreign Minister Okazaki organized under his ministry the Asian Problems Research Council (Ajia Mondai Chōsakai), which consisted of ten business leaders including Kobayashi. See Kobayashi, pp. 176–177.

44. Shirahata Tomoyoshi, private interview in Tokyo, May 9, 1972.

45. Shirahata, interview.

46. Shirahata joined the Kobayashi party in Jakarta. Both Shirahata and Kobayashi were to work together again later in that year.

47. Tokagi, interview. He recalled that Allison helped to convince Kobayashi of the need to talk about the reparations with the Indonesian government.

48. Takagi, interview.

49. For a discussion of the political developments in 1957–1959, confer Daniel Lev, *Transition to Guided Democracy* (Ithaca, N.Y.: Cornell Modern Indonesia Project, Cornell University, 1966).

50. This paragraph based on Takagi, interview.

51. Mizuno Sōhei, private interview in Tokyo, April 24, 1972. Mizuno, son of Yamashita Tarō, was secretary for Kobayashi and accompanied him to Indonesia. The three later had a successful oil business in the Middle East.

52. Takagi, interview.

53. *Antara*, November 19, 1957.

54. *Indonesian Observer*, December 3, 1957.

55. Pohan was with the Kenpeitai (Japanese military police) during the Japanese occupation, and Nishijima first met him at the outbreak of the war when both were arrested by Dutch police, Pohan as a collaborator with the Japanese military. Since the end of the war he frequently had visited Japan as an intelligence officer. In 1957 he was working as a public prosecutor in the Indonesian consulate in Singapore.

56. The Buffalo Council, formed on December 20, 1956, functioned as the local government of Central Sumatra, asserting its independence from the central government in Jakarta.

57. Shirahata, interview.

58. Shirahata, interview.

59. *Indonesian Observer*, November 29, 1957.

60. Information in the following paragraph is based on Takagi, interview.

61. *Pewarta Kemlu* 3, nos. 11/12 (1957): 826.

62. *Antara*, November 30, 1957.

63. Ibid., December 3, 1957.

64. Shirahata, interview.

65. Shirahata, interview. See also "Nihon no gaikō, minkan no hitobito: Nishijima Shigetada shi," *Sankei Shinbun*, April 8, 1958.

66. Shirahata, interview.

67. *Pewarta Kemlu* 3, nos. 11/12 (1957): 826.

68. The net reparations figure changed from $230 million to $225 million and again to $223 million. The figure changed as the amount of trade debt did, since the two figures should add to $400 million.

69. *Asahi Shinbun*, March 4, 1958; and March 14, 1958. See also Indonesia, House of Representatives (Dewan Perwakilan Rakyat), *Risalah Sementara*, session I, meetings 39–44, 1958.

70. *Asahi Shinbun*, March 8, 1958 and Shirahata, interview.

71. Shirahata, interview.

72. The full texts of the Treaty of Peace and the Reparations Agreement between Japan and Indonesia appear in *Contemporary Japan* 25 (April, 1958): 304–309; and in Indonesia, Department of Information, *The Treaty of Peace and the Reparations Agreement concluded between Indonesia and Japan* (Special Release no. 2, 1958).

73. Professor Emeritus Itagaki Yoichi, private conversation in Tokyo, April 13, 1972. After he had talked with Wajima in 1953, Itagaki wrote an article on the same subject in *Yomiuri Shinbun*, January 15, 1954. Reprinted in his *Ajia to no taiwa* (Tokyo: Shin Kigen Sha, 1968), pp. 44–48.

74. *Asahi Shinbun*, April 22, 1955.

75. Ali Sastroamidjojo, private interview in Jakarta, January 5, 1971.

76. The texts of their addresses appear in Indonesia, Foreign Ministry, *Asia-Africa Speaks from Bandung* (Jakarta n.p., 1955 [?]), pp. 19–29, and pp. 31–39, respectively. Likewise, little attention to Japan's role in the conference is given in a classic study by George M. Kahin, *The Asia-African Conference, Bandung, Indonesia, April 1955* (Ithaca, N.Y.: Cornell University Press, 1956).

Chapter 3
The Japanese-Indonesian Peace Lobby, 1951–1957

The reparations negotiations from September 1951 to December 1957 were not limited to Indonesian and Japanese government officials. Many private citizens and groups from both countries became involved, the most noticeable of which were the former officers and civilians of the Japanese army's Military Administration (Gunseikanbu) and the navy's Jakarta Liaison Office (Kaigun Bukanfu), in cooperation with their Indonesian acquaintances during that period. Usually they participated in the negotiations behind the scenes, though occasionally their informal efforts were channeled into formal positions. These negotiators formed what I will term the Peace Lobby, because their position was to urge their respective governments to hasten their peace settlement. In showing the operation of the Peace Lobby, this chapter also will disclose the cooperation among the political, industrial, and bureaucratic leaders of Japan.

These informal negotiators, or lobbyists, were essentially two types of people. One type was comprised of wartime members of the Japanese army and navy who had been sympathetic to Indonesia's early struggle for independence and who later had demonstrated their affection for Indonesia by establishing the Japan-Indonesia Association in 1947. These lobbyists had maintained contact with their wartime Indonesian friends, most of whom now were prominent figures in the society of an independent Indonesia. The goals of these lobbyists included the early payment of war reparations, the improvement of Indonesia's image of Japan and the formation of a spiritual bond between the two peoples. The other type of lobbyists were those Japanese industrialists or entrepreneurs who recognized the opportunity to tie Japan's capital and technology to Indonesia's natural resources. Most of them had had wide experience before and during the war in developing Asia's natural resources. Here the roles of both the peace lobbyists and their prewar and war-time acquaintances will be discussed.

PEACE LOBBYISTS AND THE LEGACY OF THE PACIFIC WAR

One of the Peace Lobby's first goals was to try to change the Japanese government's policy against early settlement of the war reparations. Many of the lobbyists were members of the Japan-Indonesia Association, which was annoyed especially by the Japanese Foreign Ministry's position that Japan did not have to pay compensation for war damages because it had not fought with the Indonesians. In criticizing the government's position, the association's leaders indirectly blamed a former army officer, Major General Yamamoto Moichirō, chief of staff of the Sixteenth Army and ex officio chief of the Military Administration of Java from early 1945 to August of that year.[1] He had examined Indonesia's official "Outline of Reparations Claim of Indonesia against Japan," which had been presented to the Japanese government by the Djuanda Mission in December 1951, and had asserted that the damage caused by actual fighting was minimal; that the Japanese occupation had been beneficial; that the Indonesians had confiscated most of the Japanese army's four-year supply of food, clothing, and ammunition; and that no more than 160,000 workers (*rōmusha*) had been sent outside of Java. He felt that Indonesia's claim of losing four million *rōmusha* was greatly exaggerated. Yamamoto also noted that those Indonesian workers who had been lost had mostly been volunteers. The families of the volunteers and those few recruited by force, in any case, already were being given compensation.[2] These arguments Wajima and other leaders used against Indonesia's claim of $17.5 billion.

The members of the Japan-Indonesia Association stressed that the Japanese occupation and the army of Java had obstructed rather than assisted Indonesia's attaining of independence, by prohibiting independence songs and a national flag, and by trying to impede the rise of nationalist sentiments in the immediate postwar days. In effect, they praised the Japanese navy's attempt to promote independence and criticized the army's reluctance. It was on account of these convictions that the Peace Lobby began its informal operations.

Nishijima Shigetada and Ahmad Subardjo

Two of the most important figures in the Peace Lobby were Nishijima Shigetada and his old friend Subardjo. They first became involved indirectly in the negotiations in May 1952 when Subardjo came to Tokyo to discuss the concerned matters in private capacity.

Nishijima had gone to Batavia in 1937 at the age of twenty-seven and had worked in a large Japanese department store in Bandung.[3] While at the Chiyoda Department Store, he studied Indonesian and Dutch and soon developed an interest in Java's independence movements. It was in this connection that he had come to know Subardjo.

Ahmad Subardjo Djoyoadisuryo, born in 1896, studied law at the University of Leiden. In the Netherlands he had been active in student politics with other Indonesians such as Mohammed Hatta, Iwa Kusumasumantri, and Alexander Andries Maramis. In 1919 Subardjo served as chairman of the Indonesian Association (Perkumpulan Indonesia), a student organization in The Hague. Returning to Indonesia, many of the members including Subardjo joined the independence movements.

Before the war, Nishijima and his comrades carried out underground activities against the Dutch in cooperation with the Japanese consulates in Batavia and Surabaya.[4] When the war began in December 1941, the Dutch police arrested the Japanese, including Nishijima, and expatriated them to Australia. In 1942 when they were returned to Japan, Nishijima's ship made a stopover at Singapore where he was solicited by the Southern Region Army to go back to Java, which he did.

In March 1942 the Japanese Imperial Navy controlled Borneo, Moluccas, Celebes, and West New Guinea, with its headquarters in Macassar (later in Surabaya). It established a liaison office in Jakarta, headed by Rear Admiral Maeda Tadashi, as a link with the Jakarta headquarters of the Sixteenth Army.[5] It was this liaison office which Nishijima joined at the request of one of his colleagues, Yoshizumi Tomegorō, who had been a journalist in prewar Batavia and who was a great supporter of Indonesian independence.[6] While at the liaison office Nishijima and Yoshizumi became acquainted with Subardjo and reacquainted with their old friends Sudiro, Wikana, E. Chaerudin, and Djoyopranoto, together with whom they formed the so-called Navy Group in late 1944.[7]

In October 1944 the Navy Liaison Office prepared for Indonesia's independence by creating a school, Asrama Indonesia Merdeka, where seventy youths from eighteen to twenty years old were trained for positions in the government of an independent Indonesia. This school was headed by Subardjo and was managed by Nishijima and Yoshizumi. The youths debated various problems facing their country, and Subardjo often invited Sukarno, Hatta, and Iwa Kusumasumantri, and Sjahrir to lecture.[8]

The Navy Liaison Office's most important contribution to Indonesia's independence took place from August 15 to 17, 1945 just after

Japan's surrender.[9] On this occasion, radical youth groups led by Chairul Saleh, Sukarni, Adam Malik, and Wikana demanded that Sukarno and Hatta immediately proclaim independence. When they refused, the youths kidnapped them on the night of August 15, taking them from Jakarta to the suburb of Rengasdengklok, to try to persuade them to declare independence at once.

Several navy officers, including Rear Admiral Maeda, Nishijima, Yoshizumi, and army officers Miyoshi Shunkichirō and Saitō Shizuo (who later became ambassador to Indonesia from 1964 to 1966), helped promulgate the Proclamation of Independence, despite the Japanese army's opposition. At Nishijima's and Subardjo's urging, Wikana, Adam Malik, Chairul Saleh, and the group who had abducted Sukarno and Hatta agreed to return them to Maeda's official residence in Jakarta. There, with Maeda's guarantee of safety, thirty people assembled as the "Indonesian Independence Preparatory Committee" to discuss the text of the proclamation from two o'clock in the morning of August 17 until dawn. When they could not agree on the strongly worded statement: "All existing governmental organs shall be seized by the people from the foreigners who still control them," Sukarno, Hatta, Subardjo, Maeda, Yoshizumi, Nishijima, and Miyoshi arrived at a compromise: "Matters concerning the transfer of power, and other matters, will be executed in an orderly manner and in the shortest possible time."[10]

Early that morning, when the text of the proclamation finally was drafted, Sukarno and Chairul Saleh asked Nishijima and Yoshizumi to print the proclamation with the Navy Liaison Office's printing machine. The latter made it printed without Maeda's authorization and quickly circulated by Japanese navy automobiles. Adam Malik, who had been working in the Japanese government news agency, Dōmei, used the office teletype to dispatch the news of Indonesia's declaration of Merdeka.[11] At ten o'clock a modest independence ceremony was conducted in front of Sukarno's residence, at Pengangsan Timur no. 56 (now Jalan Proklamasi).

After Japan's surrender Nishijima was arrested by the Allies as a war criminal suspect. He was released three years later in 1948 with the last group of suspects and returned to his home in Gunma prefecture.[12]

Subardjo's Visit to Tokyo, May 1952

After the failure of the Djuanda Mission in December 1951, the two governments agreed to meet again in May 1952 in Jakarta. When this was found unfeasible, Subardjo visited Tokyo for the week of May 22, 1952, not as Indonesia's foreign minister but as an advisor to Foreign

Minister Wilopo.[13] Upon his arrival Subardjo contacted Nishijima, who, in turn, introduced him to Matsunaga Yasuzaemon and other business-men.[14] After Subardjo left for home, Nishijima circulated, among political and business leaders in Tokyo, a note explaining the former foreign minister's views on the reparations issue, commercial relations between the two countries, his meeting with Matsunaga, and the importance of the spiritual bond between the two peoples.[15] Nishijima then began to press for an early peace settlement.

The Role of Certain Japanese Businessmen

Although the Japanese and Indonesian governments had not yet settled on a reparations agreement, these Japanese businessmen planned huge projects in Indonesia which would redeem Japan's past conduct and draw the countries closer. Although most of these plans never materialized, the subsequent impact of these industrialists on Indonesia was indeed real.

Matsunaga Yasuzaemon (1875–1971), president of the Electric Power Central Research Institute, chairman of the Congress for Indus-trial Development Plans, and a salient figure in the rationalization of the administration of electric power in prewar, wartime, and postwar Japan; Ayukawa Gisuke (1880–1967), president of the Manchurian Heavy Industry Development Company in 1937–1942 and of the Imperial Oil Company in 1954–1956; and Ishihara Hiroichirō (1890–1971), president of the South Seas Mining Company and of the Ishihara Industrial Company were called the "Indonesia trio" in the mid-1950s, because of their keen interest in postwar Indonesia's natural resources.[16] Matsunaga was closely associated with two experts on Indonesia's hydroelectric potential, Kudō Kōki (an acquaintance of Nishijima) and Kubota Yutaka, and with an agricultural expert, Iwata Yoshio. During the 1930s Kudō had been involved in establishing chemical industries in Manchuria and North Korea while Kubota Yutaka had built a large hydroelectric power dam on northern Korea's Amur River. Kudō and Kubota had worked under the same man, Noguchi Jun, and during the war both had taken an interest in developing Indonesia's industries and had visited Indonesia several times.[17]

After World War II Kudō became head of the Noguchi Institute, which studied and published various plans for the comprehensive in-dustrial development of postwar Japan. These publications caught the attention of Ayukawa Gisuke who, because he had been president of the Machurian Heavy Industry Development Company before the war, was now in Sugamo Prison as a war criminal. Upon his release in August 1947, Ayukawa invited Kudō to join his company. Kudō also became acquainted with Matsunaga and convinced him of Indonesia's potential for industrial development by means of Japanese capital. Kudō later introduced Nishijima to Matsunaga and Ayukawa.[18]

Kubota Yutaka, who along with Kudō Kōki had initiated Japan's prewar industrial interests in Indonesia, was one of Japan's first engineering consultants and now is with the Nippon Kōei Company. Devoted to building public works in developing countries, he is referred to as Japan's "peace corps worker" and the man "who gambles on developing nations." Before the war he helped to form the Korean Electric Power Company and the Korean-Manchurian Amur River Hydroelectric Company, which had drawn up extensive development plans for the Korean and Manchurian regions.[19] In the late 1930s, when Japan shifted its expansionist policy southward, Kubota became interested in building dams in Indonesia, using the abundant water from northeast Sumatra's Lake Toba and Asahan River. The electric power from these dams could be used also to refine aluminum from the bauxite brought in from nearby Bintan Island. The Dutch East Indies government long had regarded the region as a potential site for industrial development but never had done anything about it. Soon after the Japanese army occupied Sumatra in March 1942 Kubota was sent in June to head the Sumatran Water Resources Development Survey Mission.[20] Ensuing from this were some projects which were only partially completed at the end of the war. In 1946 Kubota and his colleagues organized the Nippon Kōei.

Iwata Yoshio had built rubber estates in Malaya and in Sumatra before the war and had traveled throughout Southeast Asia.[21] Because of his wide knowledge of the region he was commissioned during the war to do natural resources surveys in Indonesia, especially in Sumatra. After Japan's surrender Iwata became interested in renewing economic relations between Japan and Southeast Asia in the belief that private business would be their real determinant rather than the government's trade policy. His emphasis on private investment and commercial loans was shared by the Japanese government in the early 1950s and became the basis of its official position on reparations.

Ishihara Hiroichirō (1890–1971), president of the Ishihara Industrial Company, was an adventurous industrialist and a great influence on Japanese-Indonesian business relations. In 1920 he had begun iron-ore-mining operations in Malaya in competition with the British tin exploration on Bangka Island off the coast of south Sumatra. After the war Ishihara was attracted by central and north Sumatra's natural resources with an eye to exploring for oil, refining aluminum, and generating electrical power.[22] Ishihara's younger brother, Takada Gisaburō, vice-director of the Ishihara Industrial Company, was a member of the Japanese delegation to the Asia-Africa Bandung Conference in 1955. As the only nongovernment member of the delegation of thirteen, this might indicate the extent of Ishihara's influence and involvement in Indonesian matters.[23]

Nishijima's Visit to Jakarta, January 1953

While a member of the Japan-Indonesia Association, Nishijima was also head of the Sanmei Trading Company, which traded with Indonesia. In connection with his company Nishijima returned to Indonesia in March 1953 for the first time since the war. During his stay he renewed his old prewar and wartime friendships and on March 26, was even able to talk with President Sukarno.[24] He explained Japan's views on the reparations issue and recommended Shirahata Tomoyoshi, then the consul at Surabaya, as a competent diplomat. As seen already, Shirahata later played a significant role in the negotiations.

The real purpose of Nishijima's visit was to reestablish contact with old acquaintances, and upon his return, he stressed the favorable psychological effect of an early reparations settlement.

Kubota and the Asahan Development Project, 1953–1954

Not having accomplished his wartime plans for building dams on the Asahan River, Kubota Yutaka finally in September 1953 went back to Indonesia. There he talked with Djuanda, then chairman of the National Planning Board, about developing the Asahan region. Djuanda, also an engineer by training, shared many of Kubota's views and they became close friends.[25]

Djuanda wanted the project at Asahan to produce fertilizers instead of aluminum, because Indonesia had a greater need to stimulate agricultural production.[26] Kubota thus returned to Jakarta in early 1954 with a plan for the construction of an aluminum refinery and fertilizer factories in the Asahan area. Djuanda approved the plan and promised to present it at a meeting of the cabinet.[27] In the meantime Kubota met with Prime Minister Yoshida to urge the Japanese government to adopt this project and give it financial support, if possible through the reparations fund, because Japan did not yet feel ready to provide technical aid to foreign countries. Kubota argued that the reparations payments should be used to expand Japan's trade and that they should be used together with Japan's advanced technology.[28]

Although the reparations talks between Japan and Indonesia were not progressing well at that time, the Indonesian government nevertheless suggested that the Asahan projects be started with $50 million from the projected reparations fund. Earlier in December 1953 Japan had agreed to salvage sunken Indonesian ships by means of the fund even though the final reparations amount had not yet been determined. But it refused to endorse the Asahan projects. This disappointed the Indonesians, who decided not to ask Japan for assistance in the Asahan projects.[29] Kubota's almost passionate interest in Asahan thus did not bear fruit before the reparations agreement was concluded in 1958.

Matsunaga's Dispatch of the Iwata Mission to Indonesia, February–March 1954

Matsunaga, after meeting Subardjo in May 1952, began to concern himself with Asian problems. In the previous year he had personally financed the Asian Economic Research Council (Ajia Keizai Chōsakai), requesting Iwata Yoshio to head its agricultural affairs section, and in February 1954 he asked Iwata to lead the Indonesian Industries Survey Mission. Besides Iwata, the mission contained another "Indonesia expert" from the Japan-Indonesia Association, Miyoshi Shunkichirō.

Miyoshi Shunkichirō first served as a political officer in Japan's consulate in Surabaya in 1926,[30] and he moved to Batavia as vice-consul in 1940, to Macassar as consul in 1941,[31] and during the occupation he was a civil administrator (*shiseikan*) of the Sixteenth Army's military administration of Java in Jakarta. Miyoshi and Nishijima Shigetada both participated in the drama surrounding Indonesia's proclamation of independence in August 1945. With his extensive knowledge of the country and fluency in Indonesian as well as in Dutch, Miyoshi joined the Japan-Indonesia Association after the war, serving as managing director.[32]

Before going to Indonesia, Iwata drew up a plan stating the proposed amount of Japan's reparations and capital investment and their implementation. Although this was not circulated publicly, it was considered seriously by Djuanda, then director of Indonesia's Economic Planning Board. Djuanda wanted to incorporate much of the proposal into Indonesia's Five-Year Economic Development Plan for 1956–1960 but without giving credit to Iwata (fearing internal political repercussions), and so he asked Iwata to keep his proposal confidential.[33]

Iwata had proposed that Japan's total payment consist of $500 million—$250 to $300 million in reparations and $200 to $250 million in joint projects. His proposal listed various projects for Indonesia's economic development and suggested forming a binational committee to preside over the funds for these projects.[34] Although the binational committee was never formed, the list of projects proposed by Iwata was used in later negotiations. The list consisted of some sixty items, most of which were related to such primary industries as rice production and fisheries and to such light industries as factories for cement, rubber, paper, sugar, soap, and matches. This became the basis of the list of reparations projects attached to the reparations agreement of 1958.

Another of Iwata's proposed projects was the construction of hydroelectric power stations in the Asahan valley, using water from Lake Toba in northern Sumatra. This project was considered seriously by Kubota Yutaka but was never undertaken because of its high cost. Iwata also proposed a survey of natural resources, including oil in Sumatra. This idea later was adopted by Ishihara Hiroichirō and Kobayashi Ataru, the latter having formed the North Sumatra Oil Development Cooperation Company in 1960. Still another of Iwata's projects was the construction of an eight-story "Indonesia Hall" in Tokyo that would be used as an office for those doing business with Indonesia and as a hostel and hotel for students and other visitors from Indonesia. This idea materialized in 1962 under the auspices of the Tōnichi Trading Company.[35] Although it never had any office space, Indonesia Hall (Wisma Indonesia) accommodated some five hundred students and even became a political activities center for the Indonesian Students Association (Persatuan Pelajar Indonesia, or PPI). Iwata Yoshio, under Matsunaga's tutelage, unofficially contributed much to postwar Japanese-Indonesian relations, although his work did not lead to the immediate settlement of the reparations negotiations.

Adam Malik's Visit to Tokyo, 1954

When Nishijima visited Jakarta in 1953 he sensed the unfavorable image of Japan and felt a need to improve it. Nishijima and his prewar colleague, Andō Michikuni who headed Domei's Jakarta office, talked to Fujiyama Aiichirō, president of the Society for Economic Cooperation in Asia (Ajia Kyōkai)[36] and president of the Japan Chamber of Commerce and Industry, about improving Indonesia's image of Japan and persuaded him to sponsor a visit to Japan by Indonesian journalists critical of the country. This idea appealed to Fujiyama because, also being president of a large sugar company that had had a branch factory in Java since 1918,[37] he could see future business opportunities in Indonesia and the importance of good relationships with influential Indonesians.

In April 1954 Adam Malik, being with Domei during the war and a radical youth leader at the time of Indonesia's declaration of independence, as well as chief of the Indonesian government news agency, Antara; Rosihan Anwar from *Pedoman* of democratic-socialist leanings; Mochtar Lubis from *Indonesia Raya* also of a democratic-socialist bent;

Mrs. Supeni from *Suluh Indonesia*, influenced by the PNI; Sanjoto from *Business News* and others were invited to Japan. According to Nishijima it was after this trip that Malik formed a favorable opinion of Japan and began to assist, though indirectly, Indonesia's peace settlement with Japan.[38] Malik later observed that after 1954 Indonesian newspapers became more charitable toward Japan.[39] This in turn enhanced Japan's position in the 1955 Asia-Africa Bandung Conference. Thereafter Adam Malik kept in close touch with Nishijima, and the two frequently exchanged information and ideas on the reparations issues. Later in 1957 Antara's president invited to Indonesia a group of Japanese journalists, among whom was Taniguchi Gorō, a prewar journalist in Batavia.[40] Thus Malik began to reestablish contact with his old acquaintances and that year he became Antara's Tokyo Bureau chief.

Nishijima and the Matsunaga-Ayukawa Mission, June–July 1956

In January 1955 when Wajima Eiji was in Jakarta, Nishijima prepared a joint note with his colleagues from Batavia, now members of the Japan-Indonesia Association: Ishii Tarō, Satō Nobuhide, and Shibata Yaichirō.[41] In this note they proposed that a mission headed by an important and influential figure with one or two assistants be sent to Indonesia to work out a political solution. They suggested that the mission be sent before the Asia-Africa Bandung Conference and that Wajima be replaced. Although in fact he was not replaced until April 1957, the suggestion to send a high-level mission to Indonesia was acted upon in 1956 and Nishijima was a member of it.

In early 1956 when Indonesia was claiming $1 billion in reparations and Japan was thinking in terms of between $200 million and $550 million, Japan's business leaders decided to take the initiative in narrowing this gap.[42] In April 1956 the International Chamber of Commerce held a meeting in Jakarta, providing an opportunity for Japanese business leaders to go to Indonesia. A delegation of fifteen was selected, including Kanō Hisao, later governor of Chiba prefecture, and Satō Kiichirō, president of the Mitsui Bank. Taking advantage of this meeting, Matsunaga and Ayukawa found Nishijima a place in the Japanese delegation and instructed him to procure an invitation to Indonesia for them. Since Indonesia had no influential business leaders that Nishijima could approach, he went instead to the political party leaders as the only group that could sponsor a visit by Japanese business leaders. Nishijima approached the Nahdlatul Ulama party's advisor, K. H. M. Dachlan and gained his support. Dachlan then obtained the necessary funds from another leader of the NU, Djamaluddin Malik. Nishijima returned to Japan on May 9, 1956.

The Matsunaga-Ayukawa Mission thus was organized and visited Indonesia from June 19 to July 5, 1956.[43] Although the mission actually was not sent by the Japanese government, the government did lend its assistance and support, and Matsunaga was given the title of an advisor to the Japanese Foreign Ministry. Included in the mission were Yamada Katsunori from the Shikoku Electric Power Company, Kudō Kōki from the Congress for Industrial Development Plans, Sasaki Satoru from the Imperial Oil Company, Ayukawa Gisuke's son, Kinjirō, and Nishijima Shigetada. Besides discussing reparations, the mission obviously was interested in talking about hydroelectric power and oil exploration in Indonesia. It did not succeed in narrowing the gap between Indonesia's and Japan's reparations terms, nor was it able to agree on industrial development plans. Ayukawa and Matsunaga often disagreed with each other,[44] but they did manage to formulate a plan for the Asahan River development although the plan was never realized.[45] Ayukawa tried to obtain oil concessions from Indonesia but learned to his disappointment that all the important concessions already had been given to Americans and Europeans.[46]

Nishijima had another project in mind. In the previous year Indonesia had held the nation's first general elections which produced four major parties: the Masjumi, the Indonesian Nationalist party (PNI), the Nahdlatul Ulama, and the Indonesian Communist party (PKI).[47] But Indonesia's newly elected parliament already was in jeopardy, because the internal fighting was hindering its productivity. Even the Indonesian army was nurturing doubts about its efficacy. Aware of the growing political power of the Indonesian military, Nishijima secretly visited Colonel Zulkifli Lubis, then deputy chief of staff of the Indonesian army, whom many Japanese expected to become the leader of Indonesia.[48] Nishijima explained the purpose of the Matsunaga-Ayukawa Mission, hoping to elicit support from this potential presidential contender and critic of Sukarno's communist leanings and unproductive economic policy. Contrary to expectation, however, Colonel Lubis shortly thereafter resigned his post and in August 1956 became the military commander of North Sumatra. Later, he became a formidable critic of Sukarno and led the Sumatra Rebellion.

The Matsunaga-Ayukawa Mission returned to Japan on July 5, 1956. Ayukawa had lost interest in Indonesia and Kudō died within two weeks. Thus the mission appeared to have accomplished nothing, and only Matsunaga retained an active role in Indonesian affairs.

Subardjo's Second Trip to Tokyo, July 1957

Early in 1957 former Foreign Minister Subardjo was appointed as Indonesia's ambassador to Switzerland.[49] Upon hearing this Nishijima again mobilized Matsunaga and others, and they invited Subardjo to Japan to discuss the terms of the reparations payment. Matsunaga agreed to finance Subardjo's stay in Japan and then persuaded Finance Minister Ikeda Hayato to give him enough American dollars from Japan's sparse supply to purchase Subardjo's airplane ticket.

Matsunaga, befitting his eminence in both political and business circles, set up a sort of headquarters in the Japan Industrial Club building in Tokyo to which he summoned people to talk to Subardjo. Among those called in were business leaders Ayukawa Gisuke, Ishihara Hiroichirō, Fujiyama Aiichirō, Takasaki Tatsunosuke, and Kobayashi Ataru; political leaders Ichimada Hisato, Ikeda Hayato, Miki Takeo, and Kaya Okinori; and finally Takagi Hiroichi, Shirahata Tomoyoshi, and Arakawa Masaji from the Foreign Ministry.[50] During Subardjo's stay in Japan, Nishijima took him also to see former Prime Minister Yoshida Shigeru in Ōiso.

Subardjo returned on July 20 and reported to Djuanda and President Sukarno the positions of the Japanese leaders on reparations. This time Indonesia and Japan agreed on a total amount of nearly $1 billion. However, Japan insisted upon allocating only $200 million for reparations and the rest for "economic cooperation," based on loans and the cancellations of Indonesia's trade debts whereas Indonesia claimed $300 million in reparations. Subardjo's visit to Tokyo apparently helped to produce the so-called Djuanda Memorandum of July 1957, mentioned in chapter 2.

Subardjo wrote to Nishijima in August 1957 that the Indonesian government still could not approach the reparations issue with an open mind and that he had to explain the problems to them a number of times "as if he were a school teacher facing his pupils."[51] He also asserted that the two countries should not treat the reparations negotiations as street-bargaining. He added that Djuanda and Sukarno were very thankful for Matsunaga's unselfish efforts in assisting the reparations and that when the negotiations were settled the president would like to pay a visit to Japan as a gesture of friendship, hopefully while Matsunaga was still in good health. Obviously Matsunaga was greatly appreciated by Indonesia's leaders.

Ishihara, Shimizu Hitoshi, and Shimonaka Yasaburō in Jakarta, September 1957

When Wajima's successor, Takagi Hiroichi, urged the Japanese government in August 1957 to hasten its peace settlement with Indonesia, many of the informal peace lobbyists shuttled between the two capitals. Among them were Shimizu Hitoshi, Ishihara, and Shimonaka

Yasaburō, who made hurried visits to Indonesia just before the Kobayashi party arrived on September 22, 1957. All of them felt that a final settlement was near and hoped that their respective concerns, whether private or public, would be reflected in it.

Shimizu Hitoshi had been an ardent supporter of Pan-Asianism during the war and had worked in Indonesia for the Sixteenth Army's propaganda team. Since the Japanese invasion in March 1942 he had been sympathetic toward Indonesia's independence movements and hoped that the Japanese occupation could help Indonesia achieve this goal. Upon his arrival in Indonesia in 1942 Shimizu organized a propaganda team, in order to explain to the Indonesians Japan's policies and aims of "liberation" in the country. Within a month he had created the "Triple-A Movement," named for its slogan, "Nippon the Leader of Asia, Nippon the Protector of Asia, Nippon the Light of Asia."[52]

Shimizu made close contact with Indonesian leaders during the occupation and maintained it throughout the postwar years. When Sukarno and Hatta led the popular movements, Putera and Djawa Hōkōkai, they put Shimizu, Miyoshi, and Saitō Shizuo (ambassador to Indonesia, 1964–1966) on their advisory committee.[53] Shimizu also organized a group of Indonesian activists to help him with his propaganda work. Because of the location of his office on 31 Menteng Street, the group was called the "Menteng 31 Group," or the "Sendenbu (Propaganda Section) Group." It included Mohammad Yamin, Chairul Saleh, and Sukarni. Because of his "imprudent" support for Indonesia's independence, which was against the army's policy, Shimizu was ousted from Java in July 1945. All of his Indonesian colleagues assumed important positions after 1945. Yamin became minister of justice in 1951; Saleh became minister of veterans affairs in 1957; and Sukarni, with Adam Malik, organized the radical political party, Murba, in 1948.

After joining the Japan-Indonesia Association, Shimizu formed the Japanese-Indonesian Cultural Association in 1950.[54] In the early phase of the reparations talks, Shimizu recalls that he was contacted by Yamin, Saleh, Sukarni, and Adam Malik and was asked about Japan's positions on the reparations issue.

After 1955 Shimizu had visited Indonesia frequently and, on September 11, 1957, he met with President Sukarno, in Shimizu's capacities as a member of the executive board of the Japan-Indonesia Association and chairman of the Japanese-Indonesian Cultural Association, to discuss the reparations problem.[55] Sukarno indicated that he wished to settle the major points during Kobayashi's imminent visit and stated that Japan should pay at least $450 million and that Indonesia's

$170 million trade debt could be solved later. However, Sukarno subsequently did not meet with Kobayashi and did not repeat these figures while Kobayashi was in Jakarta. He also expressed a desire to visit Japan for four days in November but did not come until the following January. Shimizu's role in the negotiations thus was limited.

In September 1957 Ishihara also went to Indonesia to discuss with President Sukarno ways in which Japan's reparations and private capital would benefit Indonesia's economy. Earlier in February 1956, his company, the Ishihara Industrial Company, and the Daiwa Bank, together with Sumatran-based Indonesian businessmen, had formed a private bank in Jakarta, the Bank Perdania. Ishihara's visit to Indonesia was, this time, not favored by many Japanese. Foreign Minister Fujiyama Aiichirō, Shirahata, and Nishijima all could find no reason for Ishihara to see the Indonesian president when Kobayashi, representing Japanese government and business, was about to arrive in Indonesia with official credentials from Japan's prime minister.[56]

Shimonaka Yasaburō and his secretary Kaneko Tomokazu, also a member of the Japan-Indonesia Association, made a trip to Indonesia, too, during the week of September 25, 1957.[57] Shimonaka Yasaburō (1878–1961), president of Heibonsha, a large publishing company, first became involved in Indonesian affairs in 1932 when he met Mohammed Hatta, who had slipped away to Japan to solicit support for Indonesia's struggle against Dutch colonialism. Although Shimonaka's subsequent support of Indonesia's independence movement proved ineffectual against the Dutch police, after meeting Hatta, Shimonaka established the Japan-Indonesia Association and became its president with Hatta as vice-president. In 1954 the two had met the visiting president of Antara, Adam Malik, who had been invited to Tokyo by Fujiyama at the suggestion of Nishijima and Andō. In their talks with Adam Malik they concerned themselves with the delayed negotiations on the peace settlement. Although the two visitors could not meet with Hatta, they did discuss the reparations issue with such acquaintances as Arudj Kartawinata, speaker of the House of Representatives; Mohammad Nur, minister of social welfare; and Sanusi Hardjadinata, minister of home affairs. During Shimonaka's visit to Indonesia in September 1957, he, Ishihara, and Kobayashi all met at Consul General Takagi's residence. The discussion there ended with their support of the Kobayashi proposal and with their agreement to urge Prime Minister Kishi and Foreign Minister Fujiyama also to support it.

Omar Tusin's Visit to Tokyo, October 1957[58]

When Mohammed Hatta went to Tokyo in October 1957 for the subsequently unsuccessful reparations negotiations, he took with him

Omar Tusin, one of Indonesia's experts on economic development. Omar Tusin also was head of the Indonesian Chamber of Industry, was a good friend of Djuanda, and equally important, he had been educated in Japan. He had enrolled in Tokyo's Military Academy in November 1944 but after the war had transferred to Waseda University's department of engineering from which he was graduated in 1951. Returning to Indonesia, Omar Tusin had become acquainted with Djuanda and was active as an engineering consultant and as a member of the Masjumi party. In January 1957 Omar Tusin was asked by the Garuda Council to draw up a plan for the extensive economic development of Sumatra, but because of his association with the Buffalo Council and its secessionist movement, he was arrested and detained from February to August 1957. Soon after his release he was asked to accompany Hatta to Tokyo.

Omar Tusin described his plan for the development of Sumatra to me in 1972. He had projected several areas of intensive development ("pocket areas") along the Sumatran coast—Palembang, Padang, Medan, etc.—with land and sea routes connecting them. Both Omar Tusin and Hatta had emphasized the need for such projects outside Java, in part to avoid possible communist disturbances in Java, and had suggested financing these developments with the reparations fund and Japanese credit. Their ideas were not adopted but did serve to introduce the relevance of Indonesia's internal tensions to the reparations talks.

Nishijima and the Kobayashi Mission to Jakarta, November–December 1957

The roles that Nishijima and Shirahata, as members of the Kobayashi Mission, and Adam Malik played behind the scenes of the final phase of the reparations negotiations from November 25 through December 8, 1957 has been described in chapter 2. In this chapter, their roles should be viewed again in the context of the Peace Lobby, emphasizing the importance of Nishijima's close relationship with Adam Malik to the final breakthrough in the statement over the inclusion of the "nondiscriminatory treatment" clause.

AN ASSESSMENT OF THE PEACE LOBBY

This account of the Peace Lobby from 1951 through 1957 suggests that the central figures were Nishijima, Matsunaga, Subardjo, and Adam Malik. The others introduced here lobbied for their respective concerns but with relatively minor results. The central figures were effective primarily because they were close to the prime minister, the president, or the foreign ministry of their respective countries. During the Japanese government's delay in its decision on the war-debt payment to Indonesia and during the Indonesian government's various political troubles, including successive cabinet changes, these lobbyists, particularly Nishijima, Subardjo, and Adam Malik, maintained their friendship, believing that the Japanese and the Indonesians had a spiritual bond. Nishijima and Matsunaga served as a link between the pro-Indonesian Japanese, the Japanese industrialists, and the Indonesian leaders. In the final phase of the negotiations Matsunaga recommended sending Kobayashi to Jakarta as an official envoy. Thus Kobayashi and Shirahata functioned both formally and publicly while Nishijima and Adam Malik functioned informally and privately. All achieved their goals because they were influential in both governments.

Indeed, they often functioned somewhere between the roles of lobbyist and decision-maker. Subardjo ceased to be an official negotiator in April 1952 when he resigned as foreign minister, yet on subsequent trips to Tokyo he held the title of advisor to the foreign minister. Nishijima was an executive member of the Japan-Indonesia Association, a private organization, but in the final negotiations he held the title of a research officer of the Foreign Ministry. Adam Malik was the president of a news agency sponsored by the Indonesian government, and Matsunaga was head of the Congress for Industrial Development Plans and of the Electric Power Central Research Institute. He also held the title of advisor to the Foreign Ministry.

The activities of the Peace Lobby in the reparations negotiations seem to call into question the competence of the Japanese and Indonesian foreign ministries, but in fact it reveals that the influential leaders and actual decision-makers are to be found outside the formal negotiations teams. Although Sukarno was president of Indonesia, he did not intervene in the reparations issue until after July 1957. When governmental leaders could not agree among themselves on the reparations issues, the negotiators' functions were limited. But most of the major proposals originated with the private "experts" not in the Japanese and Indonesian Foreign Ministries. The impact of these informal negotiations on the formal settlement is evident. The prewar and wartime contacts between the Japanese and the Indonesians proved useful not only to the peace settlement but also to future Japanese-Indonesian relations.

NOTES

1. The occupation of the Indonesian archipelago was administered by different military groups: Java by the Sixteenth Army (Hq.: Jakarta); Sumatra by the Twenty-fifth Army (Hq.: Padang); Borneo (now Kalimantan), Celebes (now Sulawesi), Moluccas, and West New Guniea by the Second Southern Fleet (Hq.: Macassar, later Surabaya). For further details, see Kishi Kōichi, et al., *Indoneshia ni okeru Nihon gunsei no kenkyū* (Tokyo: Kinokuniya Shoten, 1959), pp. 109–166.

2. Based on classified material (mimeographed) prepared by the Asian Affairs Bureau of the Foreign Ministry, 1954.

3. He was expelled from Tokyo Imperial University because of his supposed membership in the Japan Communist party. For further biographical information, see "Sugao no Indoneshia" (1), *Mainichi Shinbun*, November 16, 1969; and Masuda Atō, *Indoneshia gendaishi* (Tokyo: Chūō Kōron Sha, 1971), p. 147.

4. Masuda, pp. 139, 145, 147.

5. Maeda, born in 1898, served as a navy attaché in The Hague in 1939, and in 1940 joined the Japanese delegation for trade talks with the Netherlands Indies. See ibid., p. 145.

6. For the life story of Yoshizumi (1911–1948), see ibid., pp. 138, 147; Kiyoma Kazuo [pseudonym for Nishijima Shigetada], "Ajia rōninden, Yoshizumi Tomegorō," *Shisō no Kagaku*, September 1954, 59–68; and Togawa Sachio, "Shōwa kaijintan, shishi Yoshizumi Tomegorō," *Bessatsu Bungei Shunjū*, September 1963, 192–210.

7. Masuda, p. 168; and "Sugao no Indoneshia" (2), *Mainichi Shinbun*, November 18, 1969. Sudiro became Subardjo's secretary, while Chaerudin and Djoyopranoto became employed in an intelligence body within the Navy Liaison Office.

8. Masuda, p. 168.

9. Based on Kishi, pp. 492–506; and Masuda, pp. 169–183.

10. The English translations are from Benedict R. O. Anderson, *Some Aspects of Indonesian Politics under the Japanese Occupation: 1944–1945* (Ithaca, N.Y.: Modern Indonesia Project. Cornell University, 1961), pp. 84–85. The Japanese involved claim that they played a part in finalizing the text of the Proclamation, whereas the Indonesians deny it. See Kishi Kōichi, et al., *Indoneshia ni okeru*, p. 500; and Ahmad Subardjo, *Lahirnja Republik Indonesia* (Jakarta: P. T. Kinta, 1972), p. 107.

11. Adam Malik, *Riwajat dan Perdjuangan Sekitar Proklamasi Kemerdekaan Indonesia, 17 Augustus 1945* (Jakarta: Widjaya, 1970), p. 60.

12. "Sugao no Indoneshia" (2), *Mainichi Shinbun*, November 18, 1969.

13. *Mainichi Shinbun*, May 29, 1952.

14. Nishijima Shigetada, private interview in Jakarta, February 10, 1972; and Subardjo, private interview in Jakarta, January 12, 1972.

15. Nishijima Shigetada, *Subarujo gaishō [sic] kikokugo seizaikai yōjin e no yōbōsho* (typed, no date). Possessed by Nishijima.

16. For further biographical information, see Nihon Keizai Shinbun Sha, ed., *Watakushi no rirekisho* (36 vols.; Tokyo: Nihon Keizai Shinbun Sha, 1957–1969), XXI, 285–359; XXIV, 265–358; and XXII, 7–70, respectively.

17. Matsunaga Yasuzaemon, "Isai, Ayukawa san," *Ayukawa Gisuke sensei tsuisōroku*, compiled by the Ayukawa Memoirs Publishing Committee (Tokyo: Ayukawa Memoirs Publishing Committee, 1968), p. 363.

18. Nishijima, interview.

19. Daiyamondo Sha, *Nippon Kōei* (Tokyo: Daiyamonda Sha, 1971), p. 18.

20. Ibid., p. 19.

21. For details of Iwata's career, see Kobayashi Kazuhiko, *Ajia o kakeru otoko* (Tokyo: Kokusai Kaihatsu Jānaru Sha, 1972).

22. Itasaka Isao, managing director of Bank Perdania, private interview in Jakarta, July 10, 1970.

23. For a list of the Japanese delegates, see Indonesia, Foreign Ministry, *Asia-Africa Speaks from Bandung* (Jakarta: n.p., 1955[?]), p. 232.

24. From Nishijima's letter to President Sukarno, dated September 13, 1957. A copy of this letter is possessed by Nishijima.

25. Nagatsuka Toshikazu, *Kubota Yutaka 1966* (Tokyo: Denki Jōhō Sha, 1966), p. 367.
26. Ibid., p. 305.
27. Ibid., p. 319.
28. Ibid., p. 325–326.
29. Ibid., p. 361.
30. Masuda, p. 123.
31. Japan, Foreign Ministry, *Gaimushō shokuinroku 1940*, p. 23; and *1941*, p. 27. For details of his experiences during the war, see Miyoshi Shunkichirō, "Jawa senryō gunsei kaiko roku," *Kokusai Mondai*, April 1965 to January 1967.
32. See his study report, *Indoneshia ni taisuru baishō mondai* (mimeographed, Japan-Indonesia Association, n.d.) which describes a brief history of the reparations to 1956 and Indonesia's views on the reparations.
33. Kobayashi, p. 183.
34. Ibid., pp. 181, 185–189.
35. See chapters 4 and 5.
36. The society was established in 1954 as a quasigovernmental agency under the Foreign Ministry to implement Japan's economic and technical aid to foreign countries. It absorbed Matsunaga's Asian Economic Research Council and other related Asian study groups. Later in 1961 the society was renamed as the Overseas Technical Cooperation Agency (OTCA).
37. Masuda, p. 121. In 1941 he became vice-chairman of the South Seas Association (Nanyō Kyōkai), and chairman of the Southern [Asian] Economic Affairs Society (Nanpō Keizai Kondankai). In 1942 he was appointed as a counselor to the Ministry of the Navy and traveled throughout Southeast Asia. See Fujiyama Aiichirō, "Fujiyama Aiichirō," *Watakushi no rirekisho*, ed. by Nihon Keizai Shinbun Sha (Tokyo: Nihon Keizai Shinbun Sha, 1957) 4: 359–361.
38. Nishijima, interview.
39. Foreign Minister Adam Malik, private interview in Jakarta, February 24, 1972.
40. Masuda, p. 145.
41. The joint note is entitled, *Tai Indoneshia baishō mondai kaiketsu sokushin no tame ni* (typed, January 24, 1951). In 1940 Satō went to Batavia as director of the Batavia Office of the Economic Bureau of the Tokyo Municipal Government. Working closely with the Japanese consulate general in Batavia and the navy, he was involved in anti-Dutch intelligence activities and drew up a plan to rescue the nationalist leaders Hatta and Thamrin from Dutch surveillance and send them to Japan but it was unsuccessful. Ishii was an active businessman in Batavia. Both he and Satō joined Nishijima in his anti-Dutch underground activities. See Masuda, pp. 145–147. Shibata was the commander of the Second Southern Fleet.
42. This paragraph based on Nishijima, interview.
43. *Asahi Shinbun*, June 20, 1956.
44. Matsunaga, "Isai, Ayukawa san," pp. 364–365.
45. As mentioned previously, Iwata Yoshio of the Asian Economic Research Council and Kubota Yutaka of Nippon Kōei also tried to develop the Asahan River.
46. Takagi Hiroichi, "Indoneshia to Nihon no keizai kyōryoku," *Kokusai Jihyō*, no. 79 (November, 1971): 48.
47. The 1955 general elections allocated 57 seats for the PNI, 57 for the Masjumi, 45 for the NU, and 39 for the PKI, out of a total of 257 seats.
48. Nishijima, interview. Lubis was considered as one of the best officers of the Japanese-trained voluntary army (PETA).
49. Unless otherwise mentioned, information here is based on Nishijima, interview.

50. From Subardjo's photographical records.

51. From Subardjo's letter to Nishijima, dated August 14, 1957. Possessed by Nishijima.

52. See Harry Benda, Jr., *The Crescent and the Rising Sun* (The Hague: van Hoeve, 1958), p. 112; Kishi, pp. 329–335; Machida Keiji, *Tatakau bunka butai* (Tokyo: Hara Shobō, 1967), pp. 153–166; and Nakatani Yoshio, "Ko Sukaruno Daitōryō to watakushi" (1), *Indoneshia Bungaku*, no. 3 (1972): 61–68.

53. Putera is an acronym for Pusat Tenaga Rakyat, meaning literally the Center of Popular Force, which existed from March 1943 to January 1944 when it was replaced by another mass-based organization, Djawa Hōkōkai, or the Java Popular Service Association. Both were supervised by the Japanese occupation authority. See Kishi, pp. 341–352, 383–395.

54. Shimizu Hitoshi, private interview in Tokyo, April 25, 1972.

55. *Mainichi Shinbun*, September 13, 1957.

56. From Nishijima's letter to H. A. Dachlan dated August 28, 1957. A copy of the letter is possessed by Nishijima.

57. This paragraph is based on Shimonaka Yasaburō Biography Publishing Committee, *Shimonaka Yasaburō jiten* (Tokyo: Heibon Sha, 1965), pp. 18–22. Kaneko was a civilian in the Sixteenth Army in charge of youth affairs, helping Shimizu Hitoshi with his propaganda work. In May 1945 they worked to integrate all the youth groups of Java and conducted a huge demonstration in Bandung, West Java, to call for the rise of nationalist sentiment. See Masuda, p. 165.

58. Based on Omar Tusin, private interview in Jakarta, February 9, 1972.

Chapter 4
The Reparations Payment and Its Effects, 1958–1965

Japan's reparations to Indonesia, amounting to $223.08 million, were to be paid over a period of twelve years in the form of services and capital goods. This attracted both businessmen and political leaders, in both countries, who saw great benefits in being involved in this project. The questions of how the reparations fund actually was used and by whom it was used are sensitive because they allegedly entailed manipulation of the fund and involvement therein on the part of leaders of both countries. While these questions will be explored later, this chapter provides an overall picture of the payments from 1958 to 1970 and demonstrates, on the basis of Japanese statistics, that the fund was actually used up by about 1965. This chapter also will show the major items and projects for which the fund was spent. It also demonstrates that the reparations fund had a more limited effect upon Indonesia's economy than had been expected originally and argues that many of the projects planned to enhance Sukarno's prestige were of little use to the country, and, moreover, that Indonesia's inefficient government and internal political troubles delayed the completion of many projects and left many others unfinished or inoperable.

AN OVERALL PICTURE OF THE PAYMENT AND PROGRAMS

Scheduled, Approved, and Disbursed Amounts of Payment

Under the reparations agreement Japan agreed to pay $20 million annually during the first eleven years and $3.08 million during the twelfth year. The actual payments differed considerably from this schedule, although the payments did end on April 14, 1970, exactly twelve years after the agreement took effect on April 15, 1958.[1]

Receiving reparations was a new experience for Indonesia and organizing payment schedules and projects took time. Each year the Japanese and Indonesian governments were supposed to make plans for the types of projects to be carried out with the annual fund of $20 million, but during the first year plans were not formulated until March 18, 1959,[2] only two weeks before the end of the fiscal year, a delay of eleven months. Even during the second year the planning was not as efficient as might have been hoped.[3] Plans were not the only obstacle. Even after the government had agreed on the projects and payments and contracts were concluded, their actual accomplishment often was delayed.

The annual payments can be viewed on two levels: the scheduled payments ($20 million for the first eleven years and $3.08 million for the twelfth year) and the yearly approved payments. Table 10 indicates these in both yearly and cumulative breakdowns. As this table shows, the approved payment for the fourth year, $39.52 million, went far over that year's scheduled payments, while the approved payment for the fifth year fell short of the scheduled payment amount, although the cumulated disbursed amount never exceeded the scheduled amount. The Indonesian government used the reparations fund for large projects, consuming a major portion of the yearly allocated funds and by 1963 it became obvious to Japan that Indonesia's foreign exchange debts would have to be covered by the reparations fund. A Japanese government report pointed out in 1964 that the funds were running out.[4]

The largest problem in the reparations payments came after December 1965 when Indonesia began regularly to use these payments to settle loans. Soon after the reparations agreement was put into effect, Indonesia decided on some development projects to be carried out by Japanese loans, separate from the reparations fund. On October 16, 1959 after about a year of negotiations Foreign Ministers Fujiyama Aiichirō and Subandrio drew up these loans and agreed that they would be repaid in American dollars. If Indonesia could not repay them, they would be deducted from the reparations. These loans were made to Indonesia four times between 1959 and 1963, totaling $81.7 million, or $94.76 million with interest. Such reparations-secured loans technically were separate from the reparations payments, but the programs themselves often supplemented each other financially. Repayment of these loans began in August 1961 and continued uninterrupted until November 1965, when the attempted coup of October 1965 diminished Indonesia's already scanty foreign currency holdings and prevented further repayments. Then the reparations fund had to be used to cover these outstanding loans, as shown in Table 10. Consequently, most of

TABLE 10

REPARATIONS TO INDONESIA IN YEARLY AND CUMULATIVE PAYMENTS ACCORDING TO SCHEDULE, APPROVAL, AND DISBURSEMENT BASES, 1958–1970[a]

YEAR	YEARLY PAYMENTS (in millions of $)						CUMULATIVE PAYMENTS (in millions of $)			
	Scheduled amount	Approved amount[b]	Disbursed amount				Scheduled amount	(percent)	Disbursed amount	(percent)
			capital & service	educ. & mission	drawn for loan	total				
1958–1959	20.00	14.28	12.60	0.31	—	12.91	20.00	(9.0)	12.91	(5.8)
1959–1960	20.00	17.83	15.58	0.30	—	15.88	40.00	(17.9)	28.79	(12.9)
1960–1961	20.00	19.34	14.42	0.61	—	15.03	60.00	(26.9)	43.82	(19.7)
1961–1962	20.00	39.95	30.86	2.92	0.14	33.92	80.00	(36.0)	77.74	(34.9)
1962–1963	20.00	6.31	15.62	2.59	0	18.21	100.00	(44.8)	95.95	(43.1)
1963–1964	20.00	25.28	15.56	1.80	—	17.36	120.00	(53.8)	113.31	(50.9)
1964–1965	20.00	13.24	14.14	1.34	—	15.48	140.00	(62.8)	128.79	(57.8)
1965–1966	20.00	13.00	18.09	1.19	7.40	26.68	160.00	(71.7)	155.47	(69.8)
1966–1967	20.00	0.56	5.19	0.99	17.52	23.70	180.00	(80.7)	179.17	(80.5)
1967–1968	20.00	0.65	2.91	0.77	16.66	20.34	200.00	(89.7)	199.51	(89.6)
1968–1969	20.00	2.36	4.63	0.64	12.29	17.56	220.00	(98.7)	217.07	(97.5)
1969–1970	3.08	2.95	3.83	0.60	1.18	5.61	223.08	(100.0)	222.68[c]	(100.0)
TOTAL	223.08	153.43	153.82	14.06	55.19	222.68[c]	223.08	(100.0)	222.68[c]	(100.0)

— Indicates the number is negligible.

[a] Amount of payment is expressed here in U.S. dollars ($1 = ¥360), although actual payment was made in Japanese yen.

[b] Approved amount includes only payments for capital, consumer goods, and services, and not for educational and training programs in Japan and Reparations Mission activities in Japan. Disbursed amount shows these figures separately, together with amount drawn for overdue loans secured by reparations funds. Total reparations-secured loans amounted to $81.70 million, or $94.76 million with interest. Indonesia was unable to repay the loans after December 1965 and reparations were used for payments.

[c] Totals do not add up to $223.08 million, perhaps due to statistical discrepancies.

Source: Calculated from Japan, Foreign Ministry, Economic Cooperation Bureau, *Baishō nado jisshi jōkyō, 1971-nen 7-9 gatsu,* (mimeographed, October 1, 1971), pp. 20, 55.

TABLE 11
Distribution of Reparations Fund and Reparations-Secured Loans by Categories

Major Categories	Reparations payment (in millions of $)	in percent	Rep.-Secured Loans payment (in millions of $)	in percent
Capital Goods				
a. Infrastructure projects				
1. Brantas and Riam Kanan River development	30.31	14	—	—
2. Bridge	9.39	4	6.25	8
3. Docks	6.28	3	6.60	8
Subtotal	45.98	21	12.85	16
b. Heavy industry projects				
1. Machinery and ships	74.19	33	27.35	33
Subtotal	74.19	33	27.35	33
c. Light industry projects				
1. Paper mills	17.94	8	8.50	10
2. Plywood plants	6.64	3	—	—
3. Weaving and spinning plants	9.08	4	—	—
Subtotal	33.66	15	8.50	10
Consumer Goods	9.33	4	—	—
Subtotal	9.33	4	—	—

Service Industries					
1. Hotel construction		20.78	9	22.00	27
2. Department stores		10.33	5	11.00	13
3. Office buildings		5.78	3	—	—
	Subtotal	36.89	17	33.00	40
Fellowships		8.56	4	—	—
	Subtotal	8.56	4	—	—
Reparations Mission Expenses and Miscellaneous Services		14.44	6	—	—
	Subtotal	14.44	6	—	—
	TOTAL	$223.05[a]	100	$81.70	99[b]

— Indicates the number is negligible.

[a] Figures in this column are rounded; this total does not amount to $223.08 million, which should be the official total amount of payment.

[b] The total does not add up to 100 percent, because figures of this column are rounded.

Source: Based on Japan, Ministry of International Trade and Industry, Bureau of Trade Promotion, *Keizai kyōryoku no genjō to mondaiten, 1970,* pp. 308–309.

the remaining reparations programs were terminated or suspended.

The Reparations Programs

The reparations agreement of 1958 contained a list of six categories of programs and projects for which the reparations funds would be used. These were: transportation and communications, power development, industrial development, agricultural and fisheries development, mining, and services. These embraced nearly all industries and an additional list set forth sixty-six more specific categories to be considered for reparations funding. These included medical supplies, printing of the Koran (Islamic scripture), and astronomical equipment. Exceptions were some service industries, hotels, and department stores, which later were marked for loans secured by the reparations fund.

During the entire twelve-year period, a total of twenty-six major projects were approved and financed by the reparations fund, although not all of these had been completed by the last scheduled payment in 1970.[5] All twenty-six projects totaled $77.63 million, or 35 percent of the total reparations fund of $223.08 million. Among them were an irrigation flood control project in East Java; papermills in North Sumatra, South Kalimantan, and South Sulawesi; textile factories in Bandung and Jakarta; and water-power systems in East Java. The most expensive project was a dam costing $19,237,000, which was built in Karankates on the upper part of the Brantas River in East Java.

The entire reparations fund, broken down into five categories, is shown in Table 11. As the table shows, infrastructure projects received 21 percent of the fund, heavy industries 33 percent, light industries 15 percent, service industries 17 percent, and consumer goods 4 percent. Another 4 percent of the fund was used for fellowships and training for Indonesians, and the remaining 6 percent of the fund went to services connected with these projects and to the Reparations Mission expenses in Tokyo.

When the reparations first were decided upon at the San Francisco Peace Conference in 1951, the peace treaty stipulated in Article 14 that the reparations would be paid in the form of "services of the Japanese people in production, salvaging and other work." Later Japan conceded to Indonesia's demand that capital goods also should constitute part of the compensation. The result of the actual payments was, as the table demonstrates, that the original "services" accounted for only 6 percent of the total payment and that only 4 percent was made in consumer goods, indicating considerable deviation from the initial concept.

One of the projects was an educational and training program for

Indonesian youths.[6] Approximately 100 students were to be sent to Japan each year beginning in 1960, for five to seven years of university education, and some 250 young Indonesians were to go to Japan for up to two and a half years of occupational and professional training in private firms and government offices. Altogether 500 students were to be sent in five years and 1750 trainees in seven years. Under individual contracts several dozen more Indonesians were to be given technical training in order to manage the plants and other facilities being constructed as reparations projects. In all, an estimated 2,500 Indonesians were to receive some kind of technical or educational training under the reparations agreement.

Reparations-Secured Loans

Reference already has been made to Indonesia's loans. With these Indonesia undertook ten projects: four large hotels in Jakarta, Plabuhan Ratu (West Java), Yogyakarta, and Bali; a department store in Jakarta; a port dock in Surabaya; a bridge over the Musi River in Palembang; a paper mill in Banyuwangi, East Java; and sixteen ships and ten coastal patrol boats.[7] Some of these projects were combined with reparations projects; for instance, the basic construction of the hotels was covered by reparations-secured loans of $28.05 million but certain elements of these hotels were financed by $4.5 million from the reparations fund. The Musi River bridge project was arranged similarly, with $4.28 million from the reparations fund and $7.51 million from reparations-secured loans. Table 11 examines these projects together with the reparations projects. Sixty percent of the loans projects was devoted to machines and ships (33 percent) and hotels (27 percent).

ECONOMIC EFFECTS OF THE REPARATIONS PROGRAMS

Payment of the reparations was scheduled so as not to upset the Japanese economy. Article 4 of the peace treaty between Japan and Indonesia recognized that "the resources of Japan are not sufficient, if it is to maintain a viable economy, to make complete reparation for all the damage and suffering for the Republic of Indonesia and other countries caused by Japan during the war and at the same time meet its other obligations." The binational reparations agreement then provided in Article 2 that the reparations "shall be carried out in such a manner as may not prejudice the normal trade between Japan and the Republic of Indonesia, nor impose additional exchange burden upon Japan." Throughout the periods of negotiation and payment, Japan made positive use of this understanding and used the reparations to promote their exports. This already has been mentioned and in this section we will examine more closely the economic effect of the reparations on Japan as well as on Indonesia.

The total amount of Japanese reparations to be paid to the four Southeast Asian nations of Indonesia, the Philippines, Burma, and South Vietnam, came to $1,152 million.[8] This was to be paid from 1955 through 1976, making average yearly payments of approximately $52 million. The heaviest years were to be 1960 and 1962, when, according to the schedule, $75 million was to be paid annually. The major portion of the reparations was to be paid by the end of 1968, after which the annual commitment would drop to less than $45 million.[9] These figures are based on payment schedules, but the actual payment figures differed due to Indonesia's prolonged preparations. For example, in 1960, one of the heavy years, the scheduled payment was to be $75 million but the actual payment was only $49.1 million.[10] This latter amount was 1.2 percent of Japan's total exports that year, or $4.1 billion. Thus the reparations did not prove harmful to Japan's exports to Indonesia, nor did they compete with its exports elsewhere.

According to a Japanese government survey, some of the products provided by the reparations had to be financed in foreign currency. Railroads, electric generators, trucks, and freighters, for example, required steel which Japan could manufacture only by importing iron ore and other raw materials. As another example, 30.7 percent of the railroad construction costs and 15.4 percent of the expenses for cargo vessels depended upon foreign currency.[11] Despite the reparations agreement's provision against reparations payments that might impose an "additional foreign exchange burden upon Japan," Japan had to sacrifice annually a certain amount of foreign exchange because of the reparations. According to this same survey, it was found that in 1960, some $7.5 million, or 15.3 percent of the reparations required foreign currency.[12] However, this $7.5 million constituted only 0.4 percent of Japan's foreign currency holdings of $1,824 million for that year.[13] In terms of both the percentage of total export values and of foreign currency reserves, the reparations imposed little burden upon Japan. From the Japanese standpoint the supply of reparations materials made positive demands on Japan's domestic production, providing that they did not conflict with the normal flow of exports to the claimant country,[14] as the Japanese government supplied Japanese businesses with all the necessary funds. In other words, the reparations payments stimulated domestic production in Japan which it otherwise might not have had and augmented Japan's exports to Indonesia. Table 12 compares the reparations payments to the total value of exports to Indonesia and exports of capital goods to Indonesia. The value of Japanese exports

COMPARISONS AMONG JAPAN'S REPARATIONS, ITS EXPORTS TO INDONESIA, AND ITS EXPORTS OF HEAVY MANUFACTURED GOODS, 1958–1970

YEAR	(A) REPARATIONS		(B) EXPORTS TO INDONESIA		(C) EXPORTS OF CAPITAL GOODS
	(in millions of $)	$\frac{A}{A \& B} \times 100$ (in percent)	(in millions of $)	$\frac{B}{A \& B} \times 100$ (in percent)	(in millions of $)
1958	12.91	21	49.06	79	20.19
1959	15.88	18	73.02	82	38.85
1960	15.03	12	110.82	88	32.19
1961	33.92	18	154.77	82	87.37
1962	18.21	14	116.31	86	79.81
1963	17.36	15	99.07	85	69.93
1964	15.48	11	122.09	89	74.78
1965	26.68	11	207.19	89	125.02
1966	23.70	16	118.62	84	57.43
1967	20.34	12	155.15	88	81.93
1968	17.56	10	146.60	90	91.88
1969	5.61	3	235.81	97	174.37
1970	—	—	315.78	100	219.30
Average:	18.56	11	146.48	89	81.01

— Indicates the number is negligible.

Note: Figures for Column (A) are those for fiscal years; for example, the figure for 1958 covers April 1958 through March 1959.

Sources: (A), from Table 10.
(B), from Table 3.
(C), 1958, *Tsūshō hakusho 1959*, II, pp. 240–241; 1959–1961, *Tsūshō hakusho 1962*, II, pp. 272–273; 1962–1964, *Tsūshō hakusho 1965*, II, pp. 311–312; 1965–1967, *Tsūshō hakusho 1968*, II, pp. 320–322; 1968–1970, *Tsūshō hakusho 1971*, II, pp. 341–345.

increased during the period of 1958–1970. In 1959 the reparations payment was equal to approximately one-fifth of the value of Japan's total exports to Indonesia but, on the average, reparations payments for the whole period were only about one-tenth of the total exports. After 1963, with the exception of 1966, this proportion became more or less established. Since the average yearly payment of reparations was $18.56 million, larger than the 1958 payment of $12.91 million, it is obvious that Japan's exports were increasing.

As Table 11 demonstrates, the reparations were paid primarily in capital goods. As seen in Table 4 which shows the percentage composition of Japan's trade in commodities with Indonesia, exports to Indonesia were dominated by light-manufactured (consumer) goods and heavy-manufactured (capital) goods. It can be seen that there was a larger percentage of consumer goods from 1956 to 1960 than from 1961 to 1970, and that in proportion to this change, the percentage of heavy-manufactured goods increased from an average of 34.1 percent from 1956 to 1960 to an average of 62.5 percent from 1961 to 1970. This indicates that the value of exported capital goods was not affected adversely by the reparations but rather was improved by them.

Although the reparations as a whole had relatively little effect on Japan's economy, they had a much greater effect on Indonesia's economy. Indonesia's Eight-Year Economic Plan of 1961–1968 was based on a loan of one billion dollars from abroad, a sum of $125 million annually.[15] Thus Japan's payments of $20 million each year for eight years accounted for 16 percent of Indonesia's total development budget of 1961–1968, making it an important source of foreign aid for Indonesia.

Table 13 compares Japan's reparations to Indonesia, Indonesia's total imports, and its foreign exchange reserves from 1958 to 1970. It shows, Indonesia's foreign exchange reserves deteriorated after 1960. The average amount for the period from 1958 to 1962 was some $206 million. Japan's scheduled payment of $20 million was then equivalent to about 10 percent of Indonesia's reserves. After 1963, because Indonesia's foreign exchange debts increased, the reparations became an even more important source of aid for Indonesia.

Similarly, Table 13 shows that Japan's provision of materials through reparations constituted an average 3 percent of Indonesia's imports, meaning that Indonesia got that proportion of materials from Japan without spending its own foreign exchange.

A PRELIMINARY ASSESSMENT OF REPARATIONS PROJECTS

On the whole, the reparations projects have had more negative

TABLE 13

COMPARISONS AMONG JAPAN'S REPARATIONS, INDONESIA'S TOTAL
IMPORTS, AND INDONESIA'S FOREIGN EXCHANGE RESERVES, 1958–1970

YEAR	(A) REPARATIONS (in millions of $)	(B) TOTAL INDONESIAN IMPORTS (in millions of $)	$\frac{A}{B} \times 100$ (in percent)	(C) INDONESIAN FOREIGN EXCHANGE RESERVES (in millions of $)	$\frac{A}{C} \times 100$ (in percent)
1958	12.91	513	2.5	212	6.1
1959	15.88	458	3.5	300	5.3
1960	15.03	574	2.6	301	4.9
1961	33.92	794	4.3	122	5.1
1962	18.21	647	2.8	94	19.3
1963	17.36	521	3.3	−16	—
1964	15.48	680	2.3	−49	—
1965	26.68	695	3.8	−73	—
1966	23.70	527	4.5	−77	—
1967	20.34	649	3.1	−78	—
1968	17.56	716	2.5	−74	—
1969	5.61	697	0.8	−66	—
1970	—	893	—	−52	—
Average:	18.56	642	3.0	41.85	—

— Indicates the number is negligible.

Note: (C) includes (A).

Sources: (A), from Table 10.
(B), 1958–1960, *Indoneshia Kyōwakoku benran* (1964), p. 104; 1961–1969, from Table 2.
(C), 1970, *Indonesian Financial Statistics, August 1972*, p. 130; 1958–1959, *Indoneshia Kyōwakoku benran* (1964), p. 92; 1960–1969, Japan, Overseas Technical Co-operation Agency, *Kaigai keizai kyōryoku benran* 1971, p. 101; 1970, from the Economic Section, Japanese Embassy, Jakarta, January 1972.

aspects than positive if seen only in economic terms. Many projects did not receive enough funds to be completed, largely owing to Indonesia's inflation. Other projects were suspended after December 1965 because of insufficient funds.

All the 26 major reparations projects mentioned earlier were contracted between February 1959 and October 1965, and all ten reparations-secured loans projects between August 1960 and August 1963. According to an assessment made in April 1968 by the Japanese Ministry of International Trade and Industry (MITI),[16] 11 of 36 projects were not completed. Of the 25 which were completed, 7 were found to be running inefficiently. Only 18, half of all the major projects, were in satisfactory condition. The Japanese Foreign Ministry's annual report for 1968 admitted that the reparations projects had had little effect on Indonesia's economy.[17]

Among those projects both completed and running efficiently is a bridge across the Musi River in South Sumatra which was finished in May 1965 at a cost of $11,782,000. The bridge is located in Palembang, the capital and largest city in the province, which is also an area of rich oil reserves. Before this bridge was built, sampans were used to cross the 300-meter-wide river, the trip usually taking one hour including waiting time. The bridge shortened this to ten minutes on foot or three by car.

Another successful project is the Neyama water control tunnel constructed in East Java. In order to control flooding in the lowlands of Brantas River, the tunnel diverts the flow of water into the Indian Ocean. The idea of a tunnel to divert this water first was considered during the Dutch period and was implemented during the Japanese occupation. But it was not built efficiently and soon went out of operation when the tunnel became clogged. As one of the first reparations projects, the construction of a new tunnel was contracted in 1959 and was completed in April 1961 at a cost of $1,972,000. The new tunnel, 1000 meters in length and 7 meters in diameter, can displace 500 cubic meters of water per second, contributing greatly to flood control in the locality. Since its completion some 3000 hectares of land have been free of floods, resulting in a $2 million profit in the region's agricultural production in the first year.[18]

Comprehensive development projects in the areas of the Brantas River in East Java and the Kanan River (or Riam Kanan) in South Kalimantan were the largest construction projects under the reparations and became symbolic of them. These projects contracted in 1963 were called the "3K projects," representing the names of the three rivers beginning with K.[19] The first was the Karankates River, a tributary of the Brantas River; the second the Konto River (or Kali Konto), a branch of the Brantas River; and the third the Kanan River. The Karankates project was designed to generate 100,000 kilowatts of electricity with a 100-meter-high dam, the Kali Konto project, 4,500 kilowatts of electricity with a 60-meter-high dam, and the Kanan project, 30,000 kilowatts of electricity with a 58-meter-high dam. The first two dams also were designed to control flooding, to provide irrigation, and to prevent erosion. The three dam projects used $28,352,000 from the reparations funds, but, when they could not be finished for this price, additional yen credits were supplied.[20] The Kali Konto project was completed in early 1970, the Karankates project in May 1972, and the Kanan project was to have been completed sometime in 1972. It is still too early to evaluate them. Once the dams begin operation, their water control will enable greater agricultural production and control infectious disease. Their electrical output is expected to stimulate local industrial development.

Manufacturing plants and textile and paper mills were among the top priorities of the reparations programs. Out of seventeen major Indonesian textile mills, eight were built with Japanese assistance,[21] and of those, four with reparations funds. These four plants located in Jakarta, Malang, Bandung, and Denpasar (Bali) constituted some 68,400 spindles, or 17 percent of Indonesia's total spindles. While the Jakarta and Bandung mills operated at almost full capacity, the Malang and Denpasar mills encountered difficulties even while they were being built. Although they were begun in August 1961, they were not completed until February 1967 and April 1966, respectively. Both suffered from political disorders ensuing from the Gestapu incident of 1965, and many of the parts for the plants were stolen, delaying their completion even further. When finished, however, their spindles operated at 87 percent capacity in Malang and at 60 percent capacity in Bali.

In 1968 there were seven paper mills in Indonesia, four of which were built with reparations funds. These seven mills were expected to produce 85 tons of paper daily, but in 1968 their progress was interrupted. The first plant, built in Siantar, North Sumatra, in August 1962, produced 18 tons daily under Japanese supervisors but after they left its daily production dropped to 3 tons and in early 1969 stopped completely.[22] Inefficient management and labor, lack of parts, and substitution of well water for river water are listed among the reasons for the drop in production. Another paper mill, in South Kalimantan, was to have been finished in 1961 but as of early 1969 was still far from completion. Delays were blamed on inadequate planning, shortage of funds, and poor maintenance of transported equipment. The initial reparations funds of $1,919,000 were exhausted and without further financial support from the Indonesian government, the paper mill's completion is in doubt.

Other projects included four large hotels in Jakarta, Pulabuhan Ratu (West Java), Yogyakarta, and Bali. The 14-story Hotel Indonesia built in Jakarta in 1962 originally was intended to accommodate foreign dignitaries and tourists at that year's Asian Games. Until 1969 the hotel was an important source of foreign exchange, as all guests were required to pay their bills in American dollars. As the only international hotel in Jakarta—and in the nation until 1966—the Hotel Indonesia usually operated at full capacity and became the center of Jakarta's major diplomatic and social activities. The Hotel Indonesia has therefore been successful but the other three, although of equally high quality, have run at only 20 to 30 percent capacity since opening in 1966.[23] Transportation to and from these hotels is not convenient and the absence of entertainment and services discourage tourists. These factors plus Indonesia's low standard of living have limited the use of these modern and expensive hotels to foreign tourists and rich Indonesians.

Other visible and impractical projects were the 14-story Sarinah Department Store and the 29-story Wisma Nusantara office building both located on Jakarta's new main thoroughfare, Jalan Thamrin. Opening in August 1966, the Sarinah Department Store attracted Indonesians as the site of the nation's first escalator rather than as the nation's first modern department store. Although the quality of merchandise was high, the prices were too, putting it beyond the reach of the average Indonesian. The fixed-price system adopted by Sarinah was not familiar to Jakarta shoppers, and so it was not surprising that in 1969 the top floor was set aside for a casino and that in 1972 the next three upper floors were being remodeled into a hotel. Sarinah's future as a department store remains uncertain.

The future of the Wisma Nusantara is equally questionable. The first contract was let in August 1964 for $5.8 million and construction went well until the abortive coup in October 1965. After that, with the loss of Indonesia's foreign exchange, work was halted in December 1966. The office building's huge superstructure jutting nakedly into the sky became symbolic of Indonesia's political and economic conditions. In 1971 a new contract was made with Mitsui and construction was resumed. Even if the building was completed by October 1972, as scheduled, the justification for such a large and obviously expensive office building in Jakarta can be found only in terms of prestige.

Many other reparations projects encountered similar difficulties. In February 1969 the Japanese Foreign Ministry sent a mission to Indonesia headed by Kitajima Takeo, former chairman of the Fair Trade Commission under the prime minister. The Kitajima Mission found delays in many of the reparations-related projects and attributed these partly to shortages in Indonesia's supplementary funds, inadequate maintenance and lack of equipment parts, and the political upheaval of 1965.[24] The most significant cause of delay—inefficient management—the Kitajima Mission found to be because of the political importance of many projects rather than of economic considerations—making their practicality doubtful.[25]

The scholarship and training program mentioned earlier existed only in Japan's reparations to Indonesia. No other country's reparations agreements with Japan included this sort of program. In the arrangement with Indonesia, 500 students were to come to Japan for five to seven years of study while 1,750 youths were to come for vocational and technical training in government offices and private business firms.[26] However, the actual program deviated greatly from this original plan. Only 378 students and 474 trainees could be accommodated financially,[27] because the allocated funds were spent on other items such as the expenses of the Indonesian embassy in Tokyo.[28] In addition, the selection of participants was based often on political rather than educational merit. The sons or relatives of prominent figures frequently found places in this program.

Some Indonesians selected to go to Japan under this fellowship program formed political groups there. Particularly strong was the PNI-oriented, Sukarnoist group which took over the leadership of the Indonesian Students Association (PPI) in Tokyo. The PPI became the "Sukarnoist Front" in Tokyo supporting Sukarno's West Irian campaigns in 1960–1962 and his anti-Malaysia campaigns in 1963–1965 as well as his concepts of MANIPOL, USDEK, NASAKOM.[29] Some of the students were accused of indirect complicity in the attempted coup of October 1965 and were expatriated.[30]

Although this educational program implied political success, its academic success was doubtful. Many of the students' fluency in Japanese and their academic preparation were not sufficient for their coursework, and often the trainees' positions in Indonesian government offices and business firms were inferior to those given to European- and American-trained participants. Whether the limited educational achievements of this program will have a positive or a negative effect upon Japanese-Indonesian relations is unclear, as are indeed the future roles that the graduates of this program will play, both in this regard and in Indonesian society itself.

Certainly it is too soon to make a final assessment of the reparations programs. Some of the major projects have been completed only recently and their economic results have not yet been determined. However, it is evident that most of the programs under the reparations agreement digressed from the original intention. They also were used to promote trade with Japan, which was successful insofar as it provided an essential source of "foreign aid" to Indonesia. But again, many of the projects themselves proved infeasible and thus the funds were often wasted. The questions of who originated these impractical projects and why are given closer attention in the following chapter.

NOTES

1. *Asahi Shinbun*, April 17, 1970.

2. Reparations Problems Study Group, ed., *Nihon no baishō 1963* (Tokyo: Sekai Jānaru Sha, 1963), p. 213.

3. Ibid., p. 214.

4. Japan, Foreign Ministry, *Waga gaikō no kinkyō*, no. 8 (1964): 250.

5. A list of these twenty-six projects appear in Japan, Foreign Ministry, Economic Affairs Bureau, ed., *Indoneshia* (Tokyo: Nihon Kokusai Mondai Kenkyūjo, 1972), p. 115. Confer also Table 15.

6. The sixty-fifth entry in the reparations agreement's list of projects considered for the reparations payment referred to the "training of Indonesian technicians and craftsmen in Japan and in Indonesia." On February 10, 1960 the Indonesian government officially proposed a student and trainee program and the Japanese government agreed to the proposal. The first group of students arrived in 1960. see *Nihon no baishō 1963*, pp. 130–132.

7. For a general description of these projects, see ibid., pp. 234–238; and *Indoneshia*, p. 116.

8. *Nihon no baishō 1963*, pp. 20–21.

9. Ibid., pp. 20–21.

10. Ibid., p. 30.

11. Ibid., p. 31.

12. Ibid.

13. Ibid., p. 32.

14. Ibid., p. 40.

15. Ibid., p. 66.

16. Japan, Ministry of International Trade and Industry, Trade Promotion Bureau, *En shakkan, baishō nado shihonkyōryoku jisshi jōkyō* (April, 1968).

17. Japan, Foreign Ministry, *Waga gaikō no kinkyō*, no. 12 (1968): 338.

18. Daiyamondo Sha, *Nippon Kōei* (Tokyo: Daiyamondo Sha, 1971), pp. 51–52.

19. Ibid., pp. 78–79.

20. Under the reparations programs the Karankates project was contracted for $19,237,000; the Kali Konto project for $3,441,000; and the Riam Kanan project for $5,664,000. See Japan, Foreign Ministry, *Indoneshia*, p. 115. The exact amount of additional credit extended to these projects is not known publicly but they were financed by Japanese project aid of $10 million in 1968 and $20 million in 1969. See ibid., pp. 118–119.

21. Japan, Economic Cooperation Survey Mission for Indonesia, *Indoneshia Keizai Kyōryoku Chōsadan chōsa kōkoku* (Tokyo: Foreign Ministry, Economic Cooperation Bureau, 1969), p. 47.

22. Ibid., p. 55.

23. Ibid., p. 65.

24. Ibid., p. 74. For the summary of its evaluations and suggestions for Japanese economic cooperation policies, see *Asahi Shinbun*, October 28, 1969.

25. Ibid., p. 73.

26. See note 5, this chapter.

27. Sakata Zenzaburō, *Indoneshia: genjō to mondaiten* (Tokyo: Japan Federation of Economic Organizations [Keidanren], 1968), p. 72; and *Gijutsu kyōryoku nenpō 1969*, pp. 289–293.

28. Anonymous former recipient of a reparations fellowship, private interview in Jakarta, July 1970.

29. MANIPOL stands for Political Manifesto (*Manifesto Politik*), which is the title of Sukarno's 1959 Independence Day speech. It is considered to be a basic document

of his regime. Early in 1960 the speech was said to consist of five ideas: the 1945 constitution (U); Socialism a la Indonesia (S); Guided Democracy (D); Guided Economy (E); and Indonesian Personality (K). Hence, the MANIPOL became known as USDEK. NASAKOM is another acronym for the combination of the nationalist (*Nas*ional), religious (*A*gama), and Communist (*Kom*unis) forces which represented the dominant social and political forces during the Guided Democracy period and which expressed their interests in major government agencies such as the cabinet and parliament.

30. *Yomiuri Shinbun*, August 5, 1966.

Chapter 5
The Reparations Lobbies, 1958–1965

POLITICS OF REPARATIONS

Japan's payment of reparations of $223.08 million to Indonesia attracted both business and political circles in the two countries, and stimulated lobbying activities. The prominent Indonesians and Japanese who were included in these lobbies made contacts which were an important part of Sukarno's Guided Democracy period (1958–1965) and which later were essential to the close ties between the two countries.

General Payment Arrangements

The system of payment of the reparations is described in the reparations agreement of 1958 and its annexed documents. Essentially, it was the method used in ordinary commercial contracts, in which the Indonesian government drew up contracts directly with "Japanese nationals or juridical persons controlled by Japanese nationals" (Agreement, Article 4 [1]). In many cases the Indonesian government employed a system of bidding, in which it put up for bidding those products or services it needed. After Indonesia had settled upon satisfactory terms, a contract was drawn up which had to be verified by the Japanese government before becoming effective and before the necessary funds could be transferred to the concerned supplier through the Indonesian government (Agreement, Article 4 [2]). To facilitate these reparations contracts, the Indonesian government in June 1958 established a Reparations Mission (Missi Pampasan Republik Indonesia, or MISPRI) in Tokyo, apart from the Indonesian embassy (Agreement, Article 6). The Indonesian government annually sent to the mission a list of procurement orders which the mission used to negotiate with the Japanese firms as the "sole and exclusive agent" (Agreement, Article 6 [1]).

In charge of the projects on the Indonesian side was the Reparations Implementation Committee of the Indonesian government, established on September 20, 1958.[1] The committee included officials from the Ministries of Foreign Affairs, Finance, Industry, Trade, Agriculture, and Shipping, and was chaired by the secretary-general of the Foreign Ministry and administered by the ministry's Reparations Bureau. Each year the committee filed requests made by the member ministries and formulated procurement orders. General guidelines for the projects also were supplied by the National Planning Council (Dewan Perancang Nasional), formed in August 1959, and later by its successor, the National Development Planning Board (Badan Perencanaan Pembangunan Nasional, or BAPPENAS). In charge of the reparations projects on the Japanese side was the Reparations Implementation Coordinating Committee, consisting of ten ministries and one agency, namely, the Ministries of Foreign Affairs, Finance, Education, Welfare, Agriculture and Forestry, International Trade and Industry, Transportation, Postal Services, Construction, and Labor, and the Economic Planning Agency. The committee was headed by the foreign minister and the reparations payments were administered by the Foreign Ministry's Reparations Division, which was succeeded by the Economic Cooperation Bureau.[2]

The head of the Indonesian Reparations Mission would hand over the procurement orders to the Japanese committee, which would study them and, with the head of the Indonesian mission, would decide upon the "annual payment schedule" amounting to $20 million and would specify the products and services to be supplied by Japan (Agreement, Article 3). The Japanese committee did have the option of vetoing some of the proposed procurement orders on the basis that they might interfere with the normal trade between Japan and Indonesia, or might impose an additional foreign exchange burden upon Japan (Agreement, Article 2 [3]). After agreement, there were technical experts made up of the Bank of Indonesia, the Foreign Ministry, and the Reparations Mission, which conducted further technical negotiations. The mission then would put up the procurement orders for bidding. However, in reality there was practically no bidding system. Instead the mission gathered information concerning relative merits of manufacturers and prices of the necessary materials. Technically they could use the service of Japanese consultants but they learned that there were no independent ones in Tokyo reliable enough to supply objective evaluations of what they were searching. After the mission gave the final approval on designs, specifications, and unit prices of the materials involved, a contract was then drawn up.[3] The mission likewise examined and approved the qualification of Japanese experts to be sent to Indonesia under the reparations programs and issued letters of recommendation to the visa section of the embassy. The contract then was examined by the Japanese committee to see whether it fulfilled the necessary requirements and regulations agreed upon by the two governments. After being verified by the Japanese government or, in this case, by the chief of the Reparations Division of the Foreign Ministry, the contract finally became effective. After this, the Indonesian mission inspected schedules and documents, sending them back to the original procuring agents, the so-called project owners. Upon the arrival of the products in Indonesia, the Japanese government would transfer the necessary funds to the mission, which in turn would pay the supplying firms. At this point, the Indonesian mission and the Japanese government were freed from responsibility unless claims were made by the project owners.

Political Distributions

In late November 1957, many of Indonesia's ministries already began competing for large allocations of funds for their own projects. One source discloses that the Industrial Section of the Ministry of Veteran Affairs requested from Prime Minister Djuanda $23 million for its own proposed projects, when the total scheduled amount for the year of 1958–1959 was only $20 million.[4] According to this same source, in May 1958 the same ministry was forced to reduce its request to $4 million after learning that other ministries also had submitted requests. Even then, the requests from all sixteen ministries totaled $113,927,000, almost six times as much as the scheduled amount. On July 29, 1958 in an interministerial meeting this amount was lowered to $21,318,000, to be divided among only seven ministries. But by this time the Ministry of Shipping already had made a contract with the Kinoshita Trading Company for nine ships at a cost of $7.2 million. Later in March 1959 when the payment schedule and the procurement orders finally were presented, subsequent negotiations with Japan brought the total amount down further to $14.28 million, including the big contract with Kinoshita, which left only $7.08 million for the remaining six Ministries of Agriculture, Trade, Veteran Affairs, Defense, Public Works and Energy, and Transportation.

Undoubtedly this internal competition and the disagreement over the amount and allocation of the reparations funds were major reasons for the Indonesian government's delay in presenting the first year's procurement orders to the Japanese. This competition also deprived the Reparations Mission in Tokyo of much of its effectiveness. The Reparations Implementation Committee in Jakarta also lost most of its power to Foreign Minister Subandrio, Minister of Distribution Leimena,

Minister of Basic Industries and Mining Chairul Saleh, and even to President Sukarno. After 1963, several ministries sent attachés to Tokyo. There were Ministries of Agriculture, of Communications, and of Basic Industries and Mining. The last ministry was represented by three offices, one for industry, one for mining, and one for PERTAMINA, Indonesia's state oil company. The three offices were coordinated by PERTAMINA's representative, Colonel Harjono, who in fact also worked for the interest of the Indonesian army.

Many of the large projects using reparations funds seem to have been proposed and negotiated by these Indonesian leaders.[5] The increased control by Sukarno and other Javanese leaders over the reparations may be seen in the predominance of major reparations projects and reparations-secured loan projects in Java. Table 14 gives a regional distribution of twenty-six major reparations projects and ten major reparations-secured loan projects.[6] In terms of cost, the table reveals that 60 percent of the former and 59 percent of the latter were spent in Java and Bali. From 1951 to 1957 Sumatra's Asahan electric power and oil projects were the major candidates for reparations funds. However, from 1958 to 1970 only 8 percent of the expenditures for reparations

TABLE 14

REGIONAL DISTRIBUTION OF 26 MAJOR REPARATIONS PROJECTS AND 10 MAJOR REPARATIONS-SECURED LOANS PROJECTS IN NUMERICAL AND MONETARY SIZE, 1958–1970

REGIONS	REPARATIONS PROJECTS			REP.-SECURED LOAN PROJECTS		
	No. of projects	Cost (millions of $)	In percent	No. of projects	Cost (millions of $)	In percent
Java (Bali incl.)	14	$47.21	60	7	$48.10	59
Sumatra	4	6.43	8	1	6.25	8
Kalimantan	3	8.66	11	—	—	—
Sulawesi	3	13.01	17	—	—	—
Nusatenggara	—	—	—	—	—	—
Maluku	—	—	—	—	—	—
Nonregional	2	2.32	3	2	27.35	33
TOTAL	26	$77.63	99	10	$81.70	100

— Indicates the number is negligible.

Sources: Figures on reparations projects are from Japan, Foreign Ministry, Economic Affairs Bureau, *Indoneshia*, pp. 115–116; and figures on reparations-secured loan projects from Japan, Economic Cooperation Survey Mission to Indonesia, *Indoneshia Keizai Kyōryoku Chōsadan chōsa hōkoku*, p. 40.

projects and similarly 8 percent of the reparations-secured loan projects were spent in Sumatra. Sumatra had only five projects, whereas Java had twenty-one. The overbalance of projects in Java may be attributed partly to the relatively easier communications and transportation systems there than in the Outer Islands. There is little doubt, however, that if Djuanda, who died in 1963, had lived longer and had maintained his power, and if Hatta had remained as vice-president, Sumatra would have been given a greater share of the reparations fund.

The Reparations Lobbies

The reparations were of interest to Japanese businessmen because they involved large sums of money, and because, as many told me, they could easily persuade Indonesian businessmen to overprice their products and share the large profits with them. There were rumors that some Indonesian officials, usually high-ranking, were given a cut from these profits (or *komisi* from "commission") for allowing the Japanese to overprice their products. Furthermore, the reparations business was secure because payments, even those for overpriced products, were made by the Japanese government, not by Indonesia's unstable government.

Many Japanese companies competed keenly in their bids for the reparations projects. According to news reports, company officials frequently visited the Reparations Mission office, hoping to establish good rapport and thus perhaps to receive special consideration.[7] They would go directly to Jakarta to lobby with reparations officials there. Company officials would even suggest products and services "beneficial" to Indonesia. In other words, the basic negotiations were carried out before the official requests were filed in the Reparations Mission office.

Intermediaries, or reparations lobbyists, acted for the procuring agents of the Indonesian government and for the supplying agents of the Japanese firms. Among them were overseas Chinese traders and self-styled "Indonesia experts" who had lived in prewar or wartime Indonesia and, similarly, self-styled "Japan experts." Both knew Indonesian and Japanese well, claimed to understand both countries' business methods and were well-acquainted with government leaders. Japanese firms sought these intermediaries in order to bring their needs to the attention of the top echelons of the Indonesian government. Many Japanese firms tried to establish direct communications routes with Sukarno himself, his Japanese wife, Dewi, or influential figures in the ruling Liberal Democratic party.[8]

Naturally, these prominent men came to favor certain companies, as will be seen in the case of the Kinoshita Trading Company and Prime Minister Kishi Nobusuke. This, in turn, generated speculation and charges that these companies contributed funds to them or to their party. In 1970 to 1972 I met several Japanese businessmen in Jakarta who maintained that even some of Japan's ambassadors to Indonesia had favored certain companies during the period from 1958 to 1965. The circle of those involved in the reparations lobbies had become so wide that it was difficult to differentiate between their roles as intermediaries and as official decision-makers.

A complete list of Japanese firms obtaining contracts with the Indonesian government has not been made public, nor have the details of their contracts. Often the contracting companies made subcontracts with other companies, making it nearly impossible to estimate the profit of each company. One source, published in 1968 by the Japan Federation of Economic Organizations (Keidanren), provides the names of the major Japanese firms that made contracts with Indonesia, as shown in Table 15. This indicates that the Kinoshita Trading Company had the largest share of the contracts, followed by an engineering consulting firm, Nippon Kōei Company, and such trading companies as C. Itoh, Nomura, and Tōmen (Tōyō Menka). The large established traders such as Mitsui and Mitsubishi do not seem to have been as successful as their prestige would imply. Attention should be given also to an obscure company, the Tōnichi Trading Company, which won contracts to enlarge the Indonesian embassy building in Tokyo and to construct the Wisma Indonesia (Indonesia Hall) in Tokyo.

The table represents the new actors in the reparations lobbies. Matsunaga Yasuzaemon, a chief figure in the Peace Lobby and one of the "Indonesia trio," became an advisor to the Japan-Indonesia Association but remained aloof from the reparations lobbies, as did Ayukawa Gisuke. The last of the "Indonesia trio," Ishihara Hiroichirō, seemed to have been interested in the reparations business; however he supported the anti-Sukarno Sumatra Rebellion, and thus lost Sukarno's favor. An Indonesian peace lobbyist and a "Japan expert," Omar Tusin, who used to assist the Banteng Council of Sumatra, was placed under surveillance as a possible anti-Sukarnoist and remained inactive during the Sukarno presidency.

Kubota Yutaka of Nippon Kōei remained active during the post-1958 period. He had shown intense interest in the development of Indonesia's hydroelectric power, particularly in the Asahan River in North Sumatra. But the Asahan project was given to the Soviet Union in 1960 possibly for political reasons.[9] Kubota's company, however, gained nearly an exclusive hold over Indonesia's infrastructure projects under the reparations fund. He won contracts for the "3 K" projects in East Java and South Kalimantan from 1961 to 1963. It is indicative

TABLE 15

MAJOR REPARATIONS CONTRACTS AND CONTRACTED COMPANIES

ITEMS AND PROJECTS	COST (in thousands of $)	CONTRACTING COMPANIES[a]
*51 ships	41,213	Kinoshita, Tōnichi, Nichimen, Nomura
*10 patrol boats	7,350	Ishikawajima-Harima Heavy Industry, Hitachi Shipbuilding, Uraga Dock
*Musi River Bridge (S. Sumatra)	10,525	Nichimen, Fuji Wheels, Ōbayashigumi Construction, Mitsui
*Shipbuilding Dock (E. Java)	6,600	Daiichi Bussho, Pacific Consultants
*Hotel Indonesia (Jakarta)	8,000	Kinoshita, Taisei Construction
*Bali Beach Hotel (Bali)		Kinoshita, Taisei Construction, Tōnichi
*Hotel Ambarukmo (Yogyakarta) }	18,503	Kinoshita, Taisei Construction, Tōnichi
*Samdura Beach Hotel (W. Java)		Kinoshita, Taisei Construction, Tōnichi
Wisma Nusantata building (Jakarta)	5,800	Kinoshita, Taisei Construction, Kajima Construction
*Sarinah Department Store (Jakarta)	11,000	C. Itoh, Ōbayashigumi Construction
Wisma Indonesia (Tokyo)	2,000	Tōnichi, Hasegawa Construction
Indonesian Embassy building expansion (Tokyo)	300	Tōnichi, Hasegawa Construction
Neyama Tunnel (E. Java)	1,972	Nippon Kōei, Kajima Construction
Karankates Dam (E. Java)	19,237	Nippon Kōei, Kajima Construction
Kali Konto Dam (E. Java)	3,441	Nippon Kōei, Kajima Construction
Riam Kanan Dam (S. Kalimantan)	5,664	Nippon Kōei, Hazamagumi Construction
Siantar paper mill (N. Sumatra)	1,536	Kanematsu
Makassar paper mill (Sulawesi)	6,481	Kanematsu
Martapura paper mill (S. Kalimantan)	2,022	Nomura
*Banyuwangi paper mill (E. Java)	8,500	Tōmen
Jakarta textile mill (Jakarta)	3,794	C. Itoh
Denpasar textile mill (Bali)		Tōmen
Lawang textile mill (E. Java)	4,906	Tōmen

Battery factory (W. Java)	1,278	Kinoshita, Fuji Electric
Palopo plywood factory (Sulawesi)	5,678	Japan International
5 million copies of *Koran*	1,800	Toppan Printing Co.
548 steam rollers, 166 tractors	12,636	Kinoshita, Nomura, Komatsu Steel, Tōmen
1500 trucks, 1300 jeeps	13,275	C. Itoh, Isuzu Motor, Toyota Motor, Mitsubishi
Rails, 100 railway cars	7,900	Kinoshita, Sumitomo, C. Itoh, Mitsubishi

* Reparations-secured loan projects included.

ᵃ Kinoshita merged with Mitsui after August 1964. Of the companies listed, the trading firms are C. Itoh, Daiichi Busshō, Japan International, Kanematsu, Mitsubishi, Mitsui, Nichimen, Nomura, Tōmen, Tōnichi; Nippon Kōei is an engineering consulting firm.

Sources: Based on Japan, Foreign Ministry, Economic Affairs Bureau, *Indoneshia*, pp. 115–116; and Reparations Problems Study Group, *Nihon no baishō 1963*, pp. 213–224, 234–238. Supplementary information was obtained from Sakata Zenzaburō, *Indoneshia; genjō to mondaiten*, pp. 75–78.

of Kubota's successful lobbying with high Indonesian officials, including President Sukarno and officials from the Ministry of Public Works. As an illustration, when President Sukarno was in Tokyo in 1963 for discussions with Philippine President Macapagal on the Malaysia issue, he invited Kubota to dinner one evening and offered to introduce him to President Nkrumah of Ghana.[10] Later in 1964 Nkrumah asked Nippon Kōei to conduct surveys for some extensive projects in Ghana. According to one account, Kubota also was asked occasionally by Indonesian ministers to help persuade Sukarno and Djuanda to adopt certain projects and budget appropriations.[11]

Also entering the arena of Japanese-Indonesian economic relations was the Kajima Construction Company, which built the Neyama Tunnel in East Java in 1961 and participated in two of the "3 K" dam projects in the same area. In 1964 Kajima made a joint contract with the Taisei Construction Company for the Wisma Nusantara office building in Jakarta. Kajima Morinosuke thus gained a position of influence in Indonesian matters. An indication of this is his accession in 1962 to the presidency of the Japan-Indonesia Association, which had a membership of over one hundred companies doing business with Indonesia.[12] Later in 1970 he constructed Indonesia's pavilion at the Osaka Exposition, another indication of his company's involvement in Indonesia.

Kinoshita Shigeru and Kubo Masao, who represented the Kinoshita and Tōnichi trading companies respectively, established similar powerful connections with the Indonesian president and other high-ranking officials in Jakarta as will be seen later. Both got involved in the reparations through Indonesia's internal political troubles. Their activities and the significance of their presence in Japanese-Indonesian relations will be treated in the following sections.

THE KINOSHITA TRADING COMPANY AND CESSATION OF THE DUTCH SHIPPING OPERATIONS

Kinoshita's Contract to Supply Nine Ships, 1958

A first though provisional reparations contract was signed on June 18, 1958, between Indonesia's Ministry of Shipping and the Kinoshita Trading Company.[13] The contract was later formalized by the Reparations Mission and the Japanese Foreign Ministry and was then verified by the Foreign Ministry on July 24, 1958.[14] Under this contract four new ships and five secondhand ships, each weighing 2,500 DWT and costing a total of $7.2 million, were supplied to Indonesia.

After December 2, 1957, when Indonesia had ordered the Dutch shipping company KPM (Koninklijke Packetvaart Maatschappij) to halt its operations in Indonesian waters,[15] the country desperately needed interisland ships.[16] For Indonesia to procure ships through reparations seemed an appropriate measure. Soon after the contract was signed, however, the Japan Shipowners Association raised criticism of irregularities in the contract. This charge was addressed to the Kinoshita Trading Company which had received contracts for nine out of the ten ships requested, although it had not dealt with ships previously. Later in February 1959 the opposition Socialist party used this charge to implicate Prime Minister Kishi and one of his cabinet members in their involvement in the contract. But even if the Socialist party's accusation were correct, there was nothing illegal about the contract; it simply was the outcome of successful bargaining by the Kinoshita Trading Company.

Kinoshita Shigeru (1899–1967), president of the Kinoshita Trading Company, was a shrewd businessman. He had had a successful wholesale business dealing with iron ore, scrap, and steel products in Manchuria during the prewar years and in the Philippines during the postwar years. As his company grew, he expanded his business into lumber, textiles, fertilizers, chemicals, building materials, and machinery.[17] Kinoshita's business grew through his efforts to establish personal ties with influential political and industrial figures. The Kinoshita Trading Company, established in 1932, made good use of Japan's expansionist policy, helping the Fuji Iron and Steel Company to sell steel products to Manchuria. Through his business there Kinoshita became acquainted with Nagano Shigeo, managing director of the Fuji Iron and Steel Company, and with Inayama Yoshihiro, managing director of the Yawata Steel Company. Kinoshita also came to know the ambitious vice-minister of Commerce and Industry and future prime minister, Kishi Nobusuke, who through his government position, had close contacts with the iron and steel industries.[18]

These four men—Kinoshita, Nagano, Inayama, and Kishi— maintained close relationships. At the start of the Pacific War the iron and steel companies were placed under government control. From 1943 to 1944 Kishi was state minister in General Tōjō's Cabinet, heading the government's Steel Control Council. Nagano headed the council's Raw Materials Section; Inayama was deputy chief of the Production Section of the council; and Kinoshita worked under them and obviously did not suffer from the government control of iron and steel.[19] Japan's surrender led to the arrest of Kishi as a class-A war criminal suspect. At this time Kinoshita established the Japan Steel Trading Company, and, when Kishi was released from the Sugamo Prison in 1948, Kinoshita made him president of the company as the only means of assisting financially him since he was not allowed by the Occupation authorities to assume any public office till 1952 when he reentered politics.[20]

Kinoshita's contract for ships was brought before the National Diet on February 13 and 14, 1959.[21] The opposition party's Imazumi Isamu and Yanagida Hidekazu charged that three men served in effect as lobbyists for Kinoshita: an overseas Chinese trader named C. M. Chow, his prewar and wartime acquaintance and a diplomat, Toyoshima Ataru, and Kinoshita's old friend Prime Minister Kishi Nobusuke.[22] The exact role that each played is not clear but it is possible to document some aspects of their functions from interviews and published materials.

According to an informed source, in the 1930s C. M. Chow was in Shanghai working for Japanese military intelligence when he met Toyoshima, who was working in the Japanese consulate there.[23] Toyoshima later was assigned to the consulate general in Batavia and in 1941 served as vice-consul.[24] When the military administration began in 1942, Toyoshima became head of the Overseas Chinese Affairs team within the administration's Popular Affairs Department and asked Chow to join him.[25] After the war, Chow remained in Indonesia and, while serving as an intelligence officer for the Indonesian government, became an import-export trader. He set up the Indonesian Overseas Company which dealt primarily with scrap iron and ships. Through his business Chow became acquainted with the Kinoshita Trading Company.[26] After the war Toyoshima worked in the Immigration Bureau of the Ministry of Justice until his retirement in early 1958.[27] Chow later introduced Toyoshima to Kinoshita, who made him his business representative in Jakarta.

According to a Mitsui Trading Company employee in Jakarta, Chow approached Sukarno's adjutant, Sughandi, and obtained a letter of introduction from President Sukarno which he took to Prime Minister Kishi in Japan.[28] This possibly was to impress Kishi with his relationship with Sukarno and to gain the prime minister's favor in his business efforts. In the February 13, 1959 session of the Diet, Kishi admitted that he had met Chow in Hakone "a couple of times" after he had come back from his Southeast Asian tour.[29] Imazumi claimed that Chow had told him that he had met Kinoshita in Tokyo prior to Kishi's trip in November.[30]

On December 6, 1957, as soon as the Dutch vessels had left, it is reported that the Indonesian government requested the use of Japanese freighters and tankers.[31] On December 17, Indonesian Consul General Iskandar Ishak formally requested a loan of 100,000 tons of shipping from Yamagata Katsumi, president of the Japan Shipowners Association.[32] Yamagata then met with Prime Minister Kishi and Foreign Minister Fujiyama on December 17 and 19. The Japanese Foreign Ministry decided that Japan would decline requests for the reparations funds until the peace treaty was signed.

On December 21 the Indonesian government sent a mission to Tokyo which was headed by S. E. Haznam, a representative of the Indonesian National Shipping Company (Pelayaran Nasional Indonesia, or PELNI). On December 28 he and Yamagata signed an agreement to charter 26 cargo and passenger ships, totaling 75,000 DWT, and 3 to 5 tankers. Haznam immediately received bids from 20 Japanese shipping companies.[33] However, the agreement later was deemed unworkable because Japan's demands were "too heavy." Minister of Shipping Commodore Mohammad Nazir came to Tokyo on January 4 to negotiate but had no success.[34] On January 24, 1958 Haznam declared that the negotiations were terminated and added: "I am expecting offers of ships from individual firms."[35]

Upon this statement, sixteen or seventeen Japanese trading firms that had offices in Jakarta competed fiercely to gain contracts.[36] From January 29 to February 15, 1958 Sukarno visited Tokyo, and the respected weekly journal, *Ekonomisuto*, reported on February 14, 1959 that "the competition among trading companies for ship contracts reached its climax during Sukarno's visit in late January 1958."[37] Kinoshita and Chow were active contributors to Sukarno's visit. According to Yanagida's charge in the Diet in 1959, and to the earlier mentioned *Ekonomisuto* article, Chow arranged on February 13 and 14, for Kinoshita, Kishi, and Sukarno to dine in a geisha restaurant.[38] According to the magazine article, Kishi's cabinet secretary, Akagi Munenori, admitted the February 13 gathering, but Kishi and Akagi denied it at the Diet session.[39] However, the prime minister did admit the February 14 meeting, explaining that Sukarno had asked Kishi to be present when he met Kinoshita and that the meeting had been in no way out of line.[40] While the exact content of their meeting or meetings has not been disclosed, the *Ekonomisuto* article states that soon after this meeting Kinoshita made contracts with the Indonesian government to sell nine ships on a commercial basis. This contract appeared foolhardy to many Japanese shipping companies, for Indonesia was suffering from a shortage of foreign currency reserves. The companies maintained that Indonesia could charter ships from Japan through the reparations funds, and Yamagata on February 1 had suggested this possibility to Foreign Minister Fujiyama and Vice Foreign Minister Ōno Katsumi. On February 3 Indonesian Shipping Minister Nazir, who had stayed in Tokyo to join the Sukarno party, discussed this with Minister of

Transportation Nakamura Sannōji. It was after these talks that the closed meeting among Sukarno, Kishi, and Kinoshita took place. It was reported to the Diet in 1959 by Yanagida that Murakami Tōru, managing director of the Kinoshita Trading Company, and C. M. Chow had flown to Indonesia on April 4, 1958, eleven days before the reparations agreement went into effect and that on April 8 Kinoshita also had flown to Jakarta.[41] Yanagida accused the three men of having bribed the Indonesian officials, especially Minister of Shipping Nazir, to incorporate the contract with the Kinoshita Trading Company into the first year's reparations payment program.

On April 15, 1958 Foreign Minister Subandrio came to Tokyo to exchange the ratification documents of the reparations agreement and the peace treaty. At this time he also told Foreign Minister Fujiyama that preparations for the first year's procurement order plan were delayed and requested that the first year's procurements be permitted on the basis of contracts ad libitum within the limits of $20 million. Fujiyama consented to this.

Minister of Shipping Nazir left for Tokyo on June 3, stating that he was going to Japan to make "final arrangements" for the purchase of nine ships.[42] En route in Singapore he also declared that Indonesia hoped to get ten ships from Japan as part of the war reparations programs.[43] On June 6 Basuki, who had come to Tokyo as the first chief of the Indonesian Reparations Mission, met with Foreign Minister Fujiyama to deliver a message from Foreign Minister Subandrio requesting the procurement of Japanese ships as part of the reparations.[44] On June 7 Basuki presented to Yoshida Ken'ichirō, director of the Reparations Division of the Foreign Ministry, Indonesia's plan for the use of the first year's $20 million fund which included an order for ten ships.[45] In answer to Nazir's statement in Singapore and Basuki's presentation of the Indonesian plan, the Japanese shipping and trading companies immediately tendered bids. On June 6 when Nazir's party arrived it found the hotel desk piled with bids already submitted by the shipping and trading firms for the contract of ten ships.[46] Later these firms discovered that the Kinoshita Trading Company already had received a contract for nine of these ships. On June 7 Nazir met with Foreign Minister Fujiyama and Prime Minister Kishi. His meeting with Kishi lasted for more than two hours, causing an AP correspondent to comment that it was extraordinarily long.[47] Fujiyama explained to the Diet in 1959 that both Nazir and Basuki had come to obtain his consent to purchase the ships with the reparations fund.[48] Actually there is ground to believe that Nazir could have discussed ways in which the purchase of ships from Kinoshita could have been transferred to the reparations program.

On June 12 Kishi reshuffled his cabinet and appointed Nagano Mamoru as minister of transportation.[49] Nagano, whose ministry was in charge of granting permission for the supply of ships under reparations, authorized the incorporation of Kinoshita's nine ships into the reparations plan. Fujiyama later testified on June 16 that the interministerial Reparations Implementation Coordinating Committee also had studied and approved the Indonesian request for ten ships.[50] On June 18 Nazir signed a contract with Kinoshita for the purchase of nine ships on a commercial basis.[51] According to Yoshida's remarks in the Diet, on July 16 Basuki and Yoshida signed an agreement whereby Kinoshita's nine ships would be covered by the reparations funds,[52] and the agreement was verified on July 24, 1958.[53]

Kinoshita's Business Strategy

It seems probable that Kinoshita's personal relationships with Kishi, Chow, and Toyoshima were important to his obtaining the ship contracts. The close ties between Sukarno and Kishi were manifested through these contracts. The Japan Socialist party charged that Kishi intervened in behalf of one of the bidding companies. If this charge were true, one then may argue that Kishi acted more as a lobbyist than as a prime minister.

After securing the ship contracts, Kinoshita continued his maneuvering for six or seven years until his company went bankrupt in August 1964. Until then his company made contracts to construct additional ships and patrol boats, four large hotels including the Hotel Indonesia, and the twenty-nine-story Wisma Nusantara office building in Jakarta. His company also supplied shipbuilding plants, steam rollers, and agricultural equipment (see Table 15). It is not known publicly just how much of the reparations funds his company finally received, but it is known that his business activities extended beyond the reparations projects. Kinoshita also was interested in Sumatran oil, Sulawesi nickel, and offshore fisheries. At its peak his company had a total of 2,100 employees, compared to only 60 in 1945.[54] When the Kinoshita Trading Company merged with Mitsui, it ranked seventh in sales among the trading firms.[55]

The failure of the Kinoshita Trading Company in 1964 was attributed to Kinoshita's extravagance in entertaining potential and actual customers and those whose influence might help him.[56] For example, it was claimed widely in 1958 that when Sukarno and his party came to Japan, Kinoshita spent from ¥30 million to ¥50 million ($83,000 to 139,000) to entertain them in Tokyo, Kyoto, and Hakone during the eighteen days that they stayed in Japan.[57] This entertainment also included the introduction of a pretty model to President Sukarno.[58] This introduction caused Kinoshita's business rival, Kubo Masao of the Tōnichi Trading Company, then to introduce Dewi to President Sukarno, the ramifications of which meeting will be discussed in the following section.

THE SUMATRA REBELLION AND KUBO MASAO

Until 1958 Kubo Masao was president of a new and obscure trading company called the Tōnichi Trading Company. Established in March 1954, the company handled both trade and construction.[59] Although it was small, the company had on its board of directors such leaders of the ruling Liberal Democratic party as Ōno Banboku and Kōno Ichirō and the rightist leader, Kodama Yoshio.[60] In 1958 the Tōnichi Trading Company and Kubo became involved in Indonesian affairs.

When President Sukarno planned to visit Japan in January 1958, a great problem for Indonesia's consul general in Tokyo, Iskandar Ishak, was adequate security for the president, as there were rumors that anti-Sukarnoist groups might enter Japan secretly and try to assassinate him. The Tokyo Metropolitan Police, who were responsible for security in the city, refused to assume responsibility for the president while he was on an unofficial visit on the grounds that he was reckless in his personal affairs and might not follow the schedule set in advance for him, which in turn would hamper effective security measures.

According to informed sources in Jakarta, Sukarno's confidant, Colonel Sambas Atmadinata, then assistant minister of veteran affairs, contacted his relative and wartime friend, Oguchi Masami, who suggested using a private bodyguard.[61] Following this suggestion Consul General Ishak called Kodama Yoshio, who ranked at the top of the hierarchy of rightist politicians and their affiliated underworld organizations.[62] Kodama handed over the assignment to one of his prominent followers, Kobayashi Kusuo. Kobayashi was president of Dai Nihon Kyōgyō (Greater Japan Construction Company), allegedly a front for an underworld organization known as the "Ginza Police," as it was powerful in Tokyo's Ginza area, and also was an advisor to the patriotic monarchist group, Kusunoki Kōdōtai (Kusunoki Action Command for Support of the Imperial Way).[63] Kobayashi agreed to recruit twenty members of this group to guard Sukarno.[64] Kubo Masao then was asked to act as liaison between the gangsters, the police, and the president. He was chosen probably because he spoke English and because Kobayashi's boss, Kodama, was on the board of directors of Kubo's Tōnichi Trading Company.

The extent of the Kishi government's involvement in this affair is not known. However, judging from Prime Minister Kishi's pattern of conservative behavior, from his close association with rightist organizations, and from the diplomatic importance of protecting a foreign head of state, it would not be surprising if Kishi were aware of this and might have agreed to it.[65] A political scientist, Kinoshita Hanji, writes in his *Uyoku tero* [Rightist terrors]: "Kishi willingly maintains close contacts with rightist groups and makes use of them after assuming the premiership. It is public knowledge that among Kishi's close associates are prominent rightist leaders. Recently it has become increasingly conspicuous that the Liberal Democratic party under his leadership had close relations with rightist organizations."[66]

A six-man group of Sumatran rebels secretly entered Tokyo on January 28 and stayed at the Nikkatsu Hotel, near the Imperial Hotel where the presidential party stayed.[67] During the following two weeks Kubo and his team stayed close to the president. It was ironic that Sukarno, who was criticized as being lenient toward the communists, was being protected in Japan by an anticommunist bodyguard against an anticommunist group. Kubo successfully carried out his assignment and Sukarno left Japan safely. During this time Kubo must have had a chance to observe closely the modus operandi of Kinoshita, Chow, and Toyoshima in concluding their ship contracts, and he must have seen the advantage of being in the reparations business. Kubo thus decided to use his introduction to Sukarno to become involved further in Indonesian affairs. The exact depth of Kubo's involvement is yet to be established. Major sources of information available so far are articles appearing in popular weekly magazines rather than those of a more serious nature. One should bear these limitations in mind while reading the following paragraphs.

On June 6, 1959 President Sukarno returned to Japan, and on June 16 Kubo introduced to him a nineteen-year-old cabaret hostess named Nemoto Naoko.[68] According to her own notes later made public, Miss Nemoto met with the president two more times at the Imperial Hotel before his departure.[69]

From Jakarta, Sukarno sent "affectionate" letters to Miss Nemoto through the Indonesian embassy in Tokyo.[70] They exchanged letters a few times before Sukarno, in a letter dated August 18, invited Miss Nemoto to Indonesia for a two-week trip.[71] Sukarno also notified Kubo Masao of this.[72] On September 14 Miss Nemoto left for Indonesia, disguised as an employee of Tōnichi and accompanied by Kubo himself.[73] Only after they had arrived in Jakarta on September 15 did she realize, as she wrote later, that Kubo was using her to enhance his business interests in Indonesia.[74] Kubo denied in 1966 that he had used her to gain Sukarno's favor, although he admitted that his company had provided housing for her in Jakarta where he said Sukarno had visited her.[75]

The arrival of Miss Nemoto in Indonesia was a challenge to Sukarno's third wife, who had been introduced to him by Toyoshima Ataru, and, on September 30, 1959, she committed suicide in Jakarta while Miss Nemoto and Sukarno were visiting Bali.[76]

Between 1960 and 1963 Kubo Masao received four large reparations contracts (see Table 15). One may suspect that these were a result of his introducing Miss Nemoto to Sukarno. In 1961 Kubo constructed the four-story Indonesia Hall or Wisma Indonesia in Tokyo. He also won a contract to expand the Indonesian embassy building in Tokyo under the reparations funds in 1960 as well as to provide patrol-freighter boats and some of the equipment and facilities for the three resort hotels built in Bali, Yogyakarta (Central Java), and Plabuhan Ratu (West Java).[77] In addition to these reparations contracts, Kubo obtained the rights to build a guest house in the presidential palace, the National Monument, and a television transmission tower, all in Jakarta.[78] The National Monument, or what is known as Monas (Monumen Nasional), became one of Sukarno's "prestige projects." Located at the center of Merdeka Square in front of the presidential palace, the monument is a huge obelisk topped by a golden light and illuminated from the ground at night.

The Tōnichi Trading Company appeared most active in 1961. The company invited at least fifteen high-ranking officials to Japan that year, when the total number of Indonesian visitors coming to Japan at the invitation of Japanese organizations and upon the approval of the Indonesian embassy was only thirty-one.[79] At first, Tōnichi had had only one representative in Jakarta but, within a year, its Jakarta branch had ten Japanese employees, among whom were several wartime "Indonesia experts."[80] Thus it is generally believed that the growth of the Tōnichi Trading Company was due, in large part, to the close relationship between Kubo and Sukarno.

Miss Nemoto was secluded in the Tōnichi dormitory in Jakarta away from public attention.[81] But she did accompany Sukarno on his overseas trips, traveling as one of his secretaries or as "Mrs. Kirishima." (Mr. Kirishima worked at Tōnichi's Jakarta branch.[82]) By 1962 considerable friction had built up between Miss Nemoto and Kubo. She was ambitious and not content to remain a tool for Kubo's business.[83] Also there was rivalry between Kubo and Toyoshima, who was trying to win Miss Nemoto over to his side. Finally, the journalist Ōmori

Minoru, who was close to Miss Nemoto at one time, observed that Sukarno had become dissatisfied with Kubo's business dealings and forced him to close his Jakarta office in November 1963.[84] By then Miss Nemoto was closely associated with Toyoshima.[85]

DEWI AND WISMA YASOO

The conflict between Kubo and Miss Nemoto led to changes in the reparations lobbies. After Kubo's departure Miss Nemoto sided with the Kinoshita Trading Company and helped Toyoshima. Through Toyoshima, as she wrote, she also cultivated a friendship with Japanese Ambassador Ōda Takio and gradually acquired prominence in Japan's and Indonesia's political and business circles.[86]

The date on which Sukarno married Miss Nemoto is not certain. One source states that they were wed privately on March 3, 1962 when she took the Indonesian name of Ratna Dewi Sari as well as Indonesian citizenship.[87] Another source states that she became the president's official wife as late as May 1964.[88] Nevertheless, as early as June 1961 she was introduced to the Liberal Democratic party's future vice-president Kawashima Shōjirō by a wartime propaganda officer, Shimizu Hitoshi.[89] On a 1962 trip to Japan, Dewi met Takemi Tarō, president of the Japan Medical Association and Kajima Morinosuke, president of the Kajima Construction Company, with whom she discussed plans to build a hospital in Jakarta.[90] In September 1963 she was introduced by President Sukarno himself to Prime Minister Ikeda Hayato and his wife at a private gathering during their official visit to Indonesia.

Dewi's acquaintance with these prominent figures in Japan increased her status in the Japanese-Indonesian lobby, particularly after the Kinoshita Trading Company left Indonesia in 1964 and after Dewi moved from what she called a "hideout" to a large mansion called the Wisma Yasoo.[91] Dewi emerged as the president's "First Lady," and as an influence in her own right. Japanese firms, Chinese traders, and Indonesian officials competed with each other to obtain her special favor. From early 1964 through the abortive coup in 1965, a trading company man was quoted as saying, "little business between Indonesia and Japan was transacted without first meeting her approval."[92] The *Dewi mōde* (the pilgrimage to Dewi) became a cynical term describing the businessman's necessary trip to Wisma Yasoo.[93] Dewi herself later explained this as follows:

> Frankly, there were Japanese and Indonesians who somehow had the mistaken view that their business would go well if they approached me. They tried to take advantage of me, born in Japan, whom they considered influential to Sukarno, just because I was

very close to him. They always approached me with the same line: trying to sell themselves by speaking ill of their rivals and criticizing the kinds of connections that they had had with Indonesian influentials....[94]

She also wrote:

In Jakarta alone there were over sixty Japanese trading companies. [The competition among them was so keen that] a few dozen of them had to fight just to get one contract. Their representatives maneuvered whenever possible behind the scenes in order to achieve satisfactory results. Their largest problem was to establish contacts with the important Indonesian figures concerned and to gain their support in obtaining contracts, and they willingly gave remunerations for the services of these figures. To maximize their companies' profits as well as to make high rebate from their profits, they made all sorts of schemes. For instance, I have heard that the ship building companies thinned steel plates and iron walls in building contracted vessels; construction companies reduced the amount of cement to be used; rubber tire firms made thin tires; and textile companies lowered the quality of their products, and the like. The exportation of machinery was only one example which did not involve such irregularities. It is also true that there were Indonesians who made sport of such firms by demanding high commissions.[95]

Although she denies it, many Japanese and Indonesian businessmen in Jakarta told me that Dewi, too, had received some commissions. An informed source related to me that the Wisma Nasantara office building was contracted, with Dewi's intervention, to Kinoshita instead of to Yokoi Hideki, president of the Oriental Shipping Company (Tōyō Yūsen) and a daring speculator. Another source stated that Dewi and Hartini, Sukarno's second wife, fought with each other on behalf of two rival Japanese automobile companies who sought President Sukarno's approval of their exporting vehicles to Indonesia.

As the feminine head of Wisma Yasoo, Sukarno's Japanese wife tried to strengthen her position. She seemed successful when in May 1964, with Sukarno's support, she was nominated as honorary chairman of the Indonesia-Japan Friendship Society (Lembaga Persahabatan Indonesia-Jepang, or LPIJ), with Sukarno's lifelong friend and one of Indonesia's few prominent businessmen, M. Dasaad, as the society's chairman.[96] Madame Dewi then organized the Japanese wives of Indonesians into a group of forty to fifty called the Nadeshiko Club.[97] Some of the members used the club as a means of seeking Dewi's, and eventually Sukarno's personal favor to advance their husband's positions.[98] It appears that neither the Indonesia-Japan Friendship Society nor the Nadeshiko Club functioned as lobbies for the reparations projects, but Dewi did make use of them to collect donations to build an emergency hospital in Jakarta. When Kawashima visited Jakarta as the Japanese government's representative to the tenth anniversary of the Asia-Africa Bandung Conference in April 1965, he and Sukarno agreed to $37 million in credits for Indonesia, of which $1,350,000 was to be earmarked for the construction of this hospital.[99] Using her relationship with Kawashima, the Indonesian first lady visited Japan in early January 1966 and met with Prime Minister Satō to ask him to allocate part of the reparations fund to build the hospital. With Satō's agreement, the contract for $3.3 million was signed by her and by Kajima, president of the Kajima Construction Company and president of the Japan-Indonesia Association, on January 8.[100] The political turmoil in Indonesia in 1966 prevented the actual construction of the hospital, but the events leading up to it illustrate the power she had achieved in Indonesia and the role she had played first as a lobbyist and eventually as a decision-maker.

ECONOMIC COOPERATION PROJECTS

The Economic Cooperation Agreement between Indonesia and Japan was concluded in 1958 at the same time that the reparations agreement was settled. Although the economic cooperation agreement did not involve the reparations funds, it will be discussed here because it did involve Japanese investments and loans. The agreement stated that $400 million would be spent over a period of twenty years, but further details were not specified. The capital was to be raised by the companies themselves, and Japan's business community was much less enthusiastic over private investments and credits than those connected with the more secure reparations contracts. Indonesia's political instability and its growing affinity for communism plus its aversion to foreign investment also did nothing to encourage the flow of Japanese capital into the country.

Nevertheless, with government support three major investment projects were planned for the development of three of Indonesia's natural resources; oil, nickel, and lumber. One of these projects will be discussed as an illustration of the negotiating process involved. Particular attention should be paid to the importance of personal, wartime ties to the negotiations along lines seen earlier in the reparations lobbies.

Sumatran Oil and the Kobayashi Group

Several eminent Japanese industrialists, including Iwata, Kudō, Matsunaga, Ayukawa, Yamashita,[101] and Ishihara, became interested in Sumatran oil during the reparations negotiations period of 1951–1957 and, with the establishment of diplomatic relations in April 1958, the Indonesian government permitted Japan to use its capital and technology to develop and rehabilitate north Sumatra's oil fields. Before the war, Indonesia's oil had been controlled by the international oil cartel; during the war, it had been held by the Japanese military; and after the war, most of the oil fields had been returned to the original European and American oil companies. The only exception was north Sumatra's oil fields, which had been owned by BPM (Bataafsche Petroleum Maatschappij) with Royal Dutch Petroleum providing 60 percent of the capital and Shell, 40 percent. But because of the strong local opposition to returning the north Sumatran oil to BPM, operations there were not resumed. In late 1957 the Indonesian government took over possession of the north Sumatran oil fields and established its first national oil company, PERMINA (Perusahaan Minyak Nasional), headed by Colonel Ibnu Sutowo.

Because of the Sumatra Rebellion in February 1958, Japan delayed investment in the oil fields until the situation was brought under control. At that time Japan did have great need of overseas oil concessions. From 1951 to 1960, Japan's own crude oil production was only .07 percent of the world's production,[102] and until late 1957 Japan owned no overseas oil concessions and was forced to import 97 percent of its oil.[103]

As early as June 1958 Nishijima Shigetada went to Indonesia at the request of Ishibashi Shōjirō, president of the Bridgestone Tire Company, who was interested in starting an L.P.G. (liquified petroleum gas) project.[104] Using his old contacts in Indonesia, Nishijima met with Sutowo. About the same time, the Kinoshita Trading Company also talked with Sutowo about obtaining oil concessions in exchange for supplying steel. The Maruzen Oil Company, too, was interested in that area.[105] Therefore, to allay any possible disruptions Prime Minister Kishi called upon Kobayashi Ataru to mediate among the groups.[106]

The Kobayashi group consisted of Mimura Kiichi, president of the Oil Resources Development Company (a quasi-governmental company), Ishibashi Shōjirō, and Kinoshita Shigeru. They were to serve as the core group in the negotiations with PERMINA. First, in September 1958 the group sent a survey team to explore ways in which Japanese capital might be invested in developing oil in north Sumatra. Because of Indonesia's shortage of foreign currency reserves the ensuing assessment proposed a $50 million credit over ten years in exchange for repayment in products over thirty years.[107]

In March 1959 Sutowo came to Tokyo to begin negotiations with Kobayashi, and from August 24 to September 10, Mimura, including

Nishijima in his party, went to Indonesia to continue the negotiations. In Indonesia he signed a provisional agreement with PERMINA, which both the Kishi Cabinet and Sukarno endorsed.[108] To negotiate the details of the terms of capital investment, on January 28, 1960 Kobayashi sent to Indonesia Yoshida Han'emon, an expert both on oil and on Indonesia, then an advisor to the Oil Resources Development Company.[109] Later on February 18 Nishijima also went to Indonesia as Kobayashi's personal advisor.[110] In December 1959, in order to establish an oil company, the Kobayashi group formally requested the Keidanren, Japan's business federation, to ask its member firms to contribute capital for the new oil company.[111] However, the Kobayashi group failed to collect sufficient private capital and also their request was rejected by the Export-Import Bank of Japan, a government bank which extends commercial credits to exporters and importers. The reason for the Export-Import Bank's rejection was that the Japanese government had requested $200 million from the World Bank (the International Bank for Reconstruction and Development), which then complained that Japan should not put $50 million out of this amount into north Sumatran oil development but instead should spend it internally. The Japanese press implicated the American and British oil companies in the criticism from the World Bank.[112]

The rejection by the Export-Import Bank also irritated PERMINA, which demanded that a final agreement be signed by the end of March 1960. Kobayashi upbraided the Kishi government for its half-hearted support of the oil company, declaring: "Premier Khruschev just committed a $250 million credit to Indonesia. If Japan delays committing only $50 million, it will lose the confidence of all the Southeast Asian governments."[113] Between March 1 and 11, 1960, oil lobbyists Kobayashi and Mimura deliberated with International Trade and Industry Minister Ikeda Hayato, Finance Minister Satō Eisaku, Keidanren Vice-president Uyemura Kōgorō, the Liberal Democratic party's Overseas Economic Cooperation Committee chairman Ichimada Hisato, and Prime Minister Kishi. At one point Kobayashi even threatened to withdraw from the whole business, but on March 11 Kishi, Satō, and Ikeda finally agreed to have the Export-Import Bank appropriate the funds for the oil company. Armed with the ruling party's final endorsement, Mimura went to Indonesia on March 22 and, on April 7, signed the agreement with PERMINA.[114]

The agreement was based on what Indonesia called a production-sharing system, not on the joint venture system for which Japan originally had opted. It stated that Japan would extend credit of ¥18,845 million ($52.3 million) over a ten-year period and would provide machinery, material, and technical assistance, for which Japan would receive 40 percent of the oil over a basic amount of 800,000 kl or a total of 5.6 million kl over ten years.[115] To implement the agreement, the Japanese government established the North Sumatra Oil Development Cooperation Company (NOSODECO) on June 1, 1960. The company received ¥400 million in 1961 and ¥350 million in 1962 from Japan's Overseas Economic Cooperation Fund.[116]

The leadership of NOSODECO during the next several years consisted of a mixture of former bureaucrats, businessmen, and "Indonesian experts," revealing the extent of the oil lobby in Japan. Kobayashi remained as an advisor. Among NOSODECO's executive directors were Azuma Sumio from the Ministry of International Trade and Industry, Kojima Munetaka from the Ministry of Finance, Imai Tominosuke (who later became its president) from Mitsui, Nishijima, and Yoshida Han'emon.[117] On NOSODECO's board of auditors was Takasugi Shin'ichi from Mitsubishi, who in 1967 became the chairman of Keidanren's Indonesia Committee.

Because of the important position he had had in the first Japanese-Indonesian economic cooperation project, Nishijima was asked to head NOSODECO's Jakarta office in 1963 and serve as troubleshooter, when the project was facing managerial difficulties, and, in that capacity, he had at least residual influence on the course of Japanese-Indonesian relations and even on Indonesia's internal politics. A magazine article commented that Nishijima was concerned more about the "export of spirit" than about the export of technology, suggesting that he was giving spiritual guidance and advice to the PERMINA officials and workers and that he was associating with the high-ranking officials surrounding President Sukarno, such as Minister of Basic Industries Chairul Saleh and Minister of Trade Adam Malik.[118]

Because 90 percent of Indonesia's oil was controlled by Caltex, Texaco, and Shell, Japan's entrance into this field was an important historical contribution. It should be noted that NOSODECO maintained close contact with PERMINA from 1963 to 1965, when Sukarno was leaning toward communism and the Western nations had reduced their contacts with Indonesia to a minimum. On March 19, 1965, when President Sukarno seized American and British oil properties and placed them under Indonesian government control, NOSODECO and other Japanese concerns negotiated with Indonesia to purchase crude oil directly from the government. On May 13, 1965 a joint venture, the Far East Oil Trading Company, was established and had the exclusive right to import oil from Indonesia.[119]

The unusually close relations among PERMINA, NOSODECO,

and the Far East Oil Trading Company raised doubts about the ethical conduct of this Japanese-Indonesian business concern. The *Indonesia Raya*, a leading daily newspaper in Indonesia, claimed in December 1969 that Sutowo had lowered the oil export price from $2.24 per barrel in 1957 to $1.49 per barrel for NOSODECO (after 1960) and $1.95 for the Far East Oil Trading Company (after 1965), in order to obtain credit from NOSODECO. It also reported that NOSODECO had received a commission of 4 cents per barrel in 1965–1966 and of 2 cents in 1966–1967. The article argued that PERMINA (at this time, PER-TAMINA), however, showed no record of receiving commissions from NOSODECO for the purchase of material through NOSODECO. The Indonesian press demanded to know what had happened to the so-called commissions, charging that this practice suggested corruption among the PERMINA officials.[120] Although these charges proved to be inconclusive, they left no doubt that the marriage between Indonesian oil and Japanese capital played a significant political role in maintaining the nations' close relationship and had led to Indonesia's dependence upon Japan as its principal buyer of oil.

AN ASSESSMENT OF THE REPARATIONS LOBBIES

The keen competition among Japanese companies and Indonesian government agencies to obtain the maximum share of the reparations funds rendered useless the formal structure used to determine these allocations. In effect, these companies and agencies generated an informal decision-making system in which those with political authority or influence had dominance over the selection of reparations projects and distribution of the funds.

The major components of the reparations lobby included Japanese trade offices in Jakarta, which grew from sixteen in 1958 to sixty in 1965, and included sixteen ministries of the Indonesian government and intermediaries. Among the outstanding lobbyists were wartime officers who worked either as company representatives (Toyoshima) or independently (Nishijima). There were also brokers (C. M. Chow) and political leaders (Kishi, Kawashima, and Sukarno). There were two distinct types of lobbyists: those who were decision-makers but acted as lobbyists favoring certain companies (Kishi, Kawashima, and Sukarno); and those who began as lobbyists but eventually became decision-makers in the allotment of the reparations payments. The most typical lobbyist of the latter type was Dewi.

While the decision-making process in the reparations payments revealed Japan's political style and close relationships between the conservative party leadership and the rightist groups, it also disclosed both

Japan's and Indonesia's practice of favored treatment. Combining this with his patriotic tastes, President Sukarno selected large, visible, expensive, but often impractical projects, giving the contracts to a few select companies and causing Indonesia to consume most of the funds by 1965.

Economic and personal ties between Japan and Indonesia were reinforced through implementation of the reparations funds and long-term investment in Indonesia's natural resources. This explains Indonesia's continued association with pro-Western Japan during its period of anti-Western policy and the reparations lobbies as a basis for Japan's mediation role in the Indonesian-Malaysian conflicts from 1963 to 1966, which will be discussed in the following chapter.

NOTES

1. *Yomiuri Shinbun*, September 21, 1958.
2. Reparations Problems Study Group, ed., *Nihon no baishō 1963* (Tokyo: Sekai Jānaru Sha, 1963), pp. 87–88, 100–105.
3. Indonesian Embassy, Tokyo, *Laporan Tahunan 1969*, pp. 397–398. The annual expenses for the mission and the funds for the educational training program previously mentioned required no contract.
4. Japan-Indonesia Association, *Tokubetsu shiryō*, no. 2: *I-koku seifu kakushō betsu shonendo baishō haibunhyō* (mimeographed, September 10, 1958), p. 1.
5. Little hard data on exactly who lobbied for what and who decided upon which project was available to this writer. Most of those interviewed were reluctant to reveal their knowledge, suggesting that the matter indeed was sensitive. What they did reveal still requires additional supporting evidence, which is difficult to obtain.
6. These major projects are listed in Table 15.
7. "Seishō tōjō," *Asahi Shinbun*, March 10, 1959.
8. For example, it is reported that Sukarno's frequent visits to Japan included numerous dinner parties given by important political figures and financially sponsored by trading and construction companies that had interests in Indonesia. See "Sukaruno o megutta Nihonjin," *Shūkan Shinchō*, April 2, 1966, p. 37.
9. In 1959 Kubota presented new proposals for the development of hydroelectric plants and aluminum refineries in Asahan, but in 1960 the Soviet Union extended $100 million in credit to Indonesia. See Nagatsuka Toshikazu, *Kubota Yutaka 1966* (Tokyo: Denki Jōhō Sha, 1966), p. 361. Some believe that it was Mohammed Yamin who gave Kubota's proposals to the Russians. From Omar Tusin, private interview in Jakarta, February 10, 1972. The Soviet technicians had hardly begun construction before the abortive coup in October 1965 forced the Russian withdrawal from the Asahan region. Thus in 1967 Nippon Kōei was invited again to look into this area. After two years of preliminary surveys, Kubota submitted a report to President Suharto in July 1969, and finally in May 1970 he succeeded in signing a contract for more specified studies of Asahan water system projects. See Daiyamondo Sha, *Nippon Kōei* (Tokyo: Daiyamondo Sha, 1971), pp. 102–103.
10. Nagatsuka, pp. 367–368.
11. Ibid.
12. In 1961–1962 the Association had 107 member companies. See Japan-Indonesia Association, *Jigyō narabi ni kaikei hōkoku sho 1961–1962* (mimeographed, no page

numbers).

13. *Antara*, June 20, 1958.

14. Yoshida Ken'ichirō's explanation was made in the Diet, February 14, 1959. See Japan, National Diet, House of Representatives, Budget Committee, *Dai 31-kai Kokkai Shūgiin Yosan Iinkai gijiroku*, no. 11 (February 14, 1959), pp. 4–5; hereafter cited as the "Budget Committee proceedings."

15. *Antara*, December 2, 1957. On December 3, the KPM management was taken over by the workers union. See *Antara*, December 8, 1957.

16. Japan, Foreign Ministry, *Indoneshia Kyōwakoku benran* (Tokyo: Nihon Kokusai Mondai Kenkyūjo, 1964), p. 165. This anti-Dutch measure had protested the United Nations General Assembly's voting on November 29, 1957 against Indonesia's proposal requesting the United Nations to take the initiative in resuming the Dutch-Indonesian talks on West Irian. KPM previously had controlled 80 percent of Indonesia's shipping business, with 74 freighters (totaling 11,516 tons) and 26 passenger ships (totaling 78,464 tons). Their withdrawal from Indonesian waters naturally caused an enormous inconvenience and paralyzed the nation's interisland commerce and transportation. See ibid.

17. *Nihon shokuinroku*, 10th ed. (Tokyo: Jinji Kōshinjo, 1964), section on companies, p. 1411.

18. Kunitō Yoshimasa, *Seishō makari tōru* (Tokyo: Akita Shoten, 1966), p. 104.

19. Fujishima Udai, "Kishi Nobusuke shi ni okeru 'sensō hanzai' no kenkyū," *Ushio*, July 1972, p. 322.

20. Ibid.

21. "Budget Committee proceedings," no. 10 (February 13, 1959); and no. 11 (February 14, 1959).

22. Ibid., no. 10, p. 13; and no. 11, p. 3.

23. Captain Yanagawa Tomoshige, private interview in Jakarta, January 23, 1971.

24. Japan, Foreign Ministry, *Gaimushō shokuinroku 1941*, p. 25.

25. Yanagawa, interview.

26. Anonymous Mitsui Trading Company employee, private conversation in Jakarta, February 1972. See also "Budget Committee proceedings," no. 10, p. 10.

27. Japan, Finance Ministry Printing Office, *Nihon shokuinroku, 1958-nen I-gatsu*, I, p. 186.

28. Mitsui Trading Company employee, interview.

29. "Budget Committee proceedings," no. 10, p. 13.

30. Ibid.

31. *Antara*, December 6, 1957.

32. *Antara*, December 18, 1957.

33. *Antara*, December 30, 1957.

34. Foreign Minister Fujiyama's remarks at the National Diet on February 14, 1959. See "Budget Committee proceedings," no. 11, p. 4.

35. *Antara*, January 25, 1958.

36. "Budget Committee proceedings," no. 11, p. 3; and "Seishō tōjō," *Asahi Shinbun*, March 10, 1959.

37. "Iwayuru 'baishō oshoku' no arasuji," *Ekonomisuto*, February 14, 1959, pp. 24–25.

38. "Budget Committee proceedings," no. 11, p. 2.

39. "Iwayuru 'baishō oshoku,'" p. 24.

40. "Budget Committee proceedings," no. 10, p. 13.

41. "Budget Committee proceedings," no. 11, p. 4.

42. *Antara*, June 4, 1958.

43. *Antara*, June 7, 1958.
44. *Antara*, June 9, 1958.
45. *Antara*, June 9, 1958.
46. "Budget Committee proceedings," no. 11, p. 4.
47. Quoted in *Antara*, June 20, 1958.
48. "Budget Committee proceedings," no. 10, p. 10.
49. Nagano Mamoru was the older brother of Nagano Shigeo, who was Kishi's and Kinoshita's long-time friend from their days in Manchuria.
50. "Budget Committee proceedings," no. 10, p. 10.
51. *Antara*, June 20, 1958.
52. "Budget Committee proceedings," no. 10, p. 10.
53. Ibid.
54. Kunitō, pp. 110, 114.
55. Ibid., p. 110.
56. Ibid., p. 111.
57. "Seishō tōjō," *Asahi Shinbun*, March 10, 1959; Kunitō, ibid., p. 107.
58. After she was introduced to the president in Kyoto in 1958, she went to Indonesia in November 1958 as "a tutor" for Toyoshima's daughter. She was called Mrs. Basuki since it was easier to stay in Indonesia as the wife of an Indonesian than as the wife of a Japanese. In July 1959 she became the third official wife of President Sukarno. See Kajiyama Toshiyuki, "Shūbun ni irodorareta Devi fujin hiroku," *Yangu Redi*, March 31, 1966, p. 149. Toyoshima later remarked to a magazine reporter: "I was asked by Mr. Sukarno's adjutant and Chow who worked for Kinoshita on the reparations contract, to bring her [the model]. So I had my wife, who planned to come to Jakarta a half-year later, bring her as a member of our family." See "Sukaruno o megutta," pp. 38–39.
59. *Nihon shokuinroku*, 10th ed. (Tokyo: Jinji Kōshinjo, 1964), section on companies p. 1411.
60. Kajiyama, p. 150.
61. A former wartime officer, private interview in Jakarta, January 1971; and an anonymous Japanese businessman, private interview in Jakarta, February 1972. For Oguchi's background, see Takeda Shigesaburō, ed., *Jagatara kanwa* (Nagasaki: by the editor, 1968), p. 318.
62. Kodama, born in 1911, was a patriotic activist in prewar days. During the Pacific War he cooperated with Japan's political and military maneuvers in mainland China by providing his own intelligence organization known as the "Kodama Agency." When the war ended, he served as an advisor to the first postwar cabinet formed by Prince Higashikuninomiya. Later he was detained until late 1948 as a class-A war criminal suspect. When he was released he resumed his association with the conservative wing of the ruling party and has exerted indirect influence over postwar political and economic leadership. He has demonstrated his ability to solicit financial aid and his power to deploy a sizeable number of veterans, street vendors, and members of underworld syndicates. He has promoted party leaders of nonbureaucratic origins, Hatoyama Ichirō (1883–1959), Ōno Banboku (1890–1964), Kōno Ichirō (1898–1965), Kawashima Shōjirō (1890–1970), and more recently, Nakasone Yasuhiro (b. 1918). In 1961 Kodama held a commanding position in the two most powerful rightist organizations, the Federation of All-Japan Patriotic Organizations (Zen'ai Kaigi) and the Youth Ideology Study Association (Seishikai). See Nakamura Kōji, "The Samurai Spirit," *Far Eastern Economic Review*, October 16, 1971, pp. 22–25.

63. Social Problems Study Group, *Uyoku jiten* (Tokyo: Futaba Sha, 1971), p. 33.

64. Ibid.

65. In 1960 Kishi did agree to use a right-wing bodyguard for President Eisenhower's planned visit to Tokyo. Eisenhower and Emperor Hirohito were to drive together in an open limousine from Haneda Airport to the Imperial Palace. Guarding this route would require 18,700 policemen, whereas the Tokyo police could mobilize only 15,000, so the balance was sought from among the rightist volunteers. The ruling party also sought assistance from Kodama Yoshio, who organized a plan which would deploy 18,000 *yakuza* (gangsters), 10,000 street vendors, and 10,000 veterans. Due to mounting anti-Kishi sentiment, Eisenhower was asked to cancel his visit. See Nakamura, p. 24.

66. Kinoshita Hanji, *Uyoku tero* (Kyoto: Hōritsu Bunka Sha, 1960). Quoted in David Conde, *Indoneshia no henbō*, trans. by Kasahara Yoshio (Tokyo: Kōbundō, 1966), p. 147.

67. *Antara*, February 5, 1958; *Asahi Shinbun*, February 4, 1958. The anti-Sukarno rebellion of 1958 was staged by both Sumatran and Sulawesi dissident groups. But in this study it is collectively referred to as the Sumatra Rebellion. For further details, see chapter 8.

68. Dewi Sukarno, "Daitōryō fujin e no ketsubetsu" (3), *Shūkan Gendai*, December 25, 1969, p. 118. Dewi contributed a six-part series of articles to the magazine from the December 11, 1969 through the January 22, 1970 issues. The third part was in the form of a letter to President Sukarno describing her life and experiences in Indonesia. Not all the facts given are correct.
   Nemoto Naoko was born in 1940 as the third daughter of a construction worker in Tokyo. Because her father had little money, Naoko had to work as a waitress in the Chiyoda Life Insurance Company after she graduated from junior high school in 1955, but a little over a year later she resigned to work as a nightclub hostess. The last night club in which she worked was fashionable Akasaka's Copacabana, one of the favorite night clubs of visiting foreigners. Sukarno went there on June 16, 1959. See Fujiwara Hirotatsu, et. al., *Hadaka no Devi fujin* (Tokyo: Yagumoi Shoin, 1970), pp. 11, 20, 23, 34, 36, 40.

69. Dewi, "Daitōryō fujin" (3), p. 119.

70. Ibid., p. 118.

71. Fujiwara, p. 40.

72. Ibid.

73. Ibid., p. 43.

74. Dewi, "Daitōryō fujin" (3), p. 120.

75. "Sukaruno o megutta," p. 39.

76. Kajiyama Toshiyuki, p. 148.

77. Sakata Zenzaburō, *Indoneshia; genjō to mondaiten* (Tokyo: Federation of Economic Organizations, 1968), pp. 75–78.

78. Indonesian Embassy, Tokyo, *Laporan Tahunan 1961*, pp. 188–189.

79. Ibid., pp. 154–155.

80. Kirishima Masaya, private interview in Jakarta, February 17, 1972.

81. "Sukaruno o megutta," p. 39.

82. Kirishima, interview.

83. Kirishima, interview.

84. Ōmori Minoru, *Sukaruno saigo no shinsō* (Tokyo: Shinchō Sha, 1967), p. 22.

85. Kirishima, interview.

86. "Tjatatan Pribadi Dewi," *Indonesia Raya*, March 12, 1970.

87. Mahabrata Suryadharma, *Sukarno di-tengah2 Wanita* (Kuala Lumpur: Penerbitar Pustaka Sari, 1967), p. 9.

88. "Sukaruno o megutta," p. 40. Dewi also visited Mecca to become a Haji (the title given to those making the pilgrimage to Mecca). See Dewi, "Daitōryō fujin" (4) January 1, 1970, p. 87.

89. "Neagari machigai nashi no Devi fujin no 'Kawashima Shōjirō kaisōroku'," *Shūkar Posuto*, November 27, 1970, p. 87. Shimizu had established the Japanese-Indonesiar Cultural Association and had made himself its chairman and had nominatec Kawashima as its advisor. From Shimizu Hitoshi, private interview in Tokyo April 25, 1972. For Shimizu's background, see chapter 3.

90. Dewi, "Daitōryō fujin" (4), p. 87.

91. This mansion is believed to have been built with contributions by Japanese companies. Dewi herself stated that some Japanese and Indonesians "volunteered" to build a house for her. See Dewi, "Daitōryō fujin" (1), December 11, 1969, p. 49

92. "Sukaruno o megutta," p. 40.

93. Fujiwara, p. 99.

94. Dewi, "Daitōryō fujin" (2), December 18, 1969, p. 62.

95. Dewi, "Daitōryō fujin" (1), December 11, 1969, pp. 48–49.

96. The society, established in February 1958, began modestly with only 30 member but by 1965 it had grown to over 200 members. Being an officially accreditec organization, it numbered among its members such prominent figures as Sudiro former mayor of Jakarta, Omar Tusin, former chairman of the Indonesiar Chamber of Industry, and Umar Jadi, Indonesian representative to the Unitec Nations organizations in Switzerland. Hartono, former secretary-general of the society, private interview in Jakarta, July 13, 1971.

97. The club was named after the Japanese word for the flower called pink, which symbolizes the ideal Japanese woman.

98. Anonymous former executive member of the club, private interview in Jakarta November 1970.

99. Ōmori, p. 152.

100. Conde, *Indoneshia no henbō*, p. 148. For the political implications of Dewi's visit a that time, see chapter 7.

101. Yamashita Tarō in 1957 obtained Japan's first overseas oil concessions in offshore Saudi Arabia.

102. Japan Petroleum Federation, *Naigai sekiyū shiryō 1970*, p. 9.

103. Japan, Ministry of International Trade and Industry, *Sōgō enerugī tōkei 1968*, p. 70

104. Nishijima Shigetada also was very active in the reparations negotiations; see chapter 3.

105. "Sumatora e no kyōshū," *Mainichi Shinbun*, July 31, 1959.

106. Kobayashi Ataru also was very active in the reparations negotiations; see chapter 2 and 3.

107. "Sumatora e no kyōshū."

108. The Kishi Cabinet endorsed this on September 26, 1959 and President Sukarn informed Kishi of his approval in a letter which Subandrio carried to Japan or October 14, 1959. See *Tokyo Shinbun*, January 22, 1960.

109. *Mainichi Shinbun*, January 23, 1960.

110. *Asahi Shinbun*, February 17, 1960.

111. *Tokyo Shinbun*, January 22, 1960.

112. *Sankei Shinbun*, March 2, 1960.

113. *Asahi Shinbun*, March 2, 1960.

114. *Asahi Shinbun*, March 23, 24, and April 8, 1960.
115. *Sekiyū no kaihatsu* 1, no. 1 (1968): 24.
116. *Gijutsu kyōryoku nenpō 1964*, pp. 450–451.
117. "Kita Sumatora sekiyū o gyūjiru otoko," *Jitsugyō no Sekai*, April 1965, p. 98.
118. Ibid., p. 100. NOSODECO placed in its Medan, north Sumatra, office Nakatani Yoshio, an Indonesian language expert who had worked for the occupation administration of Java during the Pacific War and had served as an interpreter for Sukarno during his frequent visits to Tokyo. Nakatani later moved to Jakarta to teach Indonesian to Dewi. According to this magazine article, Nishijima had established close contact with Dewi to reinforce his already warm relations with the members of the inner circles of President Sukarno. See ibid., p. 98.
119. Its president was Azuma Sumio, one of NOSODECO'S executive directors.
120. "Mengapa Ibnu Sutowo Turunkan Harga Minjak ke Djepang?" *Indonesia Raya*, December 26, 1969. See also an article criticizing the special relationship between PERMINA and the Kinoshita Trading Company: "Permina Beli Kapal Selalu Lewat 'Broker'—Tunas Ltd. dan Kinoshita Beli Lagi dari Orang Lain," *Indonesia Raya*, December 31, 1969.

Chapter 6
Japan's Role in the Indonesian-Malaysian Conflicts, 1963–1966

The confrontation between Indonesia and Malaysia from 1963 to mid-1966 was one of the most turbulent political events in postwar Southeast Asia, overshadowed only by the greater conflict in Indochina. Sukarno's *Konfrontasi* against the newly federated Malaysia was supported by Indonesia's Communist party (PKI) and sought backing from Peking. Sukarno's anti-Malaysia policy was also supported to a great extent by the Indonesian military who feared that they might have to be demobilized after the settlement of the West Irian issue, thus becoming incapacitated in face of the growing communist forces. Malaysia was supported by Great Britain and its Commonwealth forces of Australia and New Zealand, and Britain in turn sought American support for Malaysia in exchange for its support of American efforts in Vietnam.[1]

The confrontation officially originated with Foreign Minister Subandrio's statement on January 20, 1963, in which he declared Indonesia's policy of confrontation against the Malaysian federation of Malaya, Singapore, Sabah, Sarawak, and Brunei. Indonesia's policy continued through the Gestapu affair on September 30, 1965 and ended on August 11, 1966, when Foreign Ministers Adam Malik and Tun Razak signed a peace agreement. Despite the attention given to the confrontation itself,[2] little notice has been taken of Japan's role in this conflict. This chapter then will cover this aspect of the conflict, as well as the international significance of Japan's intervention.

Japan's part in Indonesia's confrontation with Malaysia grew partly out of its involvement with Indonesia through reparations. During this time Japan's Liberal Democratic party (LDP) was in power, headed by party President Ikeda Hayato from 1960–1964 and Vice-president

Kawashima Shōjirō from 1964–1970. Ikeda, Kawashima, and the Japanese Foreign Ministry actually were "anticonfrontationists," though they acted as mediators. Those in favor of the confrontation were the Indonesian Students Association (Persatuan Pelajar Indonesia, or PPI) in Tokyo, which succeeded in gaining the support of the Japan Socialist party (JSP) and of a less conservative and minor faction of the Liberal Democratic party led by Utsunomiya Tokuma, as well as the Japan Communist party (JCP), which had cultivated relations with Indonesia's PKI since 1960. This chapter will discuss only Japan's Foreign Ministry, Ikeda and Kawashima, all of whom were active in the reparations issue, while those in favor of confrontation will be examined in chapter 7.

During the confrontation the Foreign Ministry and the ruling Liberal Democratic party coordinated their efforts at mediation between Indonesia and Malaysia and found them to be complementary. The study of their respective efforts has been divided into three periods: (1) the pre-Malaysia period, from January 20, 1963 to September 16, 1963; (2) the post-Malaysia period, from September 16, 1963 to September 30, 1965; and (3) the post-Gestapu period, from September 30, 1965 to August 11, 1966. The Foreign Ministry's presence was most noticeable in the first and the third periods, and that of the LDP, in the second period. The emphasis on the LDP's role in the second period was due to the high-level mediation required at that time.

THE PRE-MALAYSIA PERIOD: JANUARY 20, 1963–SEPTEMBER 16, 1963

From its inception the Japanese Foreign Ministry paid close attention to the formation of Malaysia, watching for any repercussions that might obstruct Japan's economic relations with that area. Japan was in the process of paying reparations to Indonesia, Burma, the Philippines, and South Vietnam, and of extending grants to Laos and Cambodia, the latter three of which were suffering from the consequences of the Vietnam conflict. But the increasing tension among Malaysia, the Philippines, and Indonesia promised to reduce the efficacy of Japan's reparations to the latter two. Japan had hoped that the reparations eventually would lead to profitable export markets in these countries. Furthermore, Japan's first large capital investment had been in north Sumatran oil. Any showdown between Jakarta and Kuala Lumpur would occur either in the Strait of Malacca or on the Indonesian-Malaysian border in Borneo. If it were in the straits, Japan's oil development projects in north Sumatra would become primary targets of the Malaysian forces. The possibility of conflict also threatened the safe passage of Japanese oil tankers throught the Strait of Malacca.

Japan depends so much upon Middle Eastern oil that any substantial hindrance of its transportation through the strait would have an immediate and adverse effect upon its heavy industries. Yet, strange enough, this point was never articulately indicated as a motive for Japan's intervention with the confrontation. The high-ranking Japanese government officials did not seem to weigh it.[3]

At the time when Indonesia proclaimed its confrontation policy against Malaysia in January 1963, Japan was concluding a reparations agreement with South Vietnam, the last Southeast Asian claimant. From both inside and outside the Japanese government and even from the United States, there had been calls for Japan to take a more actively political position in that region.[4] However, the Foreign Ministry and the ruling party had warned against this, sensing a possibly unfavorable reaction by Southeast Asians to Japan's reentry into their affairs. Despite this, the conclusion of a reparations agreement with South Vietnam as Japan's last settlement with Southeast Asia made it easier for Japan to adopt this sort of policy.

Japan, therefore, decided on the cautious role of mediator, feeling that this might both promote peace and serve as a means of reentrance into Southeast Asian political affairs. Japan's Foreign Minister Ōhira Masayoshi thus persuaded visiting Indonesian Foreign Minister Subandrio on May 24, 1963 to invite Malaysian Prime Minister Tunku Abdul Rahman to meet with President Sukarno in Tokyo, offering them a private place for discussion.[5] On May 31, 1963 Rahman flew to Tokyo and met with President Sukarno. This first meeting after the beginning of the conflict was successful, and they met again on June 1 agreeing to observe the spirit of their 1959 friendship treaty and to strive for a peaceful settlement. In addition, Sukarno and Rahman decided that the foreign ministers of Indonesia, the Philippines, and Malaysia should meet in Manila on June 7, 1963 to set up a later summit conference of the leaders of the three countries.[6]

The foreign ministers' meeting from June 6 to June 11 was followed by a summit conference from July 30 to August 5, 1963. The summit conference proved to be only a temporary success. The three leaders, Sukarno, Rahman, and Macapagal, conceived of a federation of "Malay peoples" to be named "Maphilindo,"[7] and Rahman consented to postpone the formation of Malaysia until a United Nations survey had ascertained the wishes of North Borneo (Sabah) and Sarawak about joining the federation. Although a UN team was dispatched to North Borneo, Rahman prematurely announced on August 29, two days before Independence Day, that he would federate Malaysia on September 16 of that year. While Malaya's postponement of Malaysia Day from August 31 was humiliating for Rahman, his subsequent selection of September 16, prior to hearing the UN survey's outcome, was equally insulting to Sukarno and Macapagal. Malaysia Day, then, was less of a celebration than had been anticipated. With the refusal of Indonesia and the Philippines to recognize Malaysia, diplomatic relations were severed on the very day of its formation.

Although the summit conference ultimately failed, the fact that it took place in Tokyo signified Japan's renewed political involvement in Southeast Asia. According to a Japanese Foreign Ministry official, both Sukarno and Rahman were reluctant to meet in Tokyo and did so primarily "to save Japan's face."[8] Apparently at that time they did not feel the need for Japan's mediation—but later in 1965 when the situation worsened, they welcomed Japan's intervention.

THE POST-MALAYSIA PERIOD: SEPTEMBER 16, 1963– SEPTEMBER 30, 1965

Ikeda's Mediation Efforts

On September 16, 1963 the Malaysian and British embassies in Jakarta were attacked and, in retaliation, Tunku Rahman publicly stepped on the Indonesian flag. Malaysia's diplomatic rupture with Indonesia and the Philippines provided another item on the agenda for Prime Minister Ikeda's "goodwill tour" to the Philippines, Indonesia, Australia, and New Zealand, and marked the beginning of his personal intervention.[9] In a press conference on September 19 Ikeda remarked that he wanted to make a personal effort to mediate the issue, "even if he were not asked by the parties concerned."[10]

Several factors contributed to Ikeda's desire to mediate. First, he felt that neither the United States nor Great Britain were exerting adequate pressure upon Indonesia and Malaysia. Indeed, according to an account written by Ikeda's personal secretary, in the previous year when Ikeda visited London, he had been asked personally by Prime Minister Macmillan to "contain" Sukarno.[11] Second, it seemed that the leaders of Indonesia, Malaysia, and the Philippines harbored more emotional rather than political disagreements, and that all of them seemed to desire another summit meeting. Third, on September 19 when Subandrio stopped in Tokyo en route to New York, he gave the impression to Ōda Takio, former ambassador to Indonesia and present counselor in the Foreign Ministry, that Indonesia would appreciate Japan's mediation.[12] Fourth, it was in Japan's interest to prevent the Malaysian issue from developing into a full-fledged East-West conflict, and fifth, a stable Southeast Asia would insure the continuous export of

Japanese goods to the region. Ikeda further reasoned that the stability of the Sukarno regime was imperative to containing the advance of communist forces into Southeast Asia and that Japan's mediation would strengthen its political position in the region.[13]

This last reason, the reaffirmation of Japan's political position, coincided with the reemergence of Japanese national pride due to its economic success and was exactly what the Philippines wished to avoid. When Ikeda talked with Macapagal in Manila during his visit from September 23 to 26, 1963, he reportedly reacted coolly to Ikeda's offer of mediation, probably not wishing to appear to accept the superiority of Japan's political position.[14] Their joint communique on September 26 stated that they had had a frank exchange of views on various problems of mutual interest but it made no reference at all to the confrontation.[15]

Ikeda's subsequent visit to Jakarta from September 26–29 was more successful than his visit to Manila. His personal acquaintance with the Indonesian leaders might have been a decisive factor. He addressed Sukarno as "Brother Sukarno," which reportedly pleased the latter greatly.[16] On September 27 the parties joined to discuss economic cooperation including Ikeda's offer of $12 million in credit, and then the two leaders talked privately for forty minutes. Ikeda persuaded Sukarno to order the Indonesian flag removed from the ransacked British embassy. Sukarno had the flag taken down after dark to avoid the demonstrators' cry against the removal.[17] In their second meeting on September 28 Sukarno became more agreeable to Ikeda's emphasis on a peaceful approach to the Malaysian conflict.

Their joint communique on September 28 stated that the president and the prime minister had "agreed to cooperate closely to promote peace in the world, particularly in the Western Pacific."[18] In reference to Indonesia the communique also declared that: "In this regard the Prime Minister expressed the strong desirability of *musyawarah* (consultations) among the Maphilindo leaders in the spirit of the Manila summit to the end of contributing to the stability, peace and mutual prosperity of their region." Although the Ikeda-Sukarno communique registered Sukarno's favorable attitude toward Japan's mediation, neither this nor Ikeda's communique with Macapagal made mention of the tension among Indonesia, the Philippines, and Malaysia. Only in Canberra, following his visit to Jakarta, did Ikeda publicly state Japan's support of Malaysia, and in their joint communique on October 3, Australian Prime Minister Robert Menzies and the Japanese prime minister "expressed deep concern for the situation in that area."[19] But in Indonesia and in Manila Ikeda had been careful not to express this position publicly.

While in Jakarta Prime Minister Ikeda also talked with the British ambassador, Sir Andrew Gilchrist, and the United States ambassador, Howard Jones. The *Asahi Shinbun* on September 30, 1963 speculated that Ikeda had requested that the British ambassador persuade Malaysia to avoid violent action, while warning the United States ambassador that the American suspension of aid to Indonesia might have a negative effect.[20]

Ikeda left Indonesia with optimism over the Malaysian issue. He stated at a press conference in Australia that he would not have to mediate because the three nations concerned would settle the issue by themselves. His optimism was not long-lived for the three nations did not actually begin to move toward settlement. Most of the British businesses continued under Indonesian government control and most of the former Malayan offices, private residences and properties were confiscated by the Indonesian authorities. Indonesian armed forces and volunteers were dispatched to the Kalimantan-Sarawak borders and to north Sumatra, which faces the Malay Peninsula.

When the situation worsened, the Japanese government sent Ōda Takio to Malaysia in November. To minimize the publicity of his visit, Ōda hid himself by first joining the Japanese delegation to an ECAFE meeting in Bangkok and faterwards quietly extending his trip. He learned in Kuala Lumpur that Rahman was unhappy about the confrontation, wishing to discontinue the state of war with Indonesia if the circumstances permit.[21] Yet the situation aggravated itself. On December 12, 1963, Sukarno demanded that another survey be conducted by the United Nations to ascertain the wishes of the peoples of Sabah and Sarawak. This Malaysia rejected. Rahman's government intensified its military attack on Indonesia and the Malaysian issue appeared far from being solved.

Thus Prime Minister Ikeda again attempted to mediate in the Malaysian issue. On January 15, 1964 President Sukarno came to Japan on one of his frequent informal trips, which coincided with a visit by the then U.S. Attorney General Robert Kennedy. Kennedy stayed in Tokyo for three days beginning on January 16. On January 17 he met with Foreign Minister Ōhira, President Sukarno, and Prime Minister Ikeda, and on January 18 again with Sukarno, before visiting Manila, Kuala Lumpur, and Jakarta. In the meantime, in Tokyo, on January 16, the Japanese and Indonesians met. On the Japanese side were Prime Minister Ikeda, Foreign Minister Ōhira, the prime minister's secretary, Kurogane, Foreign Ministry Counselor Ōda, and Ambassador to Indonesia Furuuchi, and from the Indonesian side, President Sukarno,

Foreign Minister Subandrio, Ambassador to Japan Bambang Sugeng, and Army Chief of Staff Yani.[22] In this meeting Ikeda is said to have admonished the Indonesians for continuing their expensive struggle against Malaysia, pointing out that, if Indonesia did have funds sufficient to buy or build twenty warships, they could spend it far better on, for instance, a high-speed train system like Japan's. These remarks were followed by silence according to a diplomat who was present.[23]

Although their talks with the Japanese and Attorney General Kennedy led the Indonesians to agree again to seek a peaceful solution to the Malaysian issue,[24] in fact both they and the Malaysians only intensified their belligerence toward each other. Cambodia and Thailand offered mediation but with no success.[25] The Malaysian leaders carried their anti-Indonesia posture into the general elections on April 25, 1964 and on May 20, Sukarno declared that Malaysia would be "crushed" by the end of the year. The Philippines, however, in deference to internal support for Malaysia and to American pressure, modified its stand toward the issue and on May 18 reestablished consular relations with Malaysia and presented itself as a mediator. The Asian mediators in the Indonesian-Malaysian conflict now numbered four: Japan, Thailand, Cambodia, and the Philippines. The latter country's Foreign Minister Salvador Lopez shuttled back and forth between Jakarta and Kuala Lumpur and, in June 1964, finally was able to arrange another summit meeting in Tokyo.

The participants in this meeting on June 20 first agreed in principle to President Macapagal's proposal for the four Afro-Asian nations to establish a mediation commission, but then differences materialized. At the morning session of the three heads of state, Sukarno and Rahman had voiced agreement to this proposal but, at the afternoon summit session, Rahman changed his position and demanded the withdrawal of Indonesian guerilla forces from North Borneo within four weeks as a precondition to the commission.[26] Sukarno then walked out of the session, leaving the Malaysian and Philippine leaders in discussion, but, when he returned later, they had not reached a consensus.[27] Their subsequent joint statement tried to conceal the failure of the negotiations, but this was made manifest a day later when Malaysia resumed military action against the Indonesian guerillas.[28]

Japan's participation in this summit meeting was more limited than at previous meetings. Not only was the Foreign Ministry apprehensive of the results of the meeting, but also Prime Minister Ikeda did not want to take away from the Philippines the credit for arranging the meeting. Ikeda also was anxious that Japan should treat each of the countries impartially, being aware of Malaysia's and Great Britain's suspicion that it was partial to Indonesia.[29] He thus tried to avoid discussing the Malaysian issue and allotted an equal amount of time to his conferences with each head of state. Nevertheless, his underlying interest may be evidenced by the donation of his own residence for the meeting.

Ikeda's desire for mediation was never realized. By the time of his resignation in November 1964, Japan's Foreign Ministry was convinced that Sukarno had lost control of the PKI, which was the real force behind the anti-Malaysia campaign. Sukarno was seeking a solution to the campaign without losing face and privately agreed to adhere to the UN's mediation plan.[30] His pride, nonetheless, stood in the way. He had been hurt by the British and American support given to Rahman's announcement of Malaysia Day made prior to hearing the results of the UN survey. And he was hurt again when the UN General Assembly voted on December 29, 1964 to let Malaysia sit on the Security Council as a nonpermanent member. In answer to the latter action, Sukarno withdrew Indonesia from the United Nations on January 2, 1965, a decision which only further isolated his country.[31] Indonesia's withdrawal from the United Nations naturally worried the Western and neutral nations. Indonesia had drifted away from Japan's influence, and now there loomed the possibility that closer ties between Jakarta and Peking might drive away Japan altogether.

On January 6, 1965 Prime Minister Satō sent a personal letter to Sukarno, urging him to reverse his decision and offering to send a special envoy to Indonesia if that would help.[32] Although U.S. President Lyndon Johnson, during a visit by Satō in mid-January, expressed pessimism over Satō's continuing efforts at mediation, the United Nation's Secretary General U Thant expressed support.[33] Sukarno apparently wished to maintain a friendly relationship with Japan, motivated possibly by Indonesia's economic deterioration and possibly by the influence of his Japanese wife, Dewi. He therefore welcomed Satō's offer to send an envoy to Jakarta.[34] The Japanese government announced further that its relationship with Indonesia would not be altered by its withdrawal from the United Nations.

At first, the Satō Cabinet considered sending Kawashima Shōjirō, vice-president of the ruling party, as its envoy to Indonesia. But because Kawashima had had little advance preparation for the mission, it decided on a less stellar figure to ascertain Jakarta's intentions. This man was Ogasa Kōshō, a member of the Diet and vice-president of the Japan-Indonesia Association.[35] In his meeting with Sukarno on January 26, Ogasa learned that his decision to withdraw Indonesia from the UN was final but that he would be glad to have Kawashima visit and felt that Japan's mediation might be necessary at a later time.[36]

While looking for an opportune time for Kawashima's visit, the Satō Cabinet then instructed the Foreign Ministry to study the feasibility of the four-nation mediation commission proposed by Macapagal at the Tokyo summit meeting in June 1964.[37] Subandrio, in a February visit to Tokyo, agreed to a mediation commission but again these efforts came to naught.[38]

In the meantime the Satō Cabinet, the Foreign Ministry, and the ruling party leadership, particularly Kawashima, tried to keep Japanese-Indonesian relations intact and considered Indonesia's request in late January 1965 for a long-term import credit of $139 million.[39] On February 11, therefore, Foreign Minister Subandrio came to Tokyo to discuss this as well as the Malaysian issue. Japan hoped to use the credit to influence Indonesia, which was interested in purchasing generators, plants, ships, and fertilizer projects as well as consumer goods.[40] In the same month Japan planned to set up with Indonesia a joint enterprise, the Far East Oil Trading Company, which would import crude petroleum directly from the Indonesian government instead of from the big Western oil companies there.[41] Because Indonesia had just announced its seizure of American and British oil properties, wishing to sell the oil independently, Japan hoped not only to profit from this joint venture but also to prevent Indonesian oil from going to China.

The "Kawashima Lobby" and Kawashima's Role as Diplomat

Prime Minister Satō decided to send Kawashima as his personal representative to the April 1965 tenth anniversary celebration of the Asian-African Bandung conference. Satō's choice was deliberate as Kawashima was the most influential of the Japanese close to Sukarno. From mid-1964 to early 1966 he also was considered the head of Indonesia Lobby in Japan, prompting it to be termed the "Kawashima Lobby."

Kawashima's career in Indonesian affairs was a varied one. The positions that Kawashima had held in the Liberal Democratic party and in the government after 1957 provided him with many opportunities to meet with President Sukarno. From July 1957 to July 1960 Kawashima was the ruling party's secretary under Prime Minister Kishi. He also served intermittently as the party's vice-president from July 1964 until his death in November 1970. Yet what drew Kawashima into Indonesian affairs most immediately was his position as state minister in charge of the 1964 Tokyo Olympics, a post which he assumed in June 1962.

In this capacity Kawashima went to Indonesia in August 1962

for the Fourth Asian Games. Indonesia's insertion of political bias into the games precluded its future participation in the 1964 Tokyo Olympics and, on February 7, 1963, the International Olympics Committee (IOC) suspended Indonesia on the basis that it had violated IOC rules by rejecting, on political grounds, the participation of Nationalist China and Israel in the Jakarta-sponsored games.[42] Although Indonesia retaliated by withdrawing from the IOC, it later regretted the decision and sought a face-saving way to reenter the organization. In May 1963 Kawashima met in Tokyo with Sukarno to discuss ways in which Indonesia would be able to participate in the Tokyo Olympic games.[43] Among the reasons that Sukarno had chosen to confer with Kawashima, was the latter's obvious influence within the ruling party and his sympathy toward the "nonalighed" countries. However, one cannot ignore Sukarno's personal confidence in Kawashima, inspired by his wife Dewi's friendship with Kawashima, whom she addressed as "Papa" and whom Sukarno addressed as "Kakakmu" (elder brother).[44]

Later in April 1964 Sukarno invited to Indonesia nine members of the Diet and seven political journalists, whom he requested Kawashima to select by himself, which he did.[45] He included four members of his political faction, the Kōyū Club.[46] After this visit members of the Kōyū Club and Kawashima's supporters made frequent trips to Indonesia. Ogasa Kōshō's visit in January 1965 was in this context.

The so-called Kawashima Lobby acted in concert with the reparations lobby that emerged in 1960, as well as with the Foreign Ministry. The reparations lobby was centered principally on economic issues, whereas the Kawashima Lobby concentrated on political issues. Both overlapped and operated informally and confidentially. The exact membership of the lobby is yet to be identified, but one may speculate that two prominent individuals with whom Kawashima had worked in the lobby were Saitō Shizuo, ambassador to Indonesia, and Dewi.

Saitō Shizuo was head of the Planning Section of the General Affairs Department of the occupation administration during the war and, as such, one of Sukarno's close friends. That he had been on friendly terms with Sukarno was a major reason for his appointment as ambassador to Indonesia at the critical time when Sukarno was leaning more decisively toward the communist camp.[47] Upon his assignment to Jakarta in September 1964 he frequently was seen at the presidential Merdeka Palace. Saitō also cultivated Dewi's friendship. One source indicates that the ambassador routinely played bridge with her at Wisma Yasoo to gather information about Indonesia's forthcoming political moves.[48] Saitō had two other wartime Japanese colleagues stationed in Jakarta with whom he worked. Nishijima Shigetada he had known since the war when Nishijima, being in the navy's Jakarta Liaison Office, was actively promoting Indonesia's independence. The other colleague was former Captain Yanagawa Tomoshige, who was with the Beppan (Special Intelligence Task Unit) of the Sixteenth Army's staff. In 1943 Yanagawa organized an Indonesian military intelligence school in Tanggerang, West Java, which became the origin of the Indonesian voluntary army (PETA), the core of the present Indonesian army.[49] Yanagawa also was in close contact with Sukarno during the war and had a reunion with him in Tokyo in June 1959. Yanagawa served as advisor to the Japanese team for the Games for the New Emerging Forces (GANEFO) in November 1963,[50] and, in the following year, returned as a consultant to various Japanese companies.[51]

Shimizu Hitoshi was another possible helper for Kawashima's efforts. As an often-cited propaganda officer of the occupation administration in Java during the war and now president of the Japanese-Indonesian Cultural Association, he continued his wartime association with Sukarno and Indonesian friends from the Propaganda Office. He maintained his interest in and affection for Indonesia by forming the Japanese-Indonesian Cultural Association, and, after 1964, he attempted to relate his cultural association to Jakarta's Indonesia-Japan Friendship Society, which Dewi headed since May 1964.[52] According to one source, Shimizu was a frequent visitor of Dewi's Wisma Yasoo. He came to enjoy Kawashima's acquaintance through the business of the Jakarta-sponsored Asian Games of 1962 mentioned earlier and he was reportedly present at a meeting of May 1963 whom Kawashima discussed with Indonesian leaders on Indonesia's participation in the 1964 Tokyo Olympics.[53]

Saitō, Nishijima, Yanagawa, and Shimizu all had close contacts with important figures in Indonesia. Shimizu was a friend of Chairul Saleh, minister of basic industries, who used to work in Shimizu's propaganda office and now was one of Sukarno's right-hand men. Nishijima knew both Saleh and Adam Malik, both of whom had been leaders of the radical Murba party. Adam Malik worked closely with Sukarno until November 1964 when he and other Murba leaders organized a movement (BPS),[54] to prevent an alliance between Sukarno and the Communists (PKI), which failed because of Sukarno's and the PKI's opposition. Yanagawa is known to have had close contact with Indonesia's military police chief, Major General Sudirgo. Ambassador Saitō quickly established a reputation for reliable inside information. Admiring this, Japanese correspondents and even American embassy officials paid close heed to the *Saitō jōhō* (Saitō's information).[55] In addition Saitō's boss in Tokyo, Shiina Etsusaburō, foreign minister from

July 1964 to December 1966, belonged to the Kawashima faction in the ruling party.

It is against this background that the Kawashima Lobby emerged. Its members shared the view that no Indonesian but Sukarno could hold the troubled country together, considering that Japan had little choice but to support Sukarno and hope for a stable Indonesia under his leadership.

Kawashima went to Jakarta in April 1965, ostensibly as Prime Minister Satō's representative at the anniversary ceremony but, more importantly, to find out Sukarno's objectives in the confrontation against Malaysia.[56] On April 16 and 17 Kawashima met with him, proposing that he come to Tokyo early in May for another conference with Rahman who already had planned to visit at that time. Kawashima tried to enhance his proposal by telling Sukarno that Japan would support the second Afro-Asian conference to be held that June in Algiers and that he, Kawashima, would attend.[57] Japan privately hoped that this gesture would discourage Indonesia from seeking support from Peking at the conference. Kawashima agreed to Indonesia's request for $20 million to build steam-power plants on the outskirts of Jakarta.

From Jakarta Kawashima flew to Kuala Lumpur to talk with Rahman on April 20. After Kawashima related to Rahman the contents of his discussion with Sukarno, Rahman agreed to the formation of a four-nation mediation commission and to another meeting with Sukarno. Then Kawashima went to Bangkok to request the Thai government's support of Japanese mediation efforts. In Bangkok Kawashima also gathered Japan's ambassadors to Indonesia, Malaysia, and Thailand—Saitō Shizuo, Kai Fumihiko, and Kasuya Takao, respectively—to work out provisional plans for the commission. Ambassador Saitō then returned to Jakarta on April 25 to convey to Sukarno the outcome of the Kawashima-Rahman talks in Kuala Lumpur and to invite him formally to Tokyo to meet with Rahman.[58]

It was understood that Sukarno had accepted the invitation, but on May 1 he told a huge, cheering crowd of workers that he would not go to Tokyo. This was explained in part by Indonesian Coordinating Minister of Public Relations Roeslan Abdulgani, who told a *Far Eastern Economic Review* correspondent that he had received "thousands of letters" from Indonesians expressing disapproval of the visit.[59] He added that the Tunku's visit to Tokyo had been planned primarily to chair the Asian Soccer Council and to attend the games and that Indonesia considered the Malaysian dispute too important to be discussed during a sports trip.[60]

Kawashima's initial attempt at mediation thus failed. Only the

Tunku came to Tokyo as planned, yet most observers believed that Sukarno's refusal was owing to pressure from the PKI; that his personal choice had been to come. The U.S. embassy in Jakarta also felt that the PKI was trying to undermine its political rival, the Indonesian army, by creating tension first over West Irian and then Malaysia, thus dispersing the military forces outside Java.[61] The Tunku declared, too, that the communists in Indonesia were staging "hot and cold wars" against Malaysia.[62]

Japan's—and Kawashima's—second effort to mediate in Indonesian affairs centered on the second Afro-Asian conference. Kawashima believed that Japan should establish closer relations with the nonaligned nations in order to deal more effectively with the United States and the Soviet Union and stressed that an effective delegation be sent to the conference. Japan also insisted that Malaysia be asked to the conference, with which Indonesia naturally disagreed. To discuss this and economic matters, Indonesian Foreign Minister Subandrio came to Tokyo on May 19 and met with Prime Minister Satō, Foreign Minister Shiina, Ambassador Saitō, and Kawashima. Subandrio still protested Malaysia's participation in the conference but did emphasize the importance of Japan's involvement in Southeast Asia, which apparently meant that Indonesia would welcome both Japanese mediation and economic aid. The Shiina-Subandrio talks produced an additional Japanese credit of $15 million.

Japan's delegation to the second Afro-Asian conference was to number forty-six members headed by Kawashima. Ambassador Saitō also would join the delegation. However, on June 19 there was a coup d'etat against the procommunist Ben Bella regime in the host country, Algeria, and the conference was postponed first until November and then indefinitely. Sukarno and his eighty-member delegation reached Cairo on June 26, discussed the future of the conference with Nasser and Chou En-lai, then flew to Paris and returned to Indonesia.[63] His relationship with Chou became closer than ever.

Kawashima's third attempt at mediation occurred on the occasion of Indonesia's Independence Day celebration, August 17, 1965, to which he was invited by Sukarno.[64] This mediation attempt proved to be more difficult than the previous ones. Earlier, Indonesian political leaders including Ali Sastroamidjojo, president of the Indonesian Nationalist party (PNI), had criticized Japan's desire for Malaysia's participation in the Afro-Asian conference[65] and in his independence speech Sukarno had defied Japan's wishes by calling again to "crush Malaysia." Thus it was not surprising that, when Sukarno and Kawashima met on August 23, they disagreed on the second Afro-Asian conference postponed for

November, on the Southeast Asian Ministerial Conference on Economic Development that Japan had proposed in July,[66] as well as on the Vietnam issue. Sukarno refused to send an Indonesian official to any conference that Malaysia and South Vietnam would attend, reflecting his closer adherence to Peking's posture.[67] Kawashima's only remaining means of bargaining was the offer of more, much needed, economic aid. He was able to change Sukarno's mind with the deferred payment for $37 million·importation of goods, bringing Japan's commitment that year to Indonesia to $72 million, larger than that of any other country.[68]

Kawashima accomplished little. Soon after his visit to Indonesia, on September 30, 1965 the Gestapu affair was attempted by Colonel Untung and supported by Communist forces. Crushing it quickly, the Suharto-led army gradually changed Indonesia's political policies from a procommunist stance. The Gestapu affair also ended Kawashima's role as mediator.

Because the leverage in Kawashima's mediation efforts lay in his close relationship with Sukarno, it was no longer valuable after Sukarno lost political power. If Sukarno had had control over the PKI, the possibility that he and Kawashima could have found a peaceful solution to the Malaysian issue would have been a real one, and Kawashima's efforts might have been successful. In the actual situation, however, his efforts still should be judged as useful, for he did succeed in maintaining relations with Indonesia when it broke off economic (through not diplomatic) relations with the United States and Great Britain and diplomatic relations with Malaysia.[69]

That Indonesia did maintain close ties with Japan was contrary to Sukarno's "anticapitalist, antiimperialist" foreign policy and pointed to Sukarno's personal affection for the country. Although Japan supported Malaysia, as did the United States and Great Britain, the Japanese embassy was not stoned. Sukarno was not an ideologist but rather an opportunist. He took advantage of Japan's fear of a closer relationship between Indonesia and China to accept the much needed economic aid that Japan was all too willing to give.

THE POST-GESTAPU PERIOD: OCTOBER 1965 TO AUGUST 1966

Though the Gestapu affair occurred on September 30, 1965, it was not until March 12, 1966 that Japan could announce that its policy toward Indonesia would remain unchanged, and not until early May did Japan offer again to mediate in the Malaysian issue. On March 11, 1966 Lieutenant General Suharto led a bloodless coup against President Sukarno. Although Suharto then wielded the real power in Indonesia, he allowed Sukarno to retain his title of president. After the coup Indonesia began to redirect its political course. On March 27, 1966 Suharto appointed Adam Malik as foreign minister. On March 30 Malik stated that it would strive to end the confrontation, although Sukarno persisted in his argument that Malaysia would be "crushed." On August 11 Malik and Malaysia's Deputy Premier Tun Razak signed an agreement ending the confrontation with Malaysia.[70] On the Indonesian side Adam Malik officially deserved credit for the agreement but there were other, unofficial negotiators who had contributed to this success. Among them were Ali Murtopo and his subordinates, Daan Mogot and Willy Pesik, both former members of the Sumatra Rebellion.[71] In addition Shirahata Tomoyoshi, a former diplomat, and Ambassador to Malaysia Kai Fumihiko had worked secretly toward this settlement.[72]

Until the Gestapu affair, Shirahata did not feel that Indonesia's own political conditions were conducive to mediation by a third party.[73] But after September 30 he was eager to go to Indonesia to observe what changes had occurred. Although Shirahata did visit in October 1965, it was on his next trip in April 1966 that he contacted his old friend, Adam Malik. He told Shirahata that, although he had proposed to Malaysia that secret talks be held in Bangkok, Malaysia was suspicious of his desire for a peaceful settlement.[74] Adam Malik also revealed that the Sukarno forces still were strong and were frustrating his efforts.[75]

On April 6 and 7, 1966 Malaysia's Deputy Premier Tun Razak came to Tokyo for the Japanese-sponsored Southeast Asian Ministerial Conference on Economic Development and the new Indonesian ambassador, Rukmito Hendraningrat, attended as an observer. Earlier Indonesia had refused to participate on the grounds that it was in a state of conflict with Malaysia, but, in late March, General Suharto announced that Indonesia had "opened the door" to a peaceful solution to the confrontation with Malaysia and would attend the conference as an observer. Although Indonesia's partial participation was regarded as a hopeful sign, Ambassador Rukmito's later explanation on April 16 that even though Indonesia had "opened the door" it had not reversed its principle of confrontation against Malaysia brought both confusion and annoyance to Kuala Lumpur and to Adam Malik.[76]

To convince Malaysia of Indonesia's sincerity, Adam Malik asked Shirahata if he would go to Kuala Lumpur. Shirahata agreed to his request and suggested that he include Japan's ambassador to Malaysia, Kai Fumihiko.[77] Shirahata then proposed that Kai go secretly to Bangkok in late April to meet with Malik, who was planning to go there for a meeting with Philippine Foreign Secretary Marcos Ramos which Thai Foreign Minister Thanat Khoman had planned. After consulting with

Ambassador Saitō in Jakarta, Shirahata flew to Kuala Lumpur where he talked privately with Kai about the proposed trip to Bangkok. Kai then talked with Rahman, who approved it. On April 29 immediately after the Japanese emperor's birthday reception, Kai flew alone to Thailand.[78] On the evening of his arrival he met secretly with Adam Malik and returned to Malaysia on May 1.[79] His trip to Bangkok soon was discovered by the press and, despite Kai's initial denials, was confirmed publicly on May 5 by Deputy Premier Tun Razak in declaring that Indonesia sincerely desired peace with Malaysia.[80] The success of Kai's trip led to a meeting between Adam Malik and Tun Razak a month later in Bangkok, a meeting which proved to be a decisive step toward peace.

It is difficult to determine the extent of Japan's own contributions to the peace negotiations. As already mentioned, anticommunist members of Indonesia's military forces and participants in the Sumatra Rebellion also were talking with Malaysian leaders. Immediately after Kai left Bangkok in late April, Adam Malik also talked secretly with Ghazali bin Shafie, permanent secretary in Malaysia's foreign ministry.[81] The apparent importance of these informal relationships between Indonesia and Malaysia raise some question as to whether Japan's intervention really had been necessary in initiating the peace negotiations.

I elicited two favorable opinions concerning this question. First, Adam Malik stated that he believed the personal and confidential negotiations had been the most effective in the Malaysian issue. If he had held his initial discussions with the Malaysians, news of them inevitably would have been revealed and might have destroyed his efforts. Therefore, he considered the Japanese presence as having been valuable.[82] Second, Indonesian Ambassador to Thailand B. M. Diah concurred with Adam Malik, adding that he thought Japan had been appropriate as a third party.[83]

After Kai's return from Bangkok on May 1, Deputy Premier Razak announced on May 8 that Malaysia was prepared to hold peace talks with Indonesia "without help of a third party."[84] Adam Malik agreed with Razak, saying on May 12 that Indonesia needed no third party either.[85] During these negotiations Japan made clear to Indonesia that, as a condition for receiving $30 million of credit, Indonesia should end the confrontation and should return to the UN as soon as possible. These conditions do not seem to have been onerous to Indonesia as the negotiations were proceeding as hoped. After the Malik-Razak meeting in Bangkok ended successfully on May 31, Prime Minister Satō and the Japanese Foreign Ministry reiterated their willingness to mediate, if necessary, but neither Indonesia nor Malaysia sought their assistance.[86]

AN ASSESSMENT OF JAPAN'S ROLE IN THE CONFRONTATION

Japan's mediation role in the Indonesian-Malaysian conflict was the first of a political nature that it had played in postwar Southeast Asia. During the period from 1963–1966 Japan maintained good terms with both the disputing parties by providing economic aid. It helped keep Indonesia from going over completely to the Chinese side and, finally, in early May 1966, it persuaded Malaysia of Indonesia's true desire for peace. Japan's role as mediator was effective because the disputing parties found Japan's intervention politically expedient and because the United States, Great Britain, and the United Nations' U Thant encouraged Japan's action.

The Japanese government tried to obtain the maximum benefits from its economic aid to Indonesia and from personal friendships with the Indonesian leaders. This mediation cum economic aid cost Japan $124 million in credit (although not all of it was used): $12 million offered at the Ikeda-Sukarno talks in September 1963; $20 million at the Kawashima-Sukarno talks in April 1965; $15 million at the Shiina-Subandrio talks in May 1965; another $37 million at the Kawashima-Sukarno talks in August 1965; and $30 million at the Shiina-Hamengku Buwono talks in May 1966. From the total of $124 million, $72 million was promised during the five months from April to August 1965. This illustrates the extent of the efforts at mediation by the Kawashima Lobby, although they did not result in an immediate end to the confrontation.

The Kawashima Lobby and the missions of Ambassador Kai and the former diplomat Shirahata Tomoyoshi made extensive use of personal connections with the Indonesian leaders. The relationship that Saitō, Shimizu, Dewi, and Kawashima had with Sukarno proved to be effective. Although it is impossible to isolate the most efficient personal connection, the efficacy itself of friendship in solving international tensions suggests the merit of the device. Saitō's and Shimizu's contacts with Sukarno originated in the occupation period, but Kai's and Shirahata's friendship with Malik was made in the postwar period. The latter was a new kind of personal tie which was utilized in the postwar issues. Similar to those participants in the Peace Lobby and the reparations lobbies, Kawashima and Kai played roles somewhere between that of lobbyist and decision-maker. One should not underestimate the importance to Japan of Dewi's position in Indonesia's inner political circles, particularly at the time when China was rumored to be cultivating Sukarno's second wife, Hartini. It was without precedent in Japanese diplomatic history that a Japanese woman had acted as what journalists called a "spearhead of Japanese diplomacy."

The style of Japan's intervention in the Southeast Asian conflict shifted between 1965 and 1966. Under Ikeda and Kawashima, Japan's róle was to moderate Indonesia's militant stance toward Malaysia and to reduce its dependence upon Peking. Ikeda's offer of $12 million in credit and Kawashima's offer of $72 million in credit were made primarily to placate Sukarno. However, in May 1966 when Satō made an offer of $30 million in credit on the condition that Indonesia swiftly end its Konfrontasi, this could be interpreted as a form of economic pressure. This may suggest that as Japan's economic involvement in Southeast Asia increases and when it finds its economic interests in jeopardy, it may make further use of economic suasion as a means of influence.

Japan's role in ending the Konfrontasi was not decisive. Its international significance lies in the fact that it marks the beginning of Japan's political involvement in Southeast Asian affairs. This was followed by an expression of its concern over the conflict in Vietnam. In 1968 Japan indicated its willingness to serve on an international peace observation team for Indochina and, in May 1970, attended the Jakarta conference on Cambodia. In this last conference, the three Asian nations involved in Konfrontasi—Indonesia, Malaysia, and Japan—ironically were selected as a mediation team for the Vietnamese conflict. Not only had Japan again entered the political scene in Indonesia, it now had shown its interests in serving as a peacemaker.

NOTES

1. See the joint communique between President Johnson and Prime Minister Home issued on February 13, 1964. The communique reads in part: "The Prime Minister reemphasized the United Kingdom support for United States policy in South Vietnam. The President reaffirmed the support of the United States for the peaceful national independence of Malaysia...." See Peter Boyce, ed., *Malaysia and Singapore in International Diplomacy: Documents and Commentaries* (Sydney: Sydney University Press, 1968), p. 162.

2. Major official reports and scholarly works on the Confrontation include: Indonesia, Information Ministry, *Gelora Konfrontasi Mengganjang "Malaysia"* (Jakarta: Information Ministry, 1964); Indonesia, Foreign Ministry, *Kumpulan Bahan2 Mengenai Masalah "Malaysia"* (24 vols.; mimeographed, 1963–1966); Malaysia, Ministry of External Affairs, *Indonesian Agression against Malaysia* (2 vols.; Kuala Lumpur: Government Printer, 1964); Malaysia, Ministry of Internal Security, *Indonesian Intentions towards Malaysia* (Kuala Lumpur: Government Printer, 1964); Peter Boyce, ed. *Malaysia and Singapore* (see n. 1); J. M. Gullick, *Malaysia and Its Neighbours* (New York: Barnes & Noble, Inc., 1967); Donald Hindley, "Indonesia's Confrontation with Malaysia: Search for Motives," *Asian Survey* 4 (June 1964): 904–

913; George M. Kahin, "Malaysia and Indonesia," *Pacific Affairs* 37 (Fall 1964): 253–270; John O. Sutter, "Two Faces of *Konfrontasi*: 'Crush Malaysia' and the *Gestapu*," *Asian Survey* 6 (October 1966): 523–546; and Frank B. Weinstein, *Indonesia Abandons Confrontation* (Ithaca, N.Y.: Cornell Modern Indonesia Project, Cornell University, 1969); Ide Anak Agung Gde Agung, *Twenty Years Indonesian Foreign Policy, 1945–1965* (The Hague: Mouton, 1974); J. A. C. Mackie, *Confrontation; The Indonesia-Malaysia Dispute* (Oxford: Oxford University Press, 1973).

    In reality, Malaysia severed diplomatic relationships with the Philippines as well, over territorial rights on North Borneo or Sabah. Mediating efforts were therefore directed toward the three countries.

3. Ōda Takio, private interview in Tokyo, August 7, 1973.
4. Anonymous Japanese embassy official, private interview in Jakarta, November, 1970.
5. *Asahi Shinbun*, May 25, 1963.
6. *Asahi Shinbun*, June 1, 1963.
7. Sukarno's term stands for Malaya, the Philippines, and Indonesia.
8. Japanese embassy official, interview.
9. Ikeda was scheduled to visit Manila on September 23–26, Jakarta on September 26–28, Canberra on September 29–October 3, and Wellington on October 3–5. He followed this schedule. See Japan, Foreign Ministry, *Waga gaikō no kinkyō*, no. 8 (1964): 94–95, 98–99.
10. *Asahi Shinbun*, September 19, 1963.
11. Itō Masaya, *Ikeda Hayato, sono sei to shi* (Tokyo: Shiseidō, 1966), p. 158.
12. *Asahi Shinbun*, September 23, 1963.
13. *Asahi Shinbun*, September 23, 1963.
14. *Asahi Shinbun*, September 25, 1963.
15. Japan, Foreign Ministry, *Gaimusho Press Releases 1963*, p. 69.
16. *Asahi Shinbun*, September 28, 1963.
17. *Asahi Shinbun*, September 28, 1963; and Itō Masaya, p. 205; and Ōda, interview.
18. *Gaimusho Press Releases 1963*, p. 70.
19. Ibid., p. 72.
20. Gilchrist stated that it was an informal meeting initiated by the Japanese embassy as a "friendly gesture." Jones reminded the press that the visit was a courtesy call and that he and Ikeda had been friends since the time Ikeda was minister of finance (1949–1953; 1956–1957). See *Asahi Shinbun*, September 28, 1963. The United States suspended a new aid to Indonesia on September 24, 1963. See *Asahi Shinbun*, September 24, 1963.
21. Ōda, interview.
22. *Asahi Shinbun*, January 16, 1964.
23. Japanese embassy official, interview. In Tokyo, the United States attempted to work together with Japan but in vain. When in a meeting with Ikeda, Ōhira, Ōda, and U.S. Ambassador to Japan Edwin O. Reischauer, Kennedy expressed his interest in having a Japanese accompany his mediation trip, the Japanese present did not quite grasp his intention. Only after his departure did Ikeda sense at Ōda's suggestion that Kennedy had probably wished to have Ōda with him. Ōda, interview.
24. Kennedy met with Sukarno in Jakarta on January 22. The latter agreed to a ceasefire on the Kalimantan-Malaysian border. The ceasefire did not last long.
25. On February 10 and 11 Rahman and Macapagal met and discussed the territorial rights of Sabah in Phnom Peng under the auspices of Prince Sihanouk. Thai

Foreign Minister Thanat Khoman arranged for the two Maphilindo foreign ministers' meetings in Bangkok on February 5–10 and March 3–5. These meetings bore no results.

26. *Asahi Shinbun*, June 21, 1964.
27. *Asahi Shinbun*, June 21, 1964.
28. *Asahi Shinbun*, June 22, 1964.
29. *Asahi Shinbun*, June 21, 1964.
30. Ōmori Minoru, *Sukaruno saigo no shinsō* (Tokyo: Shinchō Sha, 1967), p. 112.
31. The only support Sukarno received for decision was from Communist China which approved Sukarno's proposal to replace the "capitalist-imperialist" UN with a new world organization of "new emerging forces."
32. *Asahi Shinbun*, January 11, 1965.
33. Ōmori, p. 112; and *Asahi Shinbun*, January 15, 1965.
34. *Asahi Shinbun*, January 14, 1965.
35. Ogasa also was a member of the Liberal Democratic party's Kōyū Club headed by Kawashima and as a friend of Sukarno had visited Indonesia a number of times.
36. *Asahi Shinbun*, January 27, 1965.
37. *Antara*, February 14, 1965. Reportedly Thailand, Cambodia, Algeria, Pakistan, and Japan were mentioned as possible members of the committee. See *Antara*, February 16, 1965.
38. *Antara*, February 14, 1965.
39. *Antara*, January 29, 1965.
40. *Asahi Shinbun*, February 14, 1965.
41. *Antara*, March 26, 1965. The joint firm is supported by the Oil Resources Development Company, Maruzen Oil, Nippon Mining, Kansai Electric Power, NOSODECO, and the Indonesian State Oil Company, PERMINA. The firm was established on May 14, 1965. See *Antara*, May 14, 1965.
42. *Asahi Shinbun*, February 8, 1963.
43. Nevertheless in public, Indonesia followed a defiant policy against the IOC and sponsored a huge Game for New Emerging Forces (GANEFO) in November 1963, to which Communist China was invited. Kawashima and the Tokyo Olympic Committee leaders met on May 30, 1963 with the visiting Sukarno party represented by Sports Minister Maladi, First Deputy Premier Leimena, Basic Industries Minister Saleh, State Secretary Ikusan, Yogyakarta Governor Hamengku Buwono IX, Ambassador Bambang Sugeng as well as the president. See *Asahi Shinbun*, May 30, 1963.
44. "Neagari machigainashi no Devi fujin no 'Kawashima Shōjirō kaisōroku,'" *Shūkan Posuto*, November 27, 1970, p. 48.
45. Obata Shin'ichi, *Seikai issun saki wa yami* (Tokyo: Kōho Sha, 1972), pp. 202, 206; and *Nihon Keizai Shinbun*, May 2, 1964.
46. The Kōyū Club, formed in November 1962, had some 25 members. The four selected to go to Indonesia in April 1964 were: Ogasa Kōshō, Arafune Seijūrō, Shinoda Kōsaku, and Terajima Ryūtarō. See Kobata, pp. 51–55; and Kawashima Shōjirō Memoirs Committee, ed., *Kawashima Shōjirō* (Tokyo: Kōyū Kurabu, 1972), p. 378.
47. Former Ambassador to Indonesia Ōda Takio recalls that Sukarno appeared extremely happy to learn in 1964 that Saitō was the prospective ambassador. Ōda, interview. See also Mogi Masa, "Tōnan Ajia no munazoko," *Asahi Jānaru*, April 4, 1965, p. 13.
48. Fujiwara Hirotatsu, et al., *Hadaka no Devi fujin* (Tokyo: Yagumoi Shoin, 1970),

p. 82.

49. The Tanggerang school, called Seinen Dōjō (youth training center), trained some fifty Indonesian youths, who later became leaders of the PETA (Pembela Tanah Air, or Fatherland Defense) established in 1944. Yanagawa is a graduate of the Japanese army intelligence school, popularly called the "Nakano School" due to its location in Nakano outside of Tokyo. See Yanagawa Tomoshige, *Rikugun chōhōin Yanagawa chūi* (Tokyo: Sankei Shinbun Sha, 1967), pp. 84–98; and Hatakeyama Seikō, *Hiroku Rikugun Nakano Gakkō* (Tokyo: Banchō Shobō, 1971), pp. 179–193.

50. *Asahi Shinbun*, November 2, 1963.

51. "Yanagawa, Bapak PÈTA" (3), *Berita Yudha*, October 15, 1970.

52. Shimizu Hitoshi, private interview in Tokyo, April 25, 1972. The Indonesia-Japan Friendship Society was an officially accredited organization whose comparable organization in Japan was the Japan-Indonesia Association headed by Kajima Morinosuke, president of the Kajima Construction Company.

53. Shimizu Hitoshi, president of the Japanese-Indonesian Cultural Association and Sukarno's longtime friend, was also present at the meeting of May 24, 1963, indicating their mutual relationship. See Indonesia, Foreign Ministry, Research Bureau, *Hubungan Indonesia dengan Negara-Negara 1963* (mimeographed, 1964 [?]), p. 13.

54. BPS stands for *Badan Pendukung Sukarnoisme* (the Body to support Sukarnoism).

55. Hayashi Risuke, *Urotaeruna, Nihon* (Tokyo: Jitsugyō no Nihon Sha, 1972), p. 72.

56. Kawashima had another diplomatic concern during his visit to Jakarta, which was to set up some kind of preliminary meeting with Premier Chou En-lai of the People's Republic of China, who was to head the Chinese delegation to the ceremony. The two leaders met on April 19, 1965, through Sukarno's introduction, and agreed to hold regular meetings at the ministerial level. This was the first meeting with Chou En-lai for a high-ranking Japanese government official since State Minister Takasaki Tatsunosuke had met with him at the Afro-Asian Bandung conference in April 1955. See Kawashima Memoirs Committee, pp. 399–403.

57. Since the Afro-Asian conference in 1955, Indonesia occasionally had proposed a second conference. They took a more explicit initiative in early 1961 and the Non-Aligned Nations Conference in Belgrade in September 1961 discussed the matter. However, due to the lack of interest on the part of many nations concerned, the conference was postponed indefinitely. Indonesia's continued efforts nevertheless made possible the holding of a preparatory meeting at the ministerial level which was geared toward a summit conference. Yet again this summit conference was postponed when the Sino-Indian border incidents occurred that year. It was only in April 1964 that twenty-two Afro-Asian countries gathered in Jakarta for another preparatory conference and decided to hold the second Afro-Asian conference in Africa beginning on March 10, 1965. Later the date was postponed until June 1965.

58. *Antara*, April 23, 1965.

59. Actually Abdulgani made up such explanation by himself when he was instructed by Sukarno to think out good reasons for the latter's cancellation of a trip to Tokyo. Abdulgani, interview, September 12, 1974.

60. *Antara*, April 28, 1965; and *Asahi Shinbun*, April 29, 1965.

61. Anonymous high-ranking United States embassy official, private interview in Jakarta, December 1971.

62. *Antara*, May 3, 1965.

63. *Asahi Shinbun*, June 28, 1965.

64. The Japanese government also sent Kimura Takeo to Malaysia's Independence

Day celebration on August 31. Kimura, a conservative member of the Liberal Democratic party, emerged as an influential figure in the Indonesia lobby after the Gestapu affair.

65. *Asahi Shinbun*, June 24, 1965.

66. The conference originally was proposed in July 1965 in response to the United States' request for Tokyo and Washington to join efforts to assist Southeast Asia's economic development. The request came after President Johnson made a speech in Baltimore in April 1965, in which he proposed $1 billion in aid to the region. All the Southeast Asian nations but Burma, Cambodia, and Indonesia initially responded positively to the Japanese proposal. See *Asahi nenkan 1966*, p. 318; and Japan, Foreign Ministry, *Gaimushō no hyakunen* (2 vols.; Tokyo: Hara Shobō, 1969), II, 1139.

67. *Asahi Shinbun*, August 24, 1965.

68. *Asahi Shinbun*, August 24, 1965.

69. During the major part of the confrontation period from September 1963 to September 1965, the United States suspended all aid to Indonesia. On September 24, 1963 following Indonesia's demonstrations against the formation of Malaysia, the United States refused to consider any new appropriations to Indonesia. On November 21, 1963 it halted its annual military aid of $15 million, and on August 13, 1964 the Senate adopted a resolution prohibiting any aid at all to Indonesia.

70. This period is described well in Frank Weinstein, *Indonesia Abandons Confrontation* (Ithaca, N.Y.: Modern Indonesia Project, Cornell University, 1969), pp. 43–57. The author too maintains that the negotiations to end the confrontation did not begin until April 30, 1966. However he gives virtually no reference to the Japanese role.

71. Ali Murtopo was a confidant of General Suharto and had flown secretly to Kuala Lumpur in August 1965, before the Gestapu affair to discuss a peace settlement. Many anticommunist PRRI members had lived in Kuala Lumpur after their Sumatra Rebellion failed and had made contacts with other anticommunist Indonesian army leaders as well as Malaysian leaders. Zulkifli Lubis, private interview in Jakarta, July 27, 1971; and Weinstein, p. 54.

72. Shirahata first became involved in the Malaysian conflict in August 1965 as a member of Kimura Takeo's delegation to Malaysia's Independence Day celebration. He now is executive director of the International Medical Foundation of Japan.

73. *Antara*, August 31, 1965.

74. Shirahata Tomoyoshi, private interview in Tokyo, May 9, 1972.

75. Shirahata, interview.

76. *Antara*, April 6, 1966.

77. Ambassador Kai was a very close friend of Tunku Rahman, and his affection for Malaysia was such that he had been given the title of respect, "Dato," rarely bestowed upon foreigners. According to an embassy official in Kuala Lumpur, Rahman had gone to Tokyo in 1963 and 1964 to meet with Sukarno, mostly out of his friendship with Kai. Anonymous high-ranking Japanese embassy official, private conversation in Kuala Lumpur, July 1967. Kai and Adam Malik also had known each other when Kai was Japan's consul general in Jakarta from 1952 to 1953. For the major part of this period, Shirahata served as consul under Kai.

78. Former Ambassador to Thailand B. M. Diah, private interview in Jakarta, January 11, 1972.

79. *Straits Times*, May 3, 1966.

80. *Antara*, May 4 and 5, 1966; *Straits Times*, May 5, 1966; and *Asahi Shinbun*, May 5, 1966.

81. *Antara*, May 30, 1966. Quoted in Weinstein, p. 54, n. 176.

82. Adam Malik, private interview in Jakarta, February 24, 1972.

83. B. M. Diah, interview.

84. *Straits Times*, May 9, 1966.

85. *The Malay Mail*, May 13, 1966.

86. On June 3 there was a meeting among ambassadors in the region, namely, Saitō Shizuo (Jakarta), Kai Fumihiko (Kuala Lumpur), Kasuya Takao (Bangkok), Takeuchi Harumi (Manila), Ueda Tsunemitsu (Singapore), and Vice-minister Shimoda Takezō, and Counselor Ushiba Nobuhiko. On June 6 Prime Minister Satō consulted with Saitō, Kai, Shimoda, Ogawa (director of the Asian Affairs Bureau) as well as with Foreign Minister Shiina. These two meetings confirmed the Japanese position that it would offer mediation if requested. See *Asahi Shinbun*, June 4 and 6, 1966.

Chapter 7
The "Sukarno Groups" in Japanese-Indonesian Relations, 1959–1966

The political and military forces which rallied behind Sukarno against the Outer Island rebels in 1958 made up the "pro-Sukarno groups," the "Sukarno groups," or simply the "Sukarnoists." This chapter treats the activities of the "Sukarno groups" in the area of Japanese-Indonesian relations. It is confined to the Sukarnoists' activities in Tokyo and in Jakarta in promoting Sukarnoist policies in and toward Japan. Among the Sukarnoists discussed here are the officials of the Indonesian embassy and the Indonesian Students Association (PPI) in Tokyo. Attention is given also to the West Irian issue and to the Konfrontasi against Malaysia in which the Indonesian embassy and the PPI worked with the PNI and PKI in Jakarta and the Japan Socialist party (JSP), the Japan Communist party (JCP), the ruling Liberal Democratic party (LDP), and the Japan-Indonesia Association in Tokyo. The chapter also examines the role of Dewi as a supporter of Sukarno during his presidency and during the post-Gestapu confusion. This study illustrates the rise and fall of the Sukarno group in the context of binational relations. As a preface, a brief picture of the scope and character of the Sukarno leadership is provided.

THE MEANING OF THE "SUKARNO GROUPS"

The legal basis for Sukarno's power, expressed as "Guided Democracy," was the 1945 constitution which he reactivated in his July 5, 1959 decree and which gave him more political strength than had the 1950 provisional constitution. President Sukarno then surrounded himself with a host of ideological slogans known by their acronyms, which collectively spelled out Sukarnoism. In his Independence Day speech of August 1959, Sukarno adopted a system called NASAKOM in which the three major political forces, the nationalists, the Communists, and religious followers, under his guidance could participate in the national decision-making process. He dissolved the elected House of Representatives (DPR) and the Constituent Assembly, replacing them with appointive bodies, the Gotong-Royong (GR, or mutual assistance) House of Representatives (DPR-GR) and the Provisional People's Consultative Assembly (MPRS), respectively. Keeping them weak, Sukarno then introduced a new quasi-legislative National Council and its successor, the Supreme Advisory Council, in which political party members as well as regional and functional representatives were appointed to make recommendations to the president and his cabinet. This process he called the "spirit of national *musyawarah*" (mutual consultation), a term which is still popular among the post-Sukarno leaders.

His speech of August 1959 was considered a statement of Indonesia's state ideology called MANIPOL (political manifesto). MANIPOL later was described as five pillars symbolized by another acronym, USDEK, from the 1945 constitution (U), the Indonesian style of socialism (S), Guided Democracy (D), Guided Economy (E), and the Indonesian personality (K).[1] The Guided Democracy, NASAKOM, MANIPOL, USDEK, plus Sukarno's long-time slogan of *Panca Sila* thus served as his ideological buttresses.[2] In order to disseminate these concepts, Sukarno organized and also headed, in August 1960, a nationwide mass organization called the National Front. In the ensuing years, Sukarnoism was expressed in such additional acronyms as struggles against NEKOLIM (neocolonialism), support of the GANEFO (Games of the New Emerging Forces) in 1963, and the CONEFO (Conference of the New Emerging Forces) planned for 1966.

Given increased constitutional power, Sukarno bolstered his political influence by two other means: by placing his men in major government positions and by having his men tap financial sources to support his political conducts and projects. Both measures helped to solidify the political system supporting him. His most important move may have been to appoint his two right-hand men, Subandrio and Saleh, as his deputy prime ministers in 1960 and 1963, respectively. Subandrio, who became foreign minister in 1957, was a major architect of Indonesian foreign policy and sought power beyond the Foreign Ministry by setting up the Central Intelligence Board, or BPI (Badan Pusat Intelijen), in 1960. He also was appointed as a deputy commander of the Supreme Operations Command, or KOTI (Komando Operasi Tertinggi), which functioned as a kind of private cabinet for Sukarno, and also as a deputy commander of the Supreme Economic Operations Command, or KOTOE (Komando Tertinggi Operasi Ekonomi). Thus he served not only as foreign minister but also directed Indonesia's foreign economic relations and intelligence activities. Saleh held various cabinet posts, serving as minister of basic industries after February 1960, and in November 1963 was given the additional position of coordinating minister of the Development Compartment, which supervised seven ministries. Saleh was also chairman of the Provisional People's Consultative Assembly, sat on the National Defense Council, and later headed the National Front. Sukarno stated in his autobiography: "Immediately underneath me is the presidium, a triumvirate of the Deputy Prime Ministers Subandrio, Leimena, and Saleh. They are my assistants. When trouble hits, I first call the presidium for their comments."[3]

Sukarno appears to have solicited private contributions from different parts of society in order to carry out his Indonesian Revolution. He gained the support of the private business association known as the National Private Enterprises Council, or BAMUNAS (Badan Musyawarah Pengusaha Nasional Swasta), which was established in February 1964 through Sukarno's instruction and was headed by R. M. Notohamiprodjo, a PNI leader, minister of finance between 1962 and 1963 and advisor to the president in charge of funds and forces.[4] Notohamiprodjo was succeeded by another PNI-affiliated businessman, T. D. Pardede. BAMUNAS collected considerable funds for Sukarno's personal needs under the name of the "Movement to Devote to the Revolution," or GEKEREV (Gerakan Kebaktian Revolusi).[5] In 1964 the president set up the Revolution Fund (Dana Revolusi) and instructed one of his PNI men, Jusuf Muda Dalam, governor of the Central Bank of Indonesia, to find financial backing for the fund.[6] Using his power of issuing import licenses, for instance, Jusuf collected 250 rupiahs for every U.S. dollar that he allowed traders for their imported goods.[7] Because Indonesia's foreign reserves had become depleted after 1963, Jusuf substituted foreign credit and, in this case, he used the Japanese credit that Kawashima had committed to Sukarno in an effort to placate him and to urge him not to use force in the Malaysian-Indonesian conflict.[8] The Revolution Fund was collected in Indonesian rupiahs and used for projects which Sukarno had designated—the National Monument, for example.[9]

Sukarno had still other sources for his monetary needs. Many of his trips to Japan were at least partly financed by Japanese trading companies.[10] Among Sukarno's personal friends in Indonesian business were A. Musin Dasaad and Markam. Dasaad, president of the Dasaad Musin Concern, is known to have assisted Sukarno financially since the 1930s.[11] He opened trade offices throughout the world, including Osaka, as early as 1951.[12] Dasaad's close ties with Sukarno were revealed in his appointment as chairman of the Indonesia-Japan Friendship Society in 1964 and later in 1966 as president of the Sarinah Department Store.[13] Markam was an obscure army lieutenant who built the Karkam Company into a multimillion-dollar operation in a span of three years by means of his exclusive right to export rubber to nearby Malaysia and Singapore during the confrontation period.[14] He was a familiar face at Sukarno's palace parties and was a generous participant in the closed auctions held there.[15] Markam also was given the president's special favor in obtaining certain import licenses and contracts. In March 1965 he met with Sukarno, who, as commander of the Supreme Economic Operations Command, endorsed Markam's importation of large quantities of Nissan jeeps, parts, and Asano cement from Japan.[16] In July 1965 Markam visited the palace to report to the president on the progress of the development projects assigned to the Karkam Company.[17]

The acceptance of financial donations was not monopolized by Sukarno. Dewi also asked for contributions from the Indonesia-Japan Friendship Society and the Nadeshiko Club to build her aforementioned Sari Asih Hospital.[18] Subandrio's BPI also acquired funds from unidentified sources, as disclosed in his 1966 trial. Subandrio had $250,000 in a Swiss bank for the planned second Asian-African conference in Algiers in June 1965 and an emergency BPI fund of $250,000 deposited in January 1966 under the name of James Newman in Daiwa Securities, Tokyo.[19]

No one doubted Sukarno's political power. However it is difficult to define the scope of the Sukarno groups and especially their character. Not every member of the groups could be considered as an ardent, sincere supporter of Sukarno. Many Indonesian businessmen and overseas Chinese traders supported the president as a matter of expedience; political leaders including Subandrio, Saleh, Aidit, and Army Chief of Staff Nasution must have supported Sukarno to promote their political ambitions. While they tried to utilize the benefits of Sukarno's "coattails," the president too tried to put them off balance. From late 1964 Sukarno's balancing between the PKI and the army changed gradually to a coalition between him and the PKI against the army. One of Sukarno's men, Trade Minister Adam Malik, thus became concerned about the PKI's growing influence and attempted to offset Sukarno's leaning toward the Communists by a movement started in November 1964, with the euphemistic name of "Body to Support Sukarnoism," or BPS (Badan Pendukung Sukarnoisme), a movement which was essentially an anticommunist drive.[20] The PKI immediately criticized BPS and under the PKI's pressure Sukarno himself denounced it too. Malik was removed from his post as trade minister but remained in the cabinet as minister without portfolio. Sukarno even suspended the activities of the Murba party whose leaders, including Malik, were suspected of being responsible for this anticommunist movement. Chairul Saleh, a Murba party leader who hoped to succeed Sukarno, quickly renounced his affiliation with the party and pledged loyalty to the leader of the Great Revolution. Two of Sukarno's wives, Dewi and Hartini, also competed for his political favor and were cultivated by members of the Kawashima Lobby, especially by Ambassador Saitō Shizuo, Foreign Minister Subandrio, and Chinese Ambassador Yao Chung Ming.[21] One hardly can classify all these figures as Sukarnoists, yet each declared himself to be pro-Sukarno.

These examples amply illustrate the complex character of the "Sukarno groups," which can be defined only broadly as those who wished to remain with Sukarno and under his power. With this background, focus can now be given to the work of the Sukarnoists in Tokyo.

THE INDONESIAN COMMUNITY IN TOKYO

From 1958 through 1966, Tokyo had from 300 to 900 Indonesian residents. They were predominantly Indonesian youths, students, and other trainees, who comprised some 70 percent, and the embassy staff and members of the Indonesian Reparations Mission, who comprised some 20 percent.[22] Unlike their Japanese counterparts in Jakarta, the Indonesian community in Tokyo had few businessmen. The Japanese capital accommodated a variety of Indonesian political activities, although the pro-Sukarno groups were dominant, there also were some anti-Sukarno groups, one of which was the Sumatran rebels seeking overseas refuge. In addition there was the Free Papuan Movement, or OPM (Organisasi Papua Merdeka), which secretly campaigned for the independence of the Papuans and opposed Sukarno's policy of integrating them into Indonesia. Tokyo attracted them because it offered them sources of moral and financial support.

The Indonesian Embassy

An important duty of the Indonesian embassy in Tokyo was to watch its nationals and their activities.[23] Another task assigned to the embassy was to use the Indonesian nationals to support Indonesia's political causes. The Indonesian government, in this case President Sukarno and his closest aides Saleh and Subandrio, apparently found it efficacious to send their own men to the embassy and the Reparations Mission, and also selected their own young men for the reparations fellowship program, which had conveniently started in 1960. Later Saleh dispatched his men to Tokyo to reinforce his influence over his department's share of the reparations fund and credit.

It is generally believed that the three Indonesian ambassadors from 1958 through early 1966—Asmaun (October 1958–October 1960), Bambang Sugeng (October 1960–April 1964), and Harsono Reksoat-modjo (May 1964–January 1966)—were sympathetic toward the PNI or were close to Sukarno. Asmaun is known to have been a PNI member,[24] and Bambang Sugeng was sympathetic to that party.[25] Former Major General Sugeng, Daidanchō (commander of the division) of the PETA during the Japanese occupation, had been appointed army chief of staff in 1953 through President Sukarno's support of the PETA faction of the army against Nasution's Dutch-trained faction. Harsono was classified as a "Subandrio man" and through him was close to Sukarno. A former embassy official told me in 1971 that after about 1963 the embassy was under the strong influence of the foreign minister's Central Intelligence Board (BPI). Later in 1966 it was reported that a BPI member had been assigned to the embassy,[26] and that the BPI's $250,000 fund had been deposited in Daiwa Securities with the help of Abdul Habir, who had been counselor of the embassy in 1962–1963 and in 1963 became chief of the Reparations Mission.[27] The first chief of the Reparations Mission, Basuki Djatiasmoro, was a relative of Sukarno's.[28]

The Indonesian Students Association

The Indonesian Students Association, the PPI which numbered 600 Indonesian youths in Tokyo, was considered the largest and strongest overseas Indonesian student group, second only to its counterpart encompassing all of Europe. Several factors contributed to this eminence. First, some of the leaders of the PPI were selected for their political and personal rather than their academic qualifications. Sons and relatives of government, political, and military leaders were favored.[29] According to one source, many managed to come to Tokyo only because a leader of the PNI's procommunist ASU group held an executive position in the Indonesia-Japan Friendship Society (LPIJ) and had become a member of Parliament.[30] Though they had little academic interest, they were active politically. Second, the PPI's organizational strength owed much to the presence of a large Indonesia hall called "Wisma Indonesia," built specifically to accommodate the *pampasan* (reparations) youths. Living together in huge, metropolitan Tokyo, they naturally nurtured a feeling of solidarity, facilitating agreement on joint actions. Third, this solidarity and their sense of political mission was encouraged by Sukarno's frequent visits to Tokyo and to Wisma Indonesia, for which he laid the cornerstone in September 1961 and which he officially opened in November 1962. Their sense of political duty was reinforced by the political indoctrination programs often presented by prominent Indonesian cabinet ministers. For example, from Panca Sila Day on June 1 through President Sukarno's birthday on June 6, 1965, the PPI planned an "indoctrination week" for those who just had graduated from Japanese universities and colleges.[31] For the PPI's fifth congress to be held in early August 1965, President Sukarno sent minister-coordinator for public relations and chairman for the Guidance of the Revolutionary Spirit, Roeslan Abdulgani, to give a lecture. Upon his return he is quoted as saying with satisfaction that "the Indonesian students in Japan had a high revolutionary spirit and that they know the development of all matters of state and society of their own country."[32]

Fourth, and most important of all, the organizational structure of the PPI was strengthened by the young political cadres or organizers of PNI affiliation who were selected under the reparations program for the specific purpose of using the PPI to promote the Indonesian government's policies.[33] There is evidence that the formation of PPI was guided by or at least was encouraged by the Indonesian embassy in Tokyo. The embassy's annual report for 1961 to the home office noted that:

> . . . we wish Indonesian students studying in Tokyo, while assuming their task of learning to be cadres for [national] development, would also become ambassadors reflecting the Indonesian Personality, which is to struggle for the achievement of the Revolution. One way to accomplish this is to bring uniformity to the attitudes and thoughts of every Indonesian youth in Japan. . . . After examining various and sensible instruments for implementation, the best is that which goes through the formation of PPI. . . .[34]

Another source indicates that between 1961 and 1965 there were altogether some ten Sukarnoist cadres in the PPI.[35] Some of them originally had been active in student movements in Indonesia, particularly in the PNI-directed Indonesian Nationalist Student Movement, or GMNI (Gerakan Mahasiswa Nasional Indonesia), and in the PKI-directed Indonesian Student Movement Concentration, or CGMI (Concentrasi Gerakan Mahasiswa Indonesia). But some of them had had little connection with these movements and became active politically only after they had come to Japan.

While maintaining some degree of independence, the PPI's activities often were coordinated by instructions received from the embassy or from the home government, the latter most likely directed by the PNI, the PKI, or even Subandrio's BPI. The embassy had a

Student Affairs Section which had direct contacts with the PPI.[36] Abdulgani, who had attended the PPI's fifth congress in August 1965, stated later that the Indonesian students in Japan had a high revolutionary spirit "because they had good guidance from Indonesian Ambassador Harsono Reksoatmodjo and his staff in Tokyo."[37]

Before the reparations scholarship program started in 1960, there already existed a small Indonesian student association. With the arrival of the *pampasan* youths, the association was reorganized in September 1961 and began to assume political roles. Within the PPI were two major ideological factions, the left-wing PNI and the right-wing PNI. Jul Sumartojo, PPI chairman from 1962–1963, belonged to the left-wing PNI; Dahlan, chairman from 1964–1965, was in the right-wing PNI; and Lily Satari, chairman from 1965–1966, was again in the left-wing PNI.[38] Regardless of the ruling faction, the student leaders and the embassy worked together to promote Sukarnoist ideas and to lobby with concerned Japanese groups. Their activities are described briefly.

SUKARNOISTS IN TOKYO AND THE WEST IRIAN CAMPAIGN

From the beginning of the West Irian campaign, the Japanese government took a neutral stand. It considered West Irian (then called West New Guinea) a disputed territory, the status of which Japan felt should be settled peacefully. But between 1960–1962 Japan was drawn into the conflict for a very short time. The first incident in which Japan was involved is referred to as the *Karel Doorman* Incident and the other, the KLM Incident.

The Karel Doorman Incident, 1960

In June 1960 the Dutch ambassador in Tokyo requested permission from Japan for its West Irian-bound aircraft carrier, the *Karel Doorman*, to enter a Japanese port for oil and water supplies. The Indonesian embassy and the PPI were determined to oppose the *Karel Doorman*'s visit. Earlier in June when President Sukarno had visited Tokyo, the PPI had presented him with a "resolution" which included support of his Political Manifesto of 1959 and a pledge to carry out government orders, especially those pertaining to the West Irian issue.[39] A former PPI leader told me in 1970 that the PPI approached the Socialist party and obtained support of such left-wing leaders as Sasaki Kōzō, Okada Haruo, Hozumi Shichirō, and Katsumada Seiichi. He also recalled that some members of the ruling Liberal Democratic party, such as Tokonami Tokuji and Yoshie Katsuyasu, showed sympathy for the PPI's efforts, and he stated that they felt that West New Guinea could best gain independence by joining Indonesia.[40] However, the sympathetic Socialist party and Liberal Democratic party members did not work as lobbyists in the Diet or in the Foreign Ministry and the cabinet. Nor did the Japan Communist party at this stage; all the parties were preoccupied with the bigger issue of ratifying the revised security treaty between Japan and the United States.

More effective support came from the Japan-Indonesia Association, which wished to represent Indonesian interests in Japan on this issue. On August 10, 1960 the Indonesian embassy's Minister Marjunani talked with the association's president, Tani Masayuki, stressing the importance of Japan to refuse the *Karel Doorman*'s visit.[41] On August 27 the association received an appeal by telegram from its Indonesian counterpart, the Indonesia-Japan Friendship Society in Jakarta.[42] That day the association officially conveyed its concern to the Japanese Foreign Ministry, saying that it hoped that the Netherlands would withdraw its request. However the Hague was adamant in its request and changed the original reason for the warship's visit, insisting that the visit would be planned as part of the 350th anniversary celebration of Japanese-Dutch trade contacts.[43] On August 31 Japan reluctantly consented to this on the condition that the aircraft carrier would not return to West Irian but would go straight back to the Netherlands.[44] On September 1 Foreign Minister Kosaka Zentarō gained the cabinet's endorsement, but the Indonesian government became more rigid and tensions between Tokyo and Jakarta suddenly intensified.[45] On that day Ambassador Bambang Sugeng met with the leaders of the Japan-Indonesia Association, the Japan Federation of Economic Organizations (Keidanren), and the Japan Chamber of Commerce and Industry.[46] The longshoremen's union of the port of Yokohama, into which the Dutch warship was supposed to come, and other groups possibly directed by the Socialist or Communist parties issued a statement of protest and presented it to the mayor of Yokohama and the Foreign Ministry.[47]

On September 2 the Japan-Indonesia Association held an emergency executive meeting in which it adopted a resolution requesting the Japanese government to postpone the Dutch ship's visit and submitted it to the cabinet, the Foreign Ministry, the political parties, and the Dutch embassy in Tokyo.[48] Although Foreign Minister Kosaka decided in favor of permitting the warship to enter Yokohama, Foreign Ministry officials began to doubt the wisdom of this decision.[49] They were concerned that when the Dutch ship came to Japan the Indonesian ambassador might leave in protest, which might be followed by Indonesia's suspension of economic relations with Japan. They also saw the disadvantage of Japanese-Indonesian tensions upon Japan's relations with other Afro-Asian countries. In addition, the Foreign Ministry thought that the mounting internal opposition as expressed by the labor unions and by the Japan-Indonesia Association might injure the friendly relations between Tokyo and The Hague.

On September 3 the Japanese Foreign Ministry learned that the *Karel Doorman* had left West Irian waters and was headed for Japan. The Japan Socialist party issued a strong statement demanding that the government rescind its landing permission in light of the popular desire for friendship and solidarity with the Asian and African peoples.[50] The Foreign Ministry also learned from its Ambassador Ōda in Indonesia that Indonesia certainly would break off economic relations with Japan if the Dutch warship did enter Yokohama.[51] At this point Kosaka reversed his decision, remarking that he did not want to trade an Asian friend for an aircraft carrier, and that day informed the Dutch ambassador of his new decision.[52] The *Karel Doorman* returned to Hollandia (now Jayapura) on September 9.[53]

The KLM Incident, 1962

A similar incident occurred in February 1962. On January 30 of that year the Dutch airline KLM asked the Japanese government for permission to land in the Tokyo airport three KLM planes (carrying a total of 211 "government personnel") chartered by the Dutch government and bound for Biak, West Irian. Japan refused permission, fearing renewed tensions with Jakarta. Then on February 3 the Dutch government transported its military personnel on a regular commercial KLM flight bound for Biak via Tokyo.[54] Japan had no legal basis to stop it. When a similar request was made by the Dutch to the United States and granted, the American embassy in Jakarta was attacked by mobs, and on February 5 the Japanese embassy tightened its security.[55]

Although Japan made a protest to The Hague, the latter ignored it, transporting even more Dutch soldiers (wearing civilian clothes) on February 6 and 10.[56] On February 10 the PPI submitted a protest to the Foreign Ministry and on February 15 and 16, PPI members demonstrated in front of the Dutch embassy in Tokyo.[57] On February 16 the Japanese consulate in Surabaya was stoned,[58] suggesting that the protest movements had been coordinated by Indonesian authorities behind the scenes.

Particularly strong support for the Indonesian cause in West Irian came from the Japanese Communist party (JCP), which after 1961 acted almost as a PKI agent in Japan.[59] It appears that the JCP had direct contact with the PKI rather than working through the embassy or the PPI. PKI leader Dipa Nusantara Aidit had visited Japan in 1960, and in the following year Aidit and another member of the PKI politi-buro, Njoto, came to Tokyo.[60] By 1961 the JCP supported the PKI's ideological stand on the West Irian issue. On February 10, 1962 when the KLM incident occurred, the JCP Central Executive Committee issued a special statement supporting the "struggles of the Indonesian people for the liberation of West Irian."[61] Its daily newspaper, *Akahata*, reported the PPI-sponsored demonstrations against the Dutch embassy on February 15 and the protest by the JCP-controlled Asia-Africa Solidarity Committee to the director of the Tokyo International Airport for assisting the Dutch in West Irian.[62]

The Japan-Indonesia Association also was worried about the problem. On February 17 it held an emergency executive meeting and submitted a note of concern to the cabinet and to the Foreign Ministry.[63] The Japanese government, however, had no way to prevent the Biak-bound commercial flights from carrying Dutch soldiers among the regular passengers. Finally on March 5, Dutch Foreign Minister Joseph Luns notified the Japanese foreign minister that his government no longer would embarrass Tokyo and the incident thus ended.[64]

Both incidents were short-lived. They occurred partly because the Japanese Foreign Ministry failed to appreciate the nationalist sentiment then prevailing among the Indonesians and because it gave the impression that Japan was assisting Dutch military efforts in West Irian. In reality Japan tried to maintain a neutral position but the Indonesian Foreign Ministry, the embassy in Tokyo, and the PPI tried its Japanese friendship most severely. Japan was intimidated by Indonesia's dem-onstrations, mobilization of support, and threats to break off economic ties, and caught between its European and Asian friends it chose to side with Indonesia, which had the greater economic importance to Japan. Indonesia depended economically upon Japan much more than the reverse. (In 1960, 4 percent of Indonesia's exports went to Japan and 16 percent of its imports came from Japan, whereas 2.7 percent of Japan's exports went to Indonesia and 1.5 percent of its imports came from Indonesia. See Table 3.) Yet Japan was vulnerable to Indonesia's threats and made the decision to avoid friction with the Asian neighbor with which it had negotiated so long on reparations and with which its economic ties had just begun to expand.

THE SUKARNOISTS IN TOKYO, NEKOLIM, AND CONEFO

The confrontation between Indonesia and Malaysia was another important issue for the Sukarnoists in Tokyo. It represented the key ideology opposing British "neocolonialism" or NEKOLIM. Related to this were the concepts of the new emerging forces (NEFO), which

Sukarno wished to champion by promoting the GANEFO and CONEFO.

The PPI approached Japan's major parties concerning the confrontation. The Socialist party's left-wing faction agreed with Indonesia's position toward Malaysia and in June 1965 expressed full support for Indonesia's struggle to "destroy the neo-colonial project of Malaysia."[65] It refused to join the official Japanese delegation, led by Kawashima, to the second Asia-Africa conference scheduled for late June 1965 and decided to send its own team.[66] In July of that year after the conference had been postponed until November, the party's Foreign Affairs Department head Katsumada Seiichi visited Jakarta to attend the 38th anniversary celebration of the PNI and issued a joint statement with PNI leader, Ali Sastroamidjojo supporting Indonesia's "Crush Malaysia" policy and outlining its plan to sponsor the CONEFO.[67]

During the period from 1963–1966, unlike the period from 1960–1962, the Japan-Indonesia Association gave only limited support to the PPI, as the latter had become increasingly militant and dogmatic in its Sukarnoist ideology. The association became even more apprehensive of the growth of the PKI and more disillusioned over Sukarno's lack of concern for the Indonesian economy. The association thus stood behind the Japanese government's attempts to mediate between Jakarta and Kuala Lumpur rather than behind the PPI's strong anti-Malaysia position. The association's president after December 1962, Kajima Morinosuke, advocated Japan's mediation most likely because his construction company had large dam projects in East Java under the reparations projects, and because he had interest in Japan's Asia policy as a senior Diet member of the ruling party, serving on the Foreign Affairs Committee.[68] The association's vice-president, Ogasa Kōshō, also a member of the Diet in the ruling party and a member of the Kawashima faction, served as a link between Japan's business and political interests in Indonesia, as seen in chapter 6.

In the meantime the PPI promoted Sukarno's idea of the GANEFO. When Jakarta sponsored the GANEFO in November 1963, it organized the Asian, African, and Latin American students in Tokyo into a sports festival, a mini-GANEFO.[69] The PPI also assisted in the formation of a Japanese team for the Jakarta GANEFO, consulting with a young Keiō University student, Tōyama Tatsukuni, also the head of Keiō University's Indonesia Society. Because of his grandfather's fame, Tōyama was successful in collecting donations from older people to cover the expenses of the Japanese participants. It should be noted that the Japanese team for the GANEFO also was advised by two wartime "Indonesia experts," Shimizu Hitoshi and former Captain Yanagawa

Tomoshige.[70] Shimizu had been a Sukarnoist since the occupation, and Yanagawa told me that he genuinely felt that the young people of developing nations should attempt to enhance their nationalist spirit through the sports festival. Both Shimizu and Yanagawa were members of the Japan-Indonesia Association's Advisory Council (San'yokai).[71] When it was reorganized in 1958 the association placed on its Advisory Council those individuals who had expert knowledge of and personal concern for Indonesian affairs but who had no affiliation with any of the association's member companies. Because the council had little connection with business interests, it took a more militant, pro-Indonesia position toward the West Irian issue than that of its businessman-directed leadership. For instance, in January 1962 when the Indonesian community in Tokyo established the West Irian Struggle Fund, a type of Red Cross medical service for those fighting in West Irian, the council supported it, and Shimizu Hitoshi actively supported its fund-raising campaign.[72] When the confrontation began, the association's business-directed leadership declined to support it whereas its Advisory Council was sympathetic. The association thus appeared to be two-faced, maintaining contact with both the militant Sukarnoists and the conservative Japanese business and political groups.

More active encouragement for the Sukarnoists in Tokyo came in January 1965 from a liberal wing of the ruling party. Utsunomiya Tokuma, Matsumura Kenzō, Fujiyama Aiichirō, and other Diet members of the LDP who had advocated improved relations between Japan and Asia and Africa, particularly with China, formed the Asia-Africa Problems Study Group on January 28.[73] It was a sort of "China Lobby" in the Diet as opposed to the much stronger "Taiwan Lobby." The new group, which numbered 74 members, stated that among its concerns were the Malaysia issue and Japan's position in the second Afro-Asian conference. A former PPI leader told me in 1970 that the group's interest in the Malaysia issue was the outcome of the PPI's lobbying. Later in May 1965, between Kawashima's visits in April and August, six members of the group headed by Utsunomiya were invited to Indonesia by the government and, during their week-long stay, met with President Sukarno, Subandrio, Saleh, Abdulgani, Yani, and leaders of the National Front.[74] *Antara*, which increasingly appeared to be under PKI control, called the group "a progressive-revolutionary Japanese parliamentary delegation."[75] They did show sympathy for Indonesia's withdrawal from the United Nations and for its proposal of a Conference of New Emerging Forces (CONEFO).[76] A member of the group, Tamura Hajime, was reported to declare that upon his return he would establish an "Indonesia Lobby" in the Diet.[77] However, the group's anti-American remarks were rebuffed by its own party, and thus in the end it was not able to form an effective lobby within the party.

The most direct support of Sukarnoism was extended by Japan's Communist party. After Aidit's and Njoto's visits to Japan in 1960 and 1961, the PKI and the JCP drew closer together. In late April 1962 the JCP sent its first fraternal delegates to the PKI's seventh congress, and on May 23, 1962 its chief Japanese delegate, Kurahara Korehito, and Aidit issued a joint statement which included the support of Indonesia's "antiimperialist" struggles over West Irian.[78] After Kurahara's return the JCP began to be more explicit in its admiration for the PKI's United National Front strategy and made gestures of support for Sukarnoism and the concept of NASAKOM.[79] At the opening ceremony of the Wisma Indonesia on November 12, 1962, JCP Chairman Nosaka, Secretary-General Miyamoto, and Executive Committee member Kurahara all were present, demonstrating the Indonesian embassy's friendly attitude toward the JCP.[80] On the forty-third anniversary of the PKI in June 1963 the JCP sent a long congratulatory message and one of its Executive Committee members, Kikunami Katsumi, to its celebration ceremony. On June 26 Kikunami issued a joint statement with Aidit supporting "the struggle of north Kalimantan people" (meaning the leaders of the Brunei revolt on December 8, 1962, which became the first local anti-Malaysian move) and Sukarno's and PKI's anti-Malaysia policy.[81]

The JCP was also occupied with ideological friction between the Communist parties of Moscow and Peking. The JCP and the PKI acted together in shifting from a neutral to a pro-Peking stand.[82] In September 1964 JCP leader Miyamoto himself visited Jakarta. His and Aidit's joint statement reaffirmed the JCP's approval of the anti-Malaysian campaigns.[83] While in Indonesia, Miyamoto also met Sukarno.[84] The PKI's first deputy chairman, M. H. Lukman, then came to Japan on December 1964.[85] Early in January 1965 the JCP supported Indonesia's withdrawal from the UN.[86]

It should be noted that from May 1963 through August 1965 the JCP's *Akahata* made almost no mention of the mediation efforts made by Prime Minister Ikeda and the ruling party's vice-president Kawashima. Instead it proceeded with its support of the planned Algiers Afro-Asian conference. When the Soviet Communist party proposed a consultation meeting in March 1965, the Asian Communist parties of Peking, Jakarta, Hanoi, Pyongyang as well as of Tokyo conspicuously did not attend, thus showing a clear sign of the Asian parties siding the Peking line.

In short, by April 1965 the Sukarnoists in Tokyo comprised a curious conglomeration including the embassy, the PPI, the JCP, the radical members of the Socialist party, and the liberal members of the Liberal Democratic party, all extending support to Sukarno on varying ideological grounds. Thus when Kawashima visited Jakarta that month to win over Sukarno to his terms, he had to compete with this group and the Chinese Communists who, with Subandrio's and the PKI's help, also tried to win over Sukarno. Both Kawashima and Chou En-lai, who also came to Jakarta in April 1965, planned to attend the second Afro-Asian conference in Algiers. Then the anticommunist military coup took place there on June 19, toppling the pro-Peking Ben Bella regime and causing the conference to be postponed. It was indeed a setback to the Peking-Jakarta alliance. A member of the Kawashima Lobby and a friend of Sukarno's, Shimizu Hitoshi, who had gone as far as Cairo to cover the Algiers conference for Japanese television, feared that a similar blow also could be dealt to the Sukarno regime.[87] He also sensed that an anti-Sukarno mood in Tokyo was gaining strength. Whether the Algerian coup encouraged the Indonesian military is yet to be ascertained. However the subsequent coup in Jakarta did resemble that one in Algiers. If the coup in Algeria did encourage even the anti-Sukarnoist minority in Tokyo, the evidence for it has not yet been established either. However, according to *Antara* on August 26, 1965, the PPI's fifth congress which took place in Tokyo on August 2, observed "subversive and counterrevolutionary elements" within the Indonesian community.[88]

On August 3 of that year Sukarno suffered a sudden illness, and Aidit who was then at Peking hurried back with a team of Chinese doctors.[89] Sukarno did recover but the incident generated tension between the army and the PKI.

According to Njono's confession at his trial in December 1965, the PKI leaders planned to stage a coup against the military before the military leaders on the "Council of Generals" could strike at them in an attempt to succeed the ailing Sukarno.[90] How much the PKI and the Peking regime worked together in the planned coup is not yet clear, but several facts suggest a positive relationship between the two, as a few writers have already asserted.[91] First, Chou En-lai advocated the formation of a people's army in Indonesia, which in January 1965 Aidit had urged Sukarno to do and which Sukarno endorsed in August 1965.[92] Second, on September 3, the *Jinmin Jihpao* (People's daily) of Peking printed Defense Minister Lin Piao's famous article on wars of national liberation which advocated an "adventurous" road to revolution for his communist comrades in Asia, Africa, and Latin America. The Japanese Communist party's *Akahata* of September 17 printed the full text of his article, supporting his views. One may speculate on there being some relationship between this article and Aidit's earlier visit to Peking in late July, and to Air Marshall Omar Dhani's secret flight on September 16 to Peking to arrange for a clandestine shipment of Chinese arms to Indonesia.[93] Toward the end of September the tension between the PKI and the army was heightened through their harsh criticism of each other and was felt even in Tokyo. Some Japanese involved in Indonesian affairs told me in Tokyo in 1972 that they sensed from their Indonesian acquaintances that a coup might take place in Indonesia in early October. Third, on September 24 Subandrio and Chinese Ambassador Yao Chung Ming conferred on Jakarta-Peking cooperation in "all spheres."[94]

THE IMPACT OF THE GESTAPU UPON THE SUKARNOISTS IN TOKYO

The News of the Gestapu

For the first day and a half of October, Indonesians in Tokyo were not able to obtain news of the Gestapu affair, as all communications between Tokyo and Jakarta had ceased.[95] The press and radio stations relied on the radio news coming from Kuala Lumpur, Singapore, and London, which had received broadcasts from Jakarta. Tokyo first learned of the coup in the newspapers' evening editions and in the evening radio news programs on October 1. The *Asahi Shinbun* reported the news in an Associated Press dispatch from Kuala Lumpur which was taken from a Radio Indonesia broadcast via the Malaysia Broadcasting Service. Indonesian embassy officials were obliged to listen to Japanese radio news programs,[96] and correspondents in Jakarta were not able to wire reports back to their home offices.[97]

On October 1 at 7:20 A.M. Lieutenant Colonel Untung, an officer in the presidential Palace Guard who was fiercely loyal to Sukarno,[98] had his assistant make an announcement over Radio Indonesia (which his troops had seized earlier) that in one stroke changed the power positions of Sukarno, the PKI, and the army.[99] This announcement said in brief that the September 30 Movement headed by Untung had arrested the generals of the "CIA-sponsored" and "subversive" Council of Generals who had planned a "counterrevolutionary coup" to be attempted prior to the Armed Forces Day on October 5. It stated that the movement was a military one within the army but was assisted by the other armed forces. Those generals, it said, had hoped that the president would die during his illness in the first week of August and that when he did not, they planned a coup with their troops entering Jakarta allegedly for the Armed Forces Day celebration. Therefore, it continued, a number of generals had been arrested, important communications media and other vital objects had been placed under the control of the September 30 Movement, and the president was being protected by the movement. The announcement then declared that following the September 30 Movement would be the formation of a revolutionary council representing levels from the national down to the village (*desa*).

At 9:30 A.M. the commander of the air force, Marshal Omar Dhani, issued a radio announcement supporting the coup,[100] thus making it clear that the air force was with the Gestapu. As revealed later,[101] on the morning of October 1 President Sukarno, who had spent the night of September 30 at Dewi's Wisma Yasoo, was persuaded by his aides not to go to the presidential palace, as it was in a confused state with the various troops stationed there demonstrating their loyalties. He thus proceeded to Grogol, an area west of Jakarta, where his fourth wife Harjati lived. At 9 A.M. after contacting Air Marshal Omar Dhani, the president then left for the Halim Air Force Base on the southeastern outskirts of the capital.[102]

That day at 2 P.M. the commander of the September 30 Movement and chairman of the Revolutionary Council, Untung, announced two decrees listing the forty-five members of the council and invalidating all military ranks above his rank, colonel.[103] This was the last statement to be issued by the Gestapu group. Two army leaders, both anti-PKI and reluctant supporters of Sukarno, who had missed being kidnapped by the movement's members, made a swift counterattack upon those military divisions implicated in the Gestapu. These two leaders were General Nasution, minister-coordinator for defense and security and chief of staff of the armed forces, who barely had escaped his assassination plot; and Major General Suharto, commander of the Army Strategic Reserves (KOSTRAD), who had not been on the abduction list. By 8 P.M. their troops had regained control of Jakarta, and Suharto made a radio announcement claiming that the army, navy, and police had crushed the Gestapu and the Revolutionary Council and denounced the Gestapu as a "counterrevolutionary act."[104] This statement marked the turning point in Indonesia's guided democracy.

During the day of October 1 the PKI's relationship to the Gestapu was not made clear, but the October 2 issue of *Harian Rakyat* (People's daily) supported the establishment of the Revolutionary Council. On the following day the Nasution-Suharto group claimed to have evidence that the PKI-controlled youth groups (Pemuda Rakyat), women's groups (GERWANI), and labor unions (SOBSI) had received secret military training at the Halim airbase and that they were responsible for murdering the six abducted generals and burying them in an old well in the area of Lubang Buaya (Crocodile Hole) near Halim. Thus the anticommunist military groups concluded that PKI indeed had been behind the Gestapu, and moved against it. On October 6 the PKI politburo announced that it had not been implicated in the Gestapu, but the army did not believe this. In a radio message on October 3 at 1:30 A.M., Sukarno stated that he had gone to Halim on his own initiative but that he had had no part in the coup attempt.[105] But he was equally unconvincing. In the next few months a hysterical anti-PKI emotion swept the country, causing the deaths of 150,000 to 500,000 PKI members and their families.

In Tokyo the PNI-affiliated leaders of the Indonesian Students Association were shocked at the news of the September 30 Movement, of the establishment of the Revolutionary Council, and of the disappearance of the president. An interview with a former PPI leader discloses that on October 2 when they heard on the radio that the Revolutionary Council had failed, some of those considered as PKI or pro-PKI members within the PPI disappeared from Tokyo that very day. It was rumored that they had flown to Hong Kong en route to Peking or to other communist or neutralist capitals. Later on October 3 upon learning of Sukarno's safety, the PNI-affiliated leaders of the PPI quickly issued a statement pledging "complete loyalty to Sukarno, the Great Leader of the Revolution,"[106] a clear manifestation of the PPI's strong PNI influence.

It took two weeks for the Indonesian embassy to decide on its position regarding the Gestapu. When Ambassador Harsono did make a statement on October 14, it still was ambiguous. He stated that the Indonesian people had protected President Sukarno and that his internal position now was even stronger.[107] That same day the PPI presented a more strongly pro-Sukarno and more strongly anti-Gestapu statement, calling for the president immediately to "purge the tools of the Indonesian Revolution from the Gestapu counter-revolutionary elements in all their manifestations."[108] Neither statement condemned the PKI nor supported the military, but in such an unstable situation it was safer to back the president.

The JCP and the Coup

The Japan Socialist party remained silent throughout this whole period in 1965, but the Japan Communist party expressed controlled apprehension. At the outset of the coup its daily, *Akahata*, reported the establishment of the Revolutionary Council in its October 2 issue, based on the Japan Broadcasting Corporation's (NHK) information but then no other news was given until its October 8 issue, obviously an attempt to hide the JCP's embarrassment over the abortive Revolutionary Council. In its October 8 issue *Akahata* reported the PKI politburo's statement on October 6 which insisted that the party had had no part in the September 30 Movement and that it supported President Sukarno. In its October 10 issue *Akahata* printed the first report from its Jakarta correspondent Sasaki Takeichi, who in usual communist terminology wrote that the eternal Indonesian Revolution would continue under Sukarno's impeccable leadership. However, in a speech before the JCP festival on October 17, party secretary Miyamoto had already expressed concern over the violent assault on the PKI which had been reported.[109]

The *Akahata* of October 23 contained a two-page space entitled "Data Material Concerning Indonesian Situations." It reprinted the full and/or partial texts of Colonel Untung's radio statement of October 1, President Sukarno's two radio announcements on the morning and evening of October 3, and PKI politburo's statement of October 6, Subandrio's statement of October 13, and Ambassador Harsono's statement of October 14. It also reported the Chinese response issued by the New China Agency on October 20 and the official Soviet, British, Malaysian, and Japanese reactions to the unfolding Indonesian drama. The Chinese reacted critically to the Soviet line which named Nasution "a revolutionary leader" and to the September 30 Movement "rebels." By means of this article the Japanese communist paper probably intended to demonstrate its support of the Chinese position, although *Akahata*'s editorial on October 23, the only one commenting on the Gestapu affair, took an ambivalent position. It was not until January 30 of the following year that the JCP's Central Committee issued their first and last official statement, which protested that, despite the PKI's statement on October 6, 1965 and Sukarno's repeated appeals for public order, the army and the Moslem forces were trying to suppress the PKI and its "democratic" organizations. Even this statement still hid the JCP's real emotions over the losses of the PKI.

The *Akahata*'s editorial on February 4, 1966, disagreed with the Chinese Communist party over the Vietnam issue. It argued that even if the Soviet Communist party were "revisionist," North Vietnam had just cause to seek military aid from the Soviet Union. The JCP seemed then to discharge its previously concealed anger over the failure of the coup by criticizing Lin Piao's "adventuristic" advocacy of wars of national liberation, which had led to the downfall of the PKI. From February 7 to April 4, 1966, Miyamoto and six other JCP leaders visited Hanoi, Pyongyang, and Peking. While they had constructive meetings in the first two capitals, they were not so lucky in Peking in their meeting with Chairman Mao Tse-tung.[110] Mao advocated guerrilla activities in Japan, especially in Okinawa, whereas the Japanese visitors considered such tactics as premature, which would serve only to bring about the PKI's fate. They were disappointed in Mao's high-handed attitude toward this, and from this point on the Japanese and Chinese Communist parties became antagonistic although their conflict was kept confidential. Thus the failure of the Gestapu meant to the JCP not only the loss of the PKI but also the creation of a rift with its Chinese comrades.

There are some Western scholars who argue that the PKI was in fact not responsible for the Gestapu and that it was used only as a scapegoat by anticommunist military leaders and the Moslem forces.[111] They assert that the Gestapu was basically an internal affair of the army and that there were elements to support this position. Yet Miyamoto and his party visited Peking in the spring of 1966 and returned with the conviction that the PKI had planned the coup at the suggestion of the Chinese party. At a closed meeting of the JCP of May 4, 1966, Oka Masayoshi, a member of Miyamoto's retinue, made a report which later was leaked and printed by an anticommunist publishing company. Assuming that the leaked information is correct, it is interesting to note that he stated the following:

> Last year around March 1965 Mao Tse-tung asked the Chairman of the Korean Workers Party, Kim Il Sung, to come to Peking and he reluctantly sent his deputy, Choe Yonggon. When Choe arrived he was informed that the (North) Vietnamese and Indonesian representatives also were there to discuss revolutions in Asia. Mao Tse-tung instructed Choe to direct the South Korean people to start their guerrilla struggles. Upon his return Choe reported this to the Premier, who refused to comply with these instructions. . . .
>
> It is the Indonesian Party which acted according to Mao's instructions and failed. Before we left [Japan] for Peking, we could not believe the death of PKI Chairman Aidit and Deputy Chairman Njoto. However [in Peking] we learned that it was indisputable. Not only they, but three hundred thousand Communist members had been arrested by the military and a majority of them were killed. The Indonesian Communist Party depended solely upon China. Financially too, it relied heavily upon the Chinese Party. We have learned that in recent years the Indonesian Party has received $30 million annually [from China].
>
> Mao Tse-tung strongly believes that a Sino-American war is inevitable. Because of this fear he wished to disperse American forces in Asia and scatter them [to different spots]. From this standpoint he envisions benefits from armed revolts in Indonesia and South Korea. The Indonesian Party used the Chinese doctors to collect information [on the president's condition] and relied upon their inaccurate information to assess the [revolutionary]

situation. The party staged an armed revolt without preparation and failed. When the revolt failed, they retreated in panic and therefore were [easily] pursued. Thus they were dealt a double blow. In staging the armed revolt the Indonesian Party did not even prepare a clandestine organization. How could they stage a revolt without a clandestine organization in the ready? One cause for their failure was an overly optimistic assessment of the Indonesian military; top leaders in the Navy and the Air Force had used considerable sums of money that they had received from China to bribe [their subordinates] and thought they had succeeded. How could a Communist Party dare to incite revolution by means of bribery? It will take five to ten years for the Indonesian Party to be rebuilt.[112] (Inserts in [] are mine.)

Although students of Indonesian politics tend to analyze the Gestapu affair within the context of the power struggle between the army and the PKI versus an internal conflict of the army, the Japanese Communists concluded in the spring of 1966 that the Gestapu was generated by the PKI against the army as a dimension of China's strategy against American imperialism in Asia.

The Indonesian Community in Tokyo and the Gestapu

On October 18, in the meantime, Indonesia's anticommunist military leadership banned PKI activities in the Jakarta area.[113] Perhaps related to this move, Indonesia's embassy in Tokyo began investigating the ideological positions of Indonesian residents in Tokyo as an initial step in the "red purge."[114] Informed sources remark that within the first two weeks of October, Major General Ibnu Sutowo, who was also director of Indonesia's state oil company, PERTAMINA, visited Tokyo and briefed the Indonesian embassy staff. He was a quiet but significant attempt on the part of the army to drive against the Sukarnoists. PERTAMINA's Tokyo office was then represented by another army man, Colonel Harjono, while in the embassy there was Colonel Sutarto Sigit, an army attaché. In a meeting on October 28 at Wisma Indonesia, PPI chairman Lily Satari condemned the Gestapu affair, claiming the need to continue a MANIPOL offensive against NEKOLIM.[115] This was still the Sukarnoist line, which was safe at a time when the army was gaining an upper hand over the PKI. Also attending this meeting were Ambassador Harsono and the visiting minister for Berdikari,[116] T. D. Pardede, Sukarno's trusted financial supporter. The fact that a pro-Sukarno cabinet minister visited the PPI at that time may indicate Sukarno's concern for the activities of the Sukarnoists in Tokyo. Another moderate, pro-Sukarno member of the cabinet, Minister of Veteran Affairs and Mobilization Mas Sarbini Martodihardjo, also visited

Tokyo from November 18–25.[117] While the ministers visited Japan ostensibly to improve economic cooperation between the two countries, there is reason to believe that Sukarno sent them to explain developments in the home country and to watch the moves of the Indonesian community, as army leaders apparently had begun to increase their contacts with anti-Sukarno Indonesians and Japanese (discussion in chapter 8). In mid-November Ibnu Sutowo entered Tokyo again.[118] Later on February 21, 1966 Sukarno, in his drive against the military, appointed Sarbini as minister of defense, taking Nasution's place.

However, Indonesia's military leadership favored neither the Sukarnoist line nor the PKI line. Reflecting anti-PKI and anti-Sukarnoist sentiment at home, those sympathizing with the military began to gather force in Tokyo. Ambassador Harsono left Tokyo on February 18, 1966.[119] It was announced first that he had been given a new assignment in London but upon his return to Indonesia news of his arrest was rumored and later confirmed.[120] When the March 11 affair finally brought victory to the Suharto group, right-wing PPI members are said to have roamed through the embassy building pulling down Sukarno's pictures from the walls.[121]

Soon after establishing power, the Suharto regime, in order to "clean out" Sukarnoist and PKI elements,[122] used two men in Tokyo. By then Colonel D. Hernomo succeeded Colonel Sigit as a military attaché in Tokyo, and on April 3, 1966 Major General Rukmito Hendraningrat was appointed as new ambassador. By the end of May, Colonel Hernomo had formed a five-man investigation committee, which began to "interrogate PKI members, PKI sympathizers, those sent to Japan by organizations related to the PKI, and those who have dishonored the name of Indonesia and have misused public funds."[123] By mid-June the committee had investigated some 50 Indonesians on the embassy staff, students, businessmen, and those working in Japanese offices.[124] On July 13, 1966 an embassy information officer explained that two students had already escaped to Cambodia.[125] The formation of this committee encouraged anticommunist PPI members who made up their own list of seventeen "PKI suspects" within the PPI and presented it to the committee.[126] Three of the procommunist, PNI-affiliated, PPI leaders were included among these seventeen members and were returned to Jakarta on July 29, 1966 for further interrogation.[127] The investigation committee in Tokyo replaced over one-third of the embassy staff, including a member of Subandrio's Central Intelligence Board.[128] The Hernomo team also investigated Dewi's personal assets in connection with the popular allegation of her misuse of Indonesia's public funds.[129]

The anticommunist leaders of the PPI established close contact with KAMI (Kesatuan Aksi Mahasiswa Indonesia), or University Students Command, as it quickly gained strength in Indonesian politics with the army's encouragement. KAMI was organized on October 25, 1965 and helped to topple the Sukarno regime. The PPI thus became the student front for the Suharto regime as it had been for the Sukarno regime. On May 24, 1966 when Suharto's first economic mission headed by Hamengku Buwono and Emil Salim came to Japan, the PPI offered to provide a bodyguard for the mission. This was in answer to a request by KAMI, which had heard the rumor in Jakarta that the remaining pro-Sukarnoists in Tokyo might try to obstruct the mission.[130]

DEWI AND THE GESTAPU

The Gestapu affair toppled the position that Dewi Sukarno had held in Indonesian politics and in Japanese-Indonesian relations. No sooner had the Gestapu affair occurred than she attempted to dissociate Sukarno from the abortive coup and to improve his damaged relations with Nasution and Suharto. Had her maneuver been successful, her place in Indonesian political history would be uncontested. Because she failed, though, students of Indonesian politics have paid little attention to her role in the post-Gestapu months. Thus an attempt is made here to elucidate how she acted during this tragedy.

Dewi on October 1, 1965

There have been conflicting reports on whether or not President Sukarno had advance knowledge of the September 30 Movement. The official published report, written in 1967 by Nugroho Notosusanto and Ismail Saleh,[131] carefully avoided mentioning this issue. But several writers outside the Indonesian government indicated that Sukarno indeed had known in advance of the movement.[132] These writers based their assertions on the same interrogations, investigations, and witnesses' reports that Nugroho and Saleh had used in their book. The military authorities' decision not to have Sukarno tried by its special military tribunal Mahmillub (Mahkamah Militer Luar Biasa), despite strong demands by the student groups, suggests that they wanted to avoid the most sensitive and most embarrassing issue in the affair. This is understandable, yet what remains unexplained is that Dewi, who as Sukarno's wife could be considered the closest person to him, was never summoned to the trial as a witness or as a defendant.

Dewi wrote an account of the events from October 1–14, which was translated into Indonesian and appeared in a radical anti-Sukarno KAMI newspaper, *Harian Kami*, from October 12 to 14, 1966.[133] Her intention in writing this account is not clear to me; however, it is obvious that at least in part she tried to prove the president's innocence. Nugroho and Saleh wrote that: "On the night of September 30, President Sukarno had gone to spend the night at Madame Dewi's house in Djalan Slipi. At 6:00 that morning the President was informed by one of his aides that several Army generals had been abducted during the night. The President immediately left for the Palace."[134] Dewi wrote: "We woke at 6:00 A.M. as usual, without knowing what had happened.... When he [the president] was about to leave at 6:40, he received reports from Commander Sabur, the guards, and Police Chief Mangil. The President looked tense for a moment but then relaxed and left for the Palace."[135] Dewi seems to have tried to establish not only the president's innocence but also her own.

Since Dewi's house was on the main road leading to Halim, Arnold Brackman, a journalist specializing in Indonesian affairs, wondered in his book if Sukarno might have "conferred at her house with any courier or member of the conspiracy who was en route to Halim that early morning."[136] Ōmori Minoru, a *Mainichi Shinbun* correspondent and one-time close friend of Dewi's, gives an account in which Dewi did not get up until 10 o'clock.[137] It would seem that Ōmori's account is more accurate than Dewi's because, first, she had played cards until very late on the night of September 30, making it likely that she slept late into the following morning.[138] Second, if she awoke at 6:00 A.M. as she claimed, she must have seen that Commander Sabur of the presidential Palace Guard, who usually came to pick up the president, did not come to Wisma Yasoo that morning.[139] The *Asahi Shinbun* of October 3, 1965 reported that Dewi's friend had informed newspapermen of the rumor that upon hearing of the coup Sukarno flew to the palace by helicopter "to avoid the possible danger on the night road." This implies that Sukarno had left while it still was dark. These conflicting accounts serve only to cloud the actual events at Dewi's house that early morning of October 1.

Nonetheless after the Gestapu affair had occurred, she began to play an intermediary role between Sukarno and Nasution. On the morning of October 1 when Suharto's and Nasution's troops began to counterattack the Gestapu rebels, there were frequent telephone calls to Wisma Yasoo, inquiring into the whereabouts of the president and his safety.[140] About 10 o'clock, the first contact man from the president came to Wisma Yasoo to deliver a letter to Dewi from Sukarno in which he said that he was now at the Halim Air Force Base and that she did not need to worry.[141] Learning the latest developments from the contact man, she "saw the whole thing as an internal conflict in the Army."[142]

According to Ōmori, Dewi immediately typed a reply to Sukarno and gave it to the contact man.[143] In it she urged the president to inform the nation of his safety as soon as possible. Whether her urging directly influenced Sukarno is not known, yet that afternoon Sabur, who was at Halim, issued an announcement to that effect.[144] After 10 o'clock, Dewi wrote, General Nasution sent a secret contact man to ask Dewi about the president's condition telling her that Nasution wished to contact the president.[145] According to Ōmori's account, the contact man urged her to contact the president for Nasution immediately, "before he fell into Communist hands," emphasizing that "it was you [Dewi] who could contact the President now."[146] At 5:00 P.M., Dewi wrote, the president's contact man returned with another message: "I would like to see you as soon as possible about something which cannot be mentioned in this letter."[147] She immediately sent an answer and at 8 o'clock that night Sukarno sent a jeep to Wisma Yasoo and Dewi went to Halim disguised in a black suit and scarf.[148]

Dewi wrote that at 9:00 P.M. she arrived at Halim and saw her husband accompanied by some ten men including cabinet member Leimena and Air Force Commander Omar Dhani.[149] (Subandrio then was in North Sumatra, and Chairul Saleh was in Peking.) Dewi and Sukarno excused themselves and talked for an hour in private. Dewi recalled that she insisted that the people were worried about the president's safety and wanted to hear his voice, and that she appealed to him to issue presidential orders restoring security and order.[150] Learning of his plan to fly at once to Madiun, a communist stronghold in East Java, she wrote, she asked to go along but Sukarno replied: "While I would be thankful for your company, please wait for me until the situation becomes orderly once more."[151] When their talk thus ended, the leaders who had gathered at Halim began to get into their cars to drive up to the airplanes; according to Ōmori's account, Dewi managed to step into Leimena's car and once inside she pleaded with Leimena to persuade Sukarno not to go to East Java.[152] According to Dewi, he [Leimena] said to her, "Don't worry, I'll take care of him for you."[153]

Dewi went home and did not know until the next morning that after fifteen minutes in the air President Sukarno changed his mind and returned to Halim. He was then driven to another presidential palace in Bogor, thirty miles south of Jakarta. Dewi writes that she believed that this was due to Leimina's urging.[154] If what she has described is true, it would appear that on the first day of the Untung coup she played a critical role as an intermediary between the president and the Nasution-Suharto military group, and that she had had some influence in Sukarno's decision not to fly to Madiun.

The Dewi-Subandrio Rivalry, October 1965 to March 1966

President Sukarno stayed in Bogor until October 9, with some of his cabinet members, most notably Subandrio. His second wife, Hartini, also was living in Bogor. Subandrio returned to Jakarta from North Sumatra on October 2 and Saleh arrived from Peking on October 7. At Wisma Yasoo, according to Ōmori, Dewi now believed that it was Subandrio who had tried to draw Sukarno away from the military and toward the Communists, and thus she felt the necessity to bring about a reconciliation between them.[155] In order to communicate secretly with Nasution, Dewi boldly sent one of her close Indonesian friends to call on Mrs. Nasution.[156] Through her friend, Dewi learned that General Nasution wished to bring the president from Bogor back to the capital. After Dewi's courier had gone back and forth several times between hers and the Nasutions' residence, Nasution sent a man on this mission, declaring that the job was too dangerous for a woman.[157] In the meantime Dewi wrote several letters to Sukarno, the first on October 3, then on October 7 and 9, explaining the developments in Jakarta.[158]

Sukarno came back to Jakarta on October 9 for the first time since he had left on October 1. Dewi writes that on October 9 she learned of Sukarno's return through a courier from the presidential palace.[159] She again urged that Sukarno make a settlement with Nasution.[160] Sukarno agreed, suggesting that he and Dewi meet with General and Mrs. Nasution on October 11, which they did.[161] On October 14 they invited Mrs. Yani, whose husband, the army chief of staff, had been among those six generals slain, to come and see them.[162]

Thereafter Dewi seems also to have tried to smooth out the differences between Sukarno and Suharto. A few days after Sukarno and Nasution met, according to Ōmori, Dewi and Suharto played golf together early in the morning. Ōmori reasons that Dewi had sensed that Suharto wanted to make a rapprochement with the president.[163] According to Ōmori, Dewi claimed that "She and Suharto faced a common enemy, Subandrio."[164] It was known that Subandrio had cultivated a relationship with Hartini and through her had become close to Bung Karno. There was further speculation that another woman, Harjati, the president's fourth wife, was gaining influence, aided by Sabur who wanted to increase his power within the presidential circle.[165] It is not strange that under these circumstances Dewi found the Gestapu a grave threat, that she strove for Sukarno's reestablishment, and that she tried to use the failure of the coup to crush the Subandrio-Hartini-Yao Chung Ming alliance. One also may speculate that Sukarno as well wished to use the anticommunist Dewi to impress upon the anticommunist military that he too was noncommunist, if not anticommunist. On October 19 Sukarno held a press conference with a group of Japanese journalists, at which Dewi was conspicuously present.[166] On December 10, 1965 Sukarno and Dewi held a cornerstone-laying ceremony for the Sari Asih Hospital, which she was building with contributions from various organizations including the Indonesia-Japan Friendship Society. On December 23 at the Merdeka Palace, Sukarno, Nasution, Suharto, and their wives gave a Christmas party, according to Ōmori.[167]

These maneuvers of Dewi's offended Subandrio, who felt that Sukarno and the military forces were joining against him. Ōmori infers that Subandrio then worked to separate Dewi from Sukarno.[168] At Sukarno's suggestion (which Dewi later deemed was prompted by Subandrio), she visited Japan in early January 1966 on behalf of the Indonesian government to request Japanese government aid to build her hospital. Dewi was accompanied by the minister of education, Brigadier General Sjarif Thajeb, who was considered sympathetic to the rising student unrest.[169] It is speculated that Dewi's trip was part of Subandrio's scheme to oust the promilitary elements from the Indo-nesian government. Following her stay in Japan, Dewi traveled to Europe to observe hospital facilities and conditions there. While in Rome she was told by the Indonesian embassy that she should not return home to Jakarta and this again, she thought, was conspired by Subandrio's followers.[170]

While she was away Sukarno became critical of the military and with Subandrio became sympathetic toward the PKI. Ōmori writes that Sukarno's change in attitude toward the military and toward the PKI during January and February of 1966 was affected by Subandrio and that Subandrio appeared to have spirited Dewi out of Indonesia so that he could curtail her influence over Sukarno.[171] The accurate relationship of Subandrio to Dewi's trips to Japan and Europe remains to be clarified. Nevertheless, Sukarno's change of attitude toward the military did coincide with them.

The military-backed student demonstrations intensified in mid-January, protesting economic inflation and calling for the removal of Subandrio and Chairul Saleh. The students also demanded that Sukarno be tried in connection with his alleged complicity with the Gestapu. But in a memorable January 15 cabinet session which student representatives were invited to attend, Sukarno defended Subandrio and Saleh, reiterating that he was the one to take full command of the nation.[172] In response to Sukarno's appeal, Saleh and Subandrio moved to establish the "Sukarno Front" and to "destroy the enemies of the President."[173] By January 21 it was decided that the Sukarno front would be commanded by Saleh, who also was acting chairman of the National Front. The Sukarno front expected to gather its forces primarily from the left-wing PNI and the procommunist, pro-Sukarno Indonesian party (Partindo), and its formation quickly aroused the opposition of the Islamic press as well as of the military leadership. On January 27 Subandrio's Foreign Ministry announced that Indonesia had received some 10,000 tons of rice from China, intimating that it would continue to encourage Indonesian-Chinese relations, and in a February 13 mass meeting Sukarno openly supported the PKI.[174]

Dewi returned to Jakarta on February 22, too late to exert further influence on Sukarno. On February 21 Sukarno had reshuffled his cabinet, ousting General Nasution as his defense minister. The new cabinet still included Subandrio, Saleh, and even Omar Dhani, who had been accused of supporting the Gestapu. Minister of Education Sjarif Thajeb had been promoted to the post of deputy chairman of the House of Representatives. Sukarno again expressed his will to continue the confrontation policy against Malaysia and thus on February 23 renamed the Supreme Operations Command (KOTI) as the Supreme Crush Malaysia Command (KOGAM), which he himself headed. This was a defiant challenge to the right-wing military leaders and student groups. The students, encouraged by the anti-Sukarno military, were now on the streets everyday to press their demands and were even boasting of a plan to attack the residences of Sukarno's wives, Dewi, Hartini, and Harjati.[175] The Suharto-Nasution group finally staged a bloodless coup against Sukarno on March 11, in which Sukarno, who had fled to Bogor in the wake of student demonstrations and military maneuvers, was forced to sign a decree certifying the transfer of power to Suharto in exchange for Suharto's guarantee of his safety.

Dewi's Last Attempt to Survive, March 1966

The March 11 affair changed the balance between the right-wing military and the Sukarno-Subandrio forces, and this time changed it decisively in the former's favor. The PKI was banned on March 12. In the face of this shift of power, Dewi immediately tried again to bring Sukarno and the military closer together. On March 14 she planned a party with wives of prominent military leaders at Wisma Yasoo "in commemoration of the dissolution of PKI."[176] This imprudent perform-ance reportedly angered Sukarno, who ordered her to cancel the party.[177] Later on March 19 she explained to the press that the party had been planned to squash the rumor that the president and the military were not on good terms.[178] Sukarno's two right-hand men, Subandrio and Saleh, were arrested on March 18, but Dewi continued to work toward a Suharto-Sukarno reconciliation. On March 20 she played golf with Suharto who supposedly suggested that she propose to Sukarno that he make a trip to Japan.[179] This suggests the basis for the rumor that the president might seek refuge abroad and reflects the people's feelings toward Sukarno's imminent downfall and also that of Dewi's.

Dewi failed repeatedly in her attempts to survive the political turmoil. When Sukarno finally lost power, she too lost a foundation from which to work. In November 1966 she left for Japan for the birth of their daughter, while Sukarno remained confined in Bogor. They did not meet again until June 19, 1970, one day before the first Indonesian president ended his sixty-nine years.

AN ASSESSMENT OF THE SUKARNOISTS IN JAPANESE-INDONESIAN RELATIONS

The Sukarnoists were a group with disparate motivations. They emerged in Tokyo about 1960 through the Indonesian Students Association (PPI) and the embassy which served as fronts for the PNI. From 1960–1962 the PPI and the embassy had considerable success in blocking Japanese support, albeit indirect, of Dutch efforts to retain West Irian. After 1962 the Sukarnoists, with increased influence by PKI doctrines, became more radical. Their strongest supporter among the Japanese was the Japan Communist party, and consequently their attempts to promote the anti-Malaysia policy, the GANEFO, and the CONEFO faced difficulty and gained support only outside the Japanese government.

As a modus operandi the Sukarnoists resorted mostly to street demonstrations and not to quiet persuasion through personal contacts. In this sense they cannot be termed the Sukarnoist Lobby and are better called the Sukarnoist pressure group. Unlike the Peace Lobby and reparations lobbies observed in chapters 3 and 5, the Sukarnoist groups included few "Japan experts" and were able to gather only a few "Indonesia experts" from the Japanese. The sparse use of personal contacts plus the lack of lobbying explain, in part, their limited success in gaining Japanese government support for their anti-Malaysia and other post-1963 policies.

Sukarno's charismatic leadership was supported largely by his favoritism in appointments to important government posts and by his manipulation of competing political forces. Only in competition with each other could these forces see the benefit of supporting Sukarno. This was manifested in their immediate reactions to the Gestapu, as little information was available in Tokyo, the Sukarnoists had no choice but to support Sukarno. Even the army leaders, who after October 1965 no longer supported Sukarno, still tried to maintain order in his name. But later when the army challenged Sukarno's power, the Sukarnoists quickly collapsed.

The major members of the Sukarnoist group, Subandrio, Saleh, Harsono, Sabur, Njono, Njoto, Lukman, Jusuf Muda Dalam, and Markam, were arrested and sentenced. One-third of the Indonesian embassy officials were dismissed. Dewi left Indonesia. When the PKI fell, the JCP ended its support of Sukarno. In the aftermath of the post-Gestapu trials, alleged monetary corruption among Sukarnoist leaders was revealed. Here one may imagine that part of the Japanese reparations funds and Kawashima's credits might have been used to finance the Sukarnoists' political and personal needs.

In light of the interaction between Tokyo and Jakarta, the PPI and Dewi become significant. Both rose to prominence as a result of Japan's reparations programs. The PPI's essential function was to advance Sukarnoist ideology; and using to advantage her beauty, intelligence, and ambition, Dewi involved herself in Sukarno's power politics. For a short period from early 1964 through September 1965, as seen in chapter 6, Dewi served as a link between the Japanese and the Indonesian governments, competing with Hartini and Subandrio to promote Japanese interests in Sukarno's foreign policy. In the post-Gestapu months Dewi continued to compete with Subandrio, trying to accomplish a rapprochement between Sukarno and the military but was not successful. Upon Dewi's and Sukarno's departure from Indonesian politics, Japan was obliged to replace the Kawashima Lobby, a development which will be discussed in the following chapter.

NOTES

1. In Indonesian they are respectively: Undang-Undang Dasar 1945 (U), Sosialism a la Indonesia (S), Demokrasi Terpimpin (D), Ekonomi Terpimpin (E), and Kepribadian Indonesia (K).

2. *Panca Sila* means the "five principles" which Sukarno framed in June 1945 as basic pillars of the Indonesian constitution. They are: nationalism, internationalism, democracy, social justice, and belief in God.

3. Sukarno, *Sukarno: An Autobiography as Told to Cindy Adams* (Indianapolis, Ind.: The Bobbs-Merrill Co., 1965), p. 283.

4. "BAMUNAS Alat Manipulasi Sukarno," *Harian Kami*, February 28, 1967.

5. Dewi wrote in 1969: "During the Sukarno period...there were those Indonesians who charged 3 percent commission for assisting every business deal with which they were involved and who voluntarily contributed to the state fund. They were used for the overseas travel costs of state dignitaries, the expenses for holding the Asian Games and the like, lest the national prestige be impaired." See Dewi Sukarno, "Daitōryō fujin e no ketsubetsu" (1), *Shūkan Gendai*, December 11, 1969,

p. 49.

6. Indonesia, Attorney General, *Proses Peradilan Jusuf Muda Dalam* (Jakarta: Pembimbing Masa, 1967), p. 78. For his biography, see ibid., pp. 117–118.

7. Ibid., p. 84.

8. Ibid., p. 86. In the trial Jusuf explained that for the Revolution Fund he had used
contributions of traders who were licensed to use $6 million of credit earmarked
for textile import from Japan. This $6 million was part of Kawashima's loan of
$37 million committed in August 1965. See chapter 7.

9. Ibid., pp. 92, 149.

10. "Sukaruno o megutta Nihonjin," *Shūkan Shinchō*, April 2, 1966, pp. 36–37.

11. Anonymous former Industry Ministry official, private interview in Jakarta,
November 1971.

12. An advertisement page in *Indonesia Review* 1, no. 1 (January 1951).

13. *Antara*, August 26, 1965; and *Asahi Shinbun*, February 11, 1967. Another indication
of the close association between Sukarno and Dasaad was the rumor spread in
1967 that the latter might be arranging for Sukarno's exile to Japan. See *Asahi
Shinbun*, February 11, 1967.

14. *Straits Times*, May 12, 1966.

15. Sukarno held private auctions in the presidential palace to sell his hats, paintings,
etc., to which he invited wealthy businessmen. From an *Antara* staff member,
private conversation in Jakarta, February, 1972.

16. *Antara Ichtisar 1965*, p. 1097.

17. Ibid., p. 1154. He was arrested on March 23, 1966 and detained by the military
on the charge of misuse of public funds. His company was taken over by the
military and renamed the Berdikari Company. See *Merdeka*, March 11, 1971; and
Harian Abadi, March 15, 1971.

18. Anonymous Executive Committee member of the Nadeshiko Club, private
interview in Jakarta, February 1971.

19. Indonesian Army, Justice Education Office, *G-30-S dihadapan Mahmillub 3 di
Jakarta (Perkara Dr. Subandrio)* (Jakarta: Pembimbing Masa, 1967), II, pp. 221–
223, 266–267.

20. For a background of this movement, see Howard P. Jones, *Indonesia: The Possible
Dream* (New York: Harcourt Brace Jovanovich, Inc., 1971), pp. 352–358.

21. Ibid., p. 395.

22. At the end of 1959 the total of 257 Indonesian residents included 90 government
officials, 65 students and trainees, and 14 businessmen. See Japan, Foreign Ministry,
Indoneshia Kyōwakoku benran (Tokyo: Nihon Kokusai Mondai Kenkyūjo, 1960),
p. 97. As of July 1963, the total of 851 residents were comprised of 127 embassy
and consular officials, 28 Reparations Mission officials, 130 traders and students
on private expenses, 368 reparations students, and 198 reparations trainees. See
Japan, Foreign Ministry, *Indoneshia Kyōwakoku benran* (Tokyo: Nihon Kokusai
Mondai Kenkyūjo, 1964), p. 171. Available Indonesian records show that under
the reparations programs 95 students came to Japan in 1960–1961, 100 in 1961–
1962, 115 in 1962–1963, and 58 in 1963–1964. See Indonesian Embassy, Tokyo,
Laporan Tahunan 1961, p. 119; *1962*, p. 133, and *1963*, section V, p. 19. No records
were available to me for the number of students in 1964–1965. Another source
indicates that a total of 378 students and 474 trainees came. See chapter 4
herein.

23. The Sumatran rebels who attempted to assassinate the visiting President Sukarno
in February 1958 are mentioned in chapter 5.

24. Anonymous former PPI leader, private interview in Jakarta, November 1970.
25. Herbert Feith, *The Decline of Constitutional Democracy in Indonesia* (Ithaca, N.Y.: Cornell University Press, 1962), pp. 269, 272.
26. *Yomiuri Shinbun*, May 31, 1966.
27. Indonesian Army, pp. 219–226, 239–241, 266–274.
28. Anonymous Japanese banker, private interview in Jakarta, July 1970.
29. Marzuki Arifin, "Orang2 Indonesia di Djepang," *Harian Kami*, April 18, 1967.
30. Ibid. ASU stands for the Ali Sastroamidjojo-Surachman leadership of the PNI which, because of its close ideological tie with the PKI, was ordered to dissolve after the Gestapu.
31. *Antara*, May 12, 1965.
32. *Antara*, August 14, 1965.
33. An anti-Sukarno, clandestine, anonymous pamphlet which was published by Nakajima Shinzaburō in Japanese in Tokyo in November 1967 indicates that the ministers of higher education and science from 1960 through 1965 were largely responsible for the selection of students and trainees. This hypothesis is yet to be established by me. However, Prijono, who was minister of higher education and science from July 1959 to February 1960, minister of basic education and culture from February 1960 to August 1964, and minister-coordinator of the Education and Culture Compartment from August 1964 to March 1966, was arrested and detained by the military in 1966. He was also a Stalin Peace Prize winner. See *Antara*, February 7, 1958. For anti-Sukarno activities in Tokyo, see chapter 8 herein.
34. Indonesian Embassy, Tokyo, *Laporan Tahunan 1961*, pp. 110–111.
35. Former PPI leader, interview.
36. Former PPI leader, interview.
37. *Antara*, August 14, 1965.
38. Former PPI leader, interview.
39. *Antara*, June 4, 1960.
40. Both Tokonami and Yoshie served in the Japanese occupation during the Pacific War. Tokonami was governor of the province of Pekalongan and director of internal affairs in the Japanese military administration. Yoshie was governor of Jakarta city. Both maintained their concern in Indonesian affairs after the war. Tokonami was among those who formed the Japan-Indonesia Association in 1947. He helped several Indonesian youths whom he had arranged to send to Japan for study while he was director of internal affairs and whom he saw in Japan after he returned. Among those Indonesians were Omar Tusin (one-time chairman of the Indonesian Chamber of Industry), Arifin Bey (counselor in the Indonesian embassy in Tokyo, 1967–1970), and Omar Barrak (chairman of the Indonesia-Japan Friendship Society). From 1951 to 1957 Tokonami and Yoshie attempted to promote an early peace settlement between Japan and Indonesia. Both attended the ceremonies for the signing of the peace treaty and the reparations agreement on January 20, 1958. From Tokonami Tokuji, private interview in Tokyo, April 24, 1972.
41. Japan-Indonesia Association, *Jigyō narabini kaikei hōkokusho, 1960–1961* (mimeographed, no page numbers), section on the chronological report of the association's activities.
42. Ibid.
43. Japan, Foreign Ministry, *Indoneshia Kyōwakoku benran* (Tokyo: Kokusai Mondai Kenkyūjo, 1964), p. 72.
44. *Asahi Shinbun*, September 1, 1960.

45. *Asahi Shinbun*, September 3, 1960.
46. Japan-Indonesia Association, *Jigyō narabini kaikei hōkokusho, 1960–1961*.
47. *Asahi Shinbun*, September 1, 1960.
48. Japan-Indonesia Association, *Jigyō narabini kaikei hōkokusho, 1960–1961*.
49. *Asahi Shinbun*, September 3, 1960.
50. *Asahi Shinbun*, September 3, 1960.
51. *Asahi Shinbun*, September 4, 1960; and Ōda Takio, private interview in Tokyo, August 4, 1973.
52. *Asahi Shinbun*, September 4, 1960.
53. *Asahi Shinbun*, September 10, 1960.
54. *Asahi Shinbun*, February 4, 1962.
55. *Asahi Shinbun*, February 6, 1962.
56. *Asahi Shinbun*, February 7, 1962; and *Akahata*, February 11, 1962.
57. *Akahata*, February 16, 1962.
58. *Asahi Shinbun*, February 17, 1962.
59. Since 1958 the JCP, under the leadership of Secretary Miyamoto Kenji, had begun to show an affinity for the PKI because it was impressed with the PKI's swift political comeback subsequent to its abortive Madiun Revolt of 1948 and the new leader Aidit's United National Front strategy. The JCP translated and published Aidit's works under the title of *Atarashii Indoneshia* (Tokyo: Shin Nihon Shuppan Sha) in March 1958, before it held the seventh party congress in July 1958, which selected Miyamoto as party secretary. In 1960 the party introduced another PKI publication under the title of *Yakushinsuru hyaku-gojū-man no Kyōsantō* (Tokyo: Nihon Kyōsantō, 1960). The following year the party's eighth congress firmly established Miyamoto's power in the party. The United Front strategy calls for the unity of progressive forces which would provide a basis to seize power by peaceful means. Aidit developed this strategy in 1951–1952. See Donald Hindley, *The Communist Party of Indonesia, 1956–1963* (Berkeley and Los Angeles, Calif.: University of California Press, 1964), p. 298.
60. Their visits are referred to in Miyamoto's speech on December 18, 1964, which welcomed Lukman's visit to Japan. See *Akahata*, December 30, 1964.
61. *Akahata*, February 10, 1962.
62. *Akahata*, February 11, 1962.
63. Japan-Indonesia Association, *Jigyō narabini kaikei hōkokusho 1961–1962* (mimeographed, no page numbers), section on the association's activities.
64. Japan, Foreign Ministry, p. 73.
65. *Antara*, June 16, 1965.
66. *Antara*, June 16, 1965.
67. *Antara*, July 26, 1965. Upon his return home Katsumada expressed his hope for closer ties with the PNI, See "A-A shokoku jinmin to no rentai kyōka no tame ni," *Gekkan Shakaitō*, July 1965, p. 39.
68. At the Diet session on January 28, 1965, Kajima strongly advocated Japan's effort for mediation. His remarks are printed in his *Nihon no gaikō, kako to genzai* (Tokyo: Kajima Kenkyujō Shuppankai, 1967), pp. 300–301.
69. Former PPI leader, interview.
70. Yanagawa Tomoshige, private interview in Jakarta, July 26, 1971; and *Asahi Shinbun*, November 2, 1963.
71. When the Advisory Council was established on March 20, 1959, it numbered twenty-eight. See Japan-Indonesia Association, *Jigyō narabini kaikei hōkokusho 1958–1959* (mimeographed, no page numbers).

72. Later in May 1963 when West Irian came formally under Indonesia's jurisdiction, Shimizu was invited to Sukarnopura (formerly Hollandia) to attend the ceremony. Shimizu Hitoshi, private interview in Tokyo, April 25, 1972.

73. *Asahi Shinbun*, January 28, 1965.

74. *Asahi Shinbun*, May 7 and 14, 1965; and *Antara*, May 7, 1965.

75. *Antara*, May 7, 1965.

76. *Antara*, May 8, 1965.

77. *Antara*, May 13, 1965.

78. *Akahara*, May 26, 1962. His trip to Indonesia was described later in his *Indoneshia kikō* (Tokyo: Shin Nihon Shuppan Sha, 1964).

79. See Kurahara Korehito, "Indoneshia Kyōsantō taikai no bunken kara nani o manabu ka," *Akahata*, July 6, 1962; Kurahara, "Indoneshia no minzoku tōitsu sensen," *Zen'ei*, no. 200 (August 1962), pp. 47–53; and Ide Jun'ichirō, "Indoneshia Kyōsantō no tō kensetsu ni manabu," ibid., pp. 54–62. In 1962 the JCP-affiliated publisher, Riron Sha, put out a collection of Sukarno's speeches under the title of *Waga kakumei no saihakken*.

80. *Akahata*, November 12, 1962.

81. *Akahata*, July 3, 1963.

82. Aidit visited Moscow in July 1963 in an attempt to smooth out the Moscow-Peking rifts. When this did not help, the JCP's Miyamoto in November of that year supported Peking's position and visited China from February through May 1964. After July 1964 when the disagreement between the JCP and the Communist party of the Soviet Union intensified, Miyamoto himself traveled to Jakarta in September 1964, and he and Aidit confirmed their leaning toward the Chinese party. See Sheldon W. Simon, *The Broken Triangle: Peking, Djakarta, and the PKI* (Baltimore, Md.: Johns Hopkins University Press, 1969), pp. 89–90.

83. *Zen'ei*, no. 228 (November 1964), pp. 2–5.

84. *Akahata*, September 2, 1964.

85. *Akahata*, December 30, 1964.

86. Anonymous, "Indoneshia no Kokuren dattai," *Zen'ei*, no. 233 (March 1965), pp. 131–137.

87. Shimizu, interview.

88. *Antara*, August 26, 1965.

89. Arnold Brackman, *The Communist Collapse in Indonesia* (New York: W. W. Norton & Co., 1969), pp. 54–55; and Jones, p. 379.

90. *Asahi Shinbun*, December 2, 1965.

91. For example, see Brackman, chapter 12; and Simon, chaps. 3–5.

92. Jones, pp. 378, 380.

93. Brackman, p. 67; Jones, p. 381.

94. *Antara*, September 24, 1965; quoted in Brackman, p. 236, note 8.

95. *Asahi Shinbun*, October 2, 1965.

96. *Asahi Shinbun*, October 2, 1965.

97. An *Asahi Shinbun* correspondent sent his first dispatch on October 6. See *Asahi Shinbun*, October 8, 1965.

98. Brackman, p. 62.

99. The text of the announcement is reprinted in Indonesian Army, Information Center, *Fakta2 Persoalan Sekitar "Gerakan 30 September"* (Jakarta: The Army, n.d.), pp. 19–22 (hereafter cited as Indonesian Army, *Fakta2....*).

100. Ibid., pp. 26–27.

101. Nugroho Notosusanto and Ismail Saleh, *The Coup Attempt of the "September 30*

Movement" in Indonesia (Jakarta: Pembimbing Masa, 1968), p. 35.

102. Ibid., p. 35.
103. Indonesian Army, *Fakta2...*, pp. 22–26.
104. Jones, p. 104; and Indonesian Army, *Fakta2...*, p. 30.
105. Jones, p. 388.
106. *Antara*, October 14, 1965.
107. *Akahata*, October 23, 1965.
108. *Antara*, October 14, 1965.
109. *Akahata*, October 20, 1965.
110. Oka Masayoshi's oral report to a JCP meeting of May 4, 1966, printed as "Miyamoto Mōtakutō kaidan no uchimaku," in *Nihon Kyōsantō honbu; kokode nani ga okonawarete iruka*, ed. by the Institute of Ideological Movement (Tokyo: Zenbō Sha, 1967), pp. 92–107.
111. A representative case in point may be Ruth McVey and Benedict Anderson, *A Preliminary Analysis of the October 1, 1965, Coup in Indonesia* (Ithaca, N.Y.: Modern Indonesia Project, Cornell University, 1971).
112. "Miyamoto Mōtakutō...," pp. 103–104.
113. *Asahi Shinbun*, October 19, 1965. *Asahi Shinbun* on October 27, 1965 reports an increased "red purge" taking place in government and state enterprise offices.
114. Anonymous Japanese embassy official, private interview in Jakarta, November 1971.
115. *Antara*, November 1, 1965.
116. Berdikari is an acronym for *Berdiri Atas Kaki Sendiri* or "Stand on [your] own feet," which was Sukarno's favorite term.
117. *Antara*, November 18, 1965; and November 25, 1965.
118. *Antara*, November 12, 1965.
119. *Antara*, February 19, 1966.
120. *Yomiuri Shinbun*, April 1, 1966; and *Asahi Shinbun*, April 16, 1966.
121. Anonymous *Antara* staff member, private interview in Jakarta, November 1971.
122. On April 7, 1966 the Foreign Ministry set up a Disciplinary Team (Team Penertib) to clean up its own apparatus from PKI influence. See Indonesia, Foreign Ministry, *Dua Puluh Lima Tahun Departemen Luar Negeri 1945–1970* (Jakarta: Yayasan Kesejahteraan Karyawan Deplu, 1971), p. 341.
123. *Yomiuri Shinbun*, May 31 and June 18, 1966; and *Asahi Shinbun*, June 1, 1966.
124. *Yomiuri Shinbun*, June 18, 1966.
125. *Yomiuri Shinbun*, July 14, 1966.
126. *Yomiuri Shinbun*, June 18, 1966.
127. *Yomiuri Shinbun*, August 5, 1966.
128. *Yomiuri Shinbun*, May 31, and July 20, 1966.
129. Fujiwara Hirotatsu, et al., *Hadaka no Devi fujin* (Tokyo: Yagumoi Shoin, 1970), pp. 189–191.
130. Anis Ibrahim, former KAMI leader, private interview in Jakarta, December 22, 1971.
131. *The Coup Attempt of the "September 30 Movement" in Indonesia* (Jakarta: Pembimbing Masa, 1968).
132. Jones, pp. 382–383; and Brackman, p. 35.
133. "Tjatatan Nj. Dewi Sukarno: Sekitar Insiden 30 Sept '65," *Harian Kami*, October 12–14, 1966. *Harian Kami* on October 12 writes that Dewi's account had been obtained from *Shūkan Asahi* through a man named Sueo Ōmori. Neither her account or Ōmori's have been identified in that magazine.

134. Nugroho and Saleh, p. 35.

135. *Harian Kami*, October 12, 1966.

136. Brackman, p. 86.

137. Ōmori Minoru, *Sukaruno saigo no shinsō* (Tokyo: Shinchō Sha, 1967), pp. 20, 66 (hereafter cited as Ōmori, *Sukaruno*).

138. Anonymous Japanese embassy official, private conversation in Jakarta, November 1970.

139. Sabur was in Bandung that morning. See Brackman, p. 62.

140. Ōmori, *Sukaruno*, p. 67.

141. *Harian Kami*, October 13, 1966.

142. *Harian Kami*, October 13, 1966.

143. Ōmori, *Sukaruno*, p. 67.

144. Nugroho and Saleh, p. 68.

145. *Harian Kami*, October 13, 1966. Ōmori writes that it was at 1 p.m. when Nasution sent his courier to Dewi. See Ōmori, *Sukaruno*, p. 69.

146. Ōmori, *Sukaruno*, p. 69.

147. *Harian Kami*, October 13, 1966.

148. *Harian Kami*, October 13, 1966.

149. *Harian Kami*, October 13, 1966.

150. *Harian Kami*, October 13, 1966.

151. *Harian Kami*, October 13, 1966.

152. Ōmori, *Sukaruno*, p. 82.

153. *Harian Kami*, October 13, 1966.

154. *Harian Kami*, October 13, 1966.

155. Ōmori, *Sukaruno*, pp. 92, 103.

156. Ibid., p. 108.

157. Ibid., p. 125.

158. *Harian Kami*, October 13 and 14, 1966.

159. *Harian Kami*, October 14, 1966. Ōmori writes that Sukarno returned to Wisma Yasoo directly from Bogor and that he was wearing sandals. See Ōmori, *Sukaruno*, p. 126.

160. Ōmori, *Sukaruno*, p. 126.

161. Ōmori, *Sukaruno*, p. 128; *Harian Kami*, October 14, 1966.

162. *Harian Kami*, October 14, 1966.

163. Ōmori, *Sukaruno*, pp. 138, 145.

164. Ibid., p. 145.

165. Ibid., p. 22.

166. *Asahi Shinbun*, October 20, 1965.

167. Ōmori, *Sukaruno*, p. 148.

168. Ibid., p. 150.

169. KAMI was organized with the advice and encouragement of Sjarif Thajeb. See Stephen A. Douglas, *Political Socialization and Student Activism in Indonesia* (Urbana, Ill.: University of Illinois Press, 1970), p. 155.

170. Ōmori, *Sukaruno*, p. 172.

171. Ibid., p. 148.

172. *Asahi Shinbun*, January 17, 1966.

173. *Asahi Shinbun*, January 23, 1966.

174. *Asahi Shinbun*, January 29 and February 15, 1966.

175. *Asahi Shinbun*, March 12, 1966.

176. *Asahi Shinbun*, March 15, 1966.

177.   *Asahi Shinbun*, March 15, 1966.
178.   *Asahi Shinbun*, March 23, 1966.
179.   *Asahi Shinbun*, March 23, 1966.

Chapter 8
The Indonesian Military Forces and Japan, 1955–1966

During the war, the Japanese military was responsible for training Indonesia's volunteer groups, PETA (Defenders of the Fatherland) in Java and Giyūgun (Volunteer Troops) in Sumatra, which are now the core of Indonesia's current military leadership.[1] Since then, however, Japan's constitution has limited its Self-Defense Forces' foreign contact to the United States. In 1960 Japan's armed forces, numbering 250,000, had only nine military attachés in seven of Japan's embassies, only one of which was in Asia, namely, Thailand.[2] Although an Indonesian military attaché had been in Japan since 1962, his Japanese counterpart was sent to Jakarta only after the Gestapu. Nevertheless, there was some contact between Japan and the Indonesian military both at the formal and informal levels. Japanese immigration statistics provide the number of Indonesian military men entering the country, as seen in Table 16. Although these figures are painfully misleading since they include a large number of those stopping over on their way to and from the United States, they still give some idea of the movement of foreign military personnel in relation to Tokyo.

Undoubtedly some of these military men visited Japan in connection with the reparations programs and economic cooperation projects, although no public statement has been issued concerning the amount of reparations funds given to the military. In June 1958 soon after the reparations agreement became effective, Nasution, in referring to the army's position of how the reparations fund should be used, stated that it would like to put its share of the funds into the nation's economic development and electric power projects which were necessary for general economic development and the army's communications purposes.[3] According to a document prepared by the Japan-Indonesia Association

TABLE 16

NUMBER OF FOREIGN MILITARY PERSONNEL ENTERING JAPAN,
1963–1970

COUNTRIES	1963	1964	1965	1966	1967	1968	1969	1970
Australia	—	19	25	25	28.	34	31	39
Burma	41	23	29	14	57	10	8	13
Cambodia	3	1	1	—	—	—	2	1
India	83	46	11	67	35	3	3	12
Indonesia	68	226	41	53	71	59	43	51
Laos	2	3	—	4	—	1	1	1
Malaysia	1	5	6	11	2	3	—	9
New Zealand	3	2	4	12	32	52	57	75
Pakistan	.41	13	3	39	4	—	—	—
Philippines	36	48	33	161	46	24	19	22
Singapore	—	—	—	1	— ·	1	1	4
South Korea	178	163	116	312	792	556	558	387
South Vietnam	80	94	35	43	84	67	82	406
Taiwan	51	79	44	95	84	80	93	114
Thailand	115	188	108	127	93	97	142	95
United Kingdom	54	62	60	83	40	30	158	147
United States	1,896	2,267	2,264	2,421	2,113	1,815	1,826	2,161

— Indicates the number is negligible.
Source: Japan, Justice Ministry, *Shutsunyūgoku kanri tōkei nenpō*, 1963–1970.

in 1958, the army requested in July an allocation of $1 million for steel helmets and uniforms.[4] This was a modest request, considering the annual reparations appropriation of $20 million, but it does indicate that reparations funds were used to support noncombative aspects of Indonesia's military. Other mention of this has been made sporadically, though exact evidence has not yet been established. For example, *Antara* on May 28, 1960 reported that the Indonesian navy chief of staff, Vice-admiral E. Martadinata, would be visiting Japan in connection with the navy's procurement of various equipment through the reparations programs, amounting to $17 million.[5] In September 1960 a three-man Indonesian military mission came to Japan reportedly "to purchase military material" though there was no reference to its relation to the reparations programs.[6] Another publication states that approximately 1,300 jeeps and 1,500 trucks were provided by the reparations.[7] I suspect that a major proportion of them was used by the military forces.[8]

More importantly, during the period of 1957 to 1966 there were some private contacts between Japanese individuals and the Indonesian military, particularly in the area of promoting anti-Sukarno movements in Indonesia. These contacts provided an important link in the post-Gestapu period between the Japanese government and the Suharto regime and formed the core of a new Indonesia Lobby to succeed the Kawashima Lobby. The data on this subject are still sparse, and many of the individuals involved are reluctant to talk about it. Yet without a discussion of it, the study of the interactions between Japan and Indonesia from 1951–1966 would be incomplete.

SOURCES OF JAPANESE SUPPORT FOR THE ANTI-SUKARNO LOBBY

Japanese Right-Wing Support for the Sumatra Rebellion of 1958[9]

One of the anti-Sukarnoists' first moves in Japan began in 1955 as the outcome of the Afro-Asian conference and the Indonesian republic's first general elections. The Bandung conference marked the closer ties between Sukarno and Chou En-lai, and the elections evidenced a swift comeback of the PKI after the failure of the Madiun Revolt in 1948. In addition, there were internal conflicts arising from the Outer Islands' opposition to Sukarno's Jakarta-centered leadership and to his emphasis on political rather than economic progress.

Among Sukarno's leading critics were Vice-president Mohammed Hatta, a Sumatran who had been pressing for economic development, and Deputy Chief of Staff Colonel Zulkifli Lubis (1954–1956), a well-trained intelligence officer who represented the army's PETA faction opposing the Dutch-trained Nasution group.[10] It was Colonel Lubis who initiated contacts with the potential Japanese supporters.

Lubis secretly sent several of his men to Japan, one of whom was Takai Jun'ichi, a soldier in the Pacific War who had chosen to remain in Indonesia, adopting the Indonesian name of Budiman. A captain in the Indonesian army, Budiman visited Japan after the Bandung conference to alert those concerned that Sukarno had assumed leftist leanings. Among those he contacted were Yanagawa Tomoshige, Kaneko Tomokazu, and Nakajima Shinzaburō, all of whom had been in Indonesia during the Pacific War and were affiliated with the Japan-Indonesia Association. Yanagawa, who had trained PETA officers during the war, recalls that at one time he was asked to come to Osaka to attend an anti-Sukarno meeting which he thought was sponsored by one of Japan's large trading companies.[11] Kaneko Tomokazu had been an active supporter of Indonesia's youth movements for independence and had worked in the Propaganda Section of the Japanese military administration, referred to in chapter 3. During the war Nakajima had been a navy medical corpsman in Ambon, in the Moluccas, and since has opened flowershops and the Indonesian restaurant, "Indonesia Raya," in downtown Tokyo with Indonesian as well as Japanese friends.

Lubis' criticism of Indonesia's PNI-dominated and allegedly extensively corrupt government became so vehement that on August 13, 1956 he ordered the arrest of the foreign minister but failed, and then resigned as deputy chief of staff on August 20.[12] Lubis subsequently was to go to North Sumatra to assume a post as North Sumatra's regional commander but this appointment made by Army Chief of Staff General Nasution was never carried out, because the then Ali Sastroamidjojo Cabinet did not accept Lubis' policy to achieve law and order in face of the rebellious Darul Islam, a fanatic, antigovernment Moslem movement in Aceh. So Lubis remained in West Java. That year a sympathetic colleague, Colonel J. F. Warrouw, then a military attaché at the Indonesian embassy in Peking, visited Japan.[13] Through the "Indonesian experts" Warrouw met Kuhara Fusanosuke (1869–1965), a former president of Seiyūkai (a major prewar political party) who had exerted indirect influence over Japan's postwar politics, to request assistance in the anti-Sukarno movement.

Kuhara agreed and assembled several of his followers also concerned about Japan's relations with Indonesia. Among them were Iwakuro Takeo, Obata Tadayoshi, Nakata Fusahide, and Tanaka Tatsuo.[14] The amount and type of assistance that Kuhara and his group actually gave to the anti-Sukarnoists are not known, but in November 1956 Lubis led an unsuccessful coup.[15] Lubis continued his efforts to build up a force which would eliminate the "evil establishment" in Jakarta. In December of that year Vice-president Hatta resigned, and on December 21, 1956 the anti-Sukarnoists organized the Banteng Council (Buffalo Council), which assumed power in Central Sumatra. On March 2, 1957 dissident military elements in Makassar, led by Colonel Warrouw's followers including Lieutenant Colonel Ventje Sumual, proclaimed a *permesta* (eternal) struggle for "a just Indonesia."[16] This anti-Sukarno move led to the fall of the second Ali Sastroamidjojo Cabinet.

Prime Minister Djuanda's succeeding cabinet tried in vain to reconcile Sukarno and Hatta. Soon after, in May 1957, Sumitro Djojohadikusumo, an Indonesian Socialist party (PSI) leader who had served as minister of finance (1952–1953; 1955–1956), left Jakarta and joined the dissident Sumatran group.[17] Sumitro was then a member of parliament and in that capacity visited Japan. Through his party affiliation he was introduced to several leaders of the Japan Socialist party. Nakajima, who knew the Socialist party chairman, Kawakami Jōtarō, was asked to serve the Kawakami-Sumitro meeting as their interpreter.

Sumitro's introduction to Nakajima led in turn to an introduction to Kuhara. Kuhara then introduced Sumitro to Fukuda Takeo, the then little-known member of the ruling party.[18] From this maze of introductions, the meeting between Sumitro and Fukuda proved to be the most significant to Japanese-Indonesian relations in the 1960s. In 1957 Sumitro volunteered to raise funds to promote the anti-Sukarno groups and established businesses in Singapore and possibly in the Netherlands where he earlier had studied economics.[19] It is known that Fukuda contributed his financial support.

In October 1957 Hatta visited Peking and then Tokyo, accompanied by Omar Tusin, president of the Indonesian Chamber of Industry. The latter was affiliated with the Garuda Council. In Peking, Colonel Warrouw joined Hatta on his way to Tokyo. Omar Tusin recalls that while Hatta and his party discussed ways in which to settle the reparations issue, they also talked with prominent industrialists and political leaders with the hope of turning the reparations funds in the direction of developing Sumatra rather than Java, the scene of incipient communist uprisings.[20] Omar Tusin also recalls that Ishii Mitsujirō of the ruling party and Takasugi Shin'ichi were among those individuals particularly sympathetic toward Indonesia's anti-Sukarnoist drive.[21] Aware of the increased tension between Sukarno and the anti-Sukarno forces, Nishijima stopped in Singapore en route to Jakarta and secretly met with E. S. Pohan of the Indonesian consulate, as discussed in chapter 2. Pohan was critical of Sukarno's leadership and acted as a link between foreign supporters and the Sumatra group.[22] Nishijima recalls that he felt that political changes in Indonesia were imminent.[23]

On November 30, 1957, two days after Prime Minister Kishi's visit, the Cikini incident occurred, an unsuccessful plot to assassinate President Sukarno at the Cikini schoolyard in Jakarta. Responsibility for the plot was attributed to Lubis after the government discovered on January 6, 1958 a document dated June 6, 1957, entitled "Towards a Just and Prosperous Indonesia" which had been prepared by Lubis.[24] Although he had failed again, the anti-Sukarno movement did not retreat. On January 9, 1958 a secret meeting took place in Sungei Dareh, West Sumatra and was attended by the dissident regional commanders of Sumatra: Z. Lubis, Maludin Simbolon, Dahlan Djambek, Achmad Hussein, Ventje Sumual; as well as former Prime Minister Mohammed Natsir of the Masjumi party; former Governor of the Bank of Indonesia Sjafruddin Prawiranegara; and former Finance Minister Sumitro Djojohadikusumo.[25] There were also Barlian, Nawawi, and Alamsjah from Palembang. This meeting, as soon known, became a starting point of the Sumatra Rebellion. From January 23 to 26, Army

Chief of Staff Nasution toured East and North Sumatra and State Police Chief Sukamto visited West Sumatra in order to gain the loyalty of the local military leaders.[26] But their efforts were useless and rebellion became inevitable.

Soon after January 20, 1958 when the reparations agreement with Japan was signed, Sukarno made plans to visit Japan. A rumor arose that the Sumatran rebel leaders might try to enter Tokyo and assassinate Sukarno.[27] Earlier they had demanded to meet with him but he had refused. President Sukarno and his party arrived in Tokyo on January 29, 1958. A day earlier Colonel Ventje Sumual and five men dressed as businessmen had secretly come to Tokyo and reserved rooms at the Nikkatsu Hotel, close to the Imperial Hotel where the Sukarno party was to stay.[28] Sumual carried a British passport which gave his name as Herman Nicholas Sumual.[29] His presence in Tokyo was not known publicly until *Antara*, on February 3, 1959, reported from Bangkok that Sumual had flown to Tokyo via Singapore and Bangkok. On that same day Colonel Warrouw flew secretly to Tokyo in order to mediate between Sumual and Sukarno.[30] He met Sukarno at the Japanese government's guest house but achieved nothing. It was believed then that either Warrouw or Sumual had presented Sukarno with an ultimatum, but in my interview with Maludin Simbolon he disclosed that no ultimatum was submitted to Sukarno at that time.[31] After this attempt, Warrouw and Sumual met in Nakajima's office and on February 5, Warrouw secretly left Tokyo.[32] On February 6 "Herman Nicholas Sumual" held an unexpected press conference in which he revealed his true identity and stated that he was on a mission representing the antigovernment forces in Padang to persuade Sukarno to dissolve the Djuanda Cabinet and change his procommunist policies.[33] Sumual added that on February 10 the provisional government in Padang would declare its independence. After Sumual's statement, he and President Sukarno's party exchanged messages, the details of which are not yet known. The British journalist James Mossman commented on the matter thus.

> Several days Jakarta was silent while a somewhat farcical exchange of messages took place in Tokyo between army officers travelling in Sukarno's entourage and rebel army officers who had been dispatched to Japan to sound out the President's reactions to the ultimatum. Sukarno and his entourage were savouring the many delights of Tokyo and spent a good deal of their time in geisha houses and various of the steam baths for which Japan is justly famous. So did the rebel officers, to whom the opportunity to mix business with pleasure had seemed too good to miss. Consequently, there ensued what one senior Japanese security official described as a 'fantastic traffic' in secret notes and verbal messages between

one place of entertainment and another. The Japanese police were terrified lest Sukarno be assassinated while the guest of their Emperor, so they too spent days and nights being scrubbed and pommelled by dainty massagueses alongside the Indonesian rebel officers, or yawning into the small hours with them in smoky night clubs or tastefully appointed brothels...[34]

The rebel leaders, most of whom in 1972 were in Jakarta, have declined to discuss this incident in detail. Lubis only would explain in general terms that they had appealed to Japanese businessmen and political leaders not to use the reparations funds to strengthen Sukarno's political position.[35] Nakajima told me that he and Kuhara had assisted the rebels and the fact that Warrouw and Sumual met in his office is some indication of this. I speculate that Tanaka and Fukuda also were approached, although being part of Kishi's faction they were not able to help the rebels openly, as the Kishi Cabinet and the Foreign Ministry were trying to consolidate Sukarno's power position by means of the reparations funds.

However, Nishijima Shigetada and Adam Malik, once sympathetic to Sumatra's anti-Sukarno group, withdrew their support after learning that the rebels meant to form a separate government in Sumatra rather than replace the Sukarno regime, and opposed the move to break up the territorial unity of the nation.[36] At Nishijima's suggestion, Adam Malik, in March of that year, wrote several articles published in Japanese newspapers, which criticized the rebels' secessionist stand.[37] The withdrawal of his anti-Sukarnoist support proved to strengthen Sukarno's position. In October 1959 Adam Malik was appointed as ambassador to Warsaw and Moscow and there he was able to procure military aid which Sukarno used against the Sumatran rebels and for his West Irian campaign.[38]

On February 7, 1958 *Antara* reported that, according to "authoritative Indonesian sources," the rebels were buying freighters from Japan and that they were maintaining agents in Tokyo and Osaka. A *Mainichi Shinbun* correspondent, Oku Genzō, saw the rebels talking to Japanese and Chinese trading companies and felt that they wanted to buy weapons and military equipment.[39] Sukarno appeared to agree with him. Soon after his return from Japan, the president visited Makassar and stated on March 14 that he had evidence showing that Sumual had failed to purchase military weapons from shady speculators in Japan.[40] In an interview with Lubis in 1971, he admitted that the rebels had negotiated in Japan to purchase ships. However, he denied that the ships were intended for war purposes but rather were for exporting Sulawesi's copra.

By February 15, 1958 the rebels had left Tokyo, reportedly having gone to various destinations.[41] That day their headquarters in Padang announced the establishment of the Revolutionary Government of the Republic of Indonesia, PRRI (Pemerintah Revolusioner Republik Indonesia). That evening, curtailing his visit by one day, Sukarno left for Indonesia.

The Japanese Right-Wing Nationalists and Anti-Sukarnoists

Despite the dramatic beginning and initial overseas support of the Sumatra Rebellion, it was not successful and by early 1959 had diminished into guerilla activities. In June 1959 Sukarno made another visit to Japan, and again there arose the rumor that the rebels might try to deliver an ultimatum to him and, if it were rejected, to assassinate him.[42] But there were no incidents during his two-week sojourn and Sudibjo, the minister of information who accompanied Sukarno, stated upon his return on June 19 that: "There is no room for rebels in Japan since the Japanese government desires to maintain good relations with Indonesia."[43]

On June 17, while Sukarno was in Tokyo, he met with one of his old wartime acquaintances, Yanagawa Tomoshige.[44] Sukarno asked if he would mediate with the rebels, as Lubis had been under Yanagawa at the Tanggerang training center. Yanagawa therefore wrote a letter to Lubis and asked the president's secretary to see that it was delivered to him, but he later learned that Lubis had never received it. The content of the letter has not been revealed but it is difficult to imagine that it could have had a significant impact. Yanagawa opposed communism but felt that only Sukarno could maintain Indonesia's unity.

That year, according to Yanagawa, Japanese anticommunist, right-wing leaders met in Tokyo to discuss ways in which to assist the Sumatran rebels. These men were Inoue Akira (alias Inoue Nisshō), Onuma Tadashi (alias Onuma Hiroaki), Miura Giichi, Migami Taku, Tamai Kenji, Nakajima Shinzaburō, Fujiwara Iwaichi, and Yanagawa.[45] Inoue, Miura, Migami, Tamai, and Onuma were extreme nationalists who all had had a part in plotting the assassinations of political and business leaders. Inoue and Onuma had been among the fourteen-member Blood Brotherhood Corps (Ketsumeidan) responsible for the assassinations, in 1932, of Finance Minister Inoue Junnosuke and the president of Mitsui, Dan Takuma.[46] Miura (1898–1970) had been convicted of complicity in the assassination attempt of Nakajima Chikuhei, a former president of Seiyūkai.[47] Migami (1905–1970) was one of the principal figures in the May 15th incident in 1932 in which Prime

Minister Inukai Tsuyoshi was shot to death.[48] Tamai had been involved in the July 15th incident in 1940.[49] In 1954 Inoue, Onuma, Migami, Tamai, and others formed the National Guardian Corps (Gokokudan), an anticommunist shock force. Fujiwara had been a celebrated army intelligence major in Burma, India, and north Sumatra and had headed the intelligence organization known as the "F Agency," after the first initial of his name.[50] He had organized local anticolonialist and independence movements at the beginning of the Pacific War and created indigenous armies against the British in India and Burma, in particular the Indian National Army (INA). In Aceh, north Sumatra, Fujiwara had directed local anti-Dutch underground movements and in the postwar period served as a division commander of the Self-Defense Forces while maintaining contact with those who had worked for him in the past.

In 1959 the emergence of a communist Indonesia appeared imminent to these individuals, and they felt that it posed a great threat to the rest of Asia. Although they agreed on this conviction, their group was not unified. Yanagawa told me that he had stressed the unfeasibility of assisting the rebels, and indeed, nothing materialized out of this secret meeting. Nevertheless it is significant that these prominent radical nationalists met with the "Indonesia experts" and that a Japanese officer met with rightist figures and former wartime officers to examine the political and military situation of another Asian country.

Anticommunist Military Leaders in Japan, 1961–1965

The Sumatra Rebellion failed and by mid-1961 even the guerillas surrendered. Hussein was detained for a few months, while Lubis and Simbolon were imprisoned until August 1966 when they were released by Suharto. Sumitro and others chose exile in Singapore, Kuala Lumpur, Hong Kong, and Tokyo. Nakajima gave shelter in Tokyo to some of the rebels, issued anti-Sukarno pamphlets and assisted the anti-Sukarnoist members of the Indonesian Students Association.[51] Fukuda maintained contact with Sumitro and assisted him financially.[52]

When Sukarno's procommunist leanings became even more pronounced during his West Irian campaign, the anticommunist military leaders who had put down the anticommunist Sumatra Rebellion also became alarmed and sought assistance from the Japanese.

Nakajima's anti-Sukarno pamphlet, published in 1965,[53] claims that anti-Sukarno military leaders had sought collaborators in Japan during the Guided Democracy period and that, between 1961 and 1965, Major General Achmad Yani, chief of staff of the army, and General Nasution, chief of staff of the armed forces and minister of defense and security, visited Japan several times either independently or with the presidential entourage. It is certain that Yani came to Tokyo in 1961, 1962, 1964, and 1965, and that Nasution came in 1961, 1962, 1963, and 1964.[54] Nakajima's pamphlet indicates that Yani sent a special envoy to Tokyo in August 1964 and that he himself came in May 1965, although this has not been established by any other source. It also states that Yani knew that 30 percent of the army were Communist members or sympathizers, and that during his 1964 and 1965 visits to Japan he had secretly solicited collaborators in case of emergency. The pamphlet adds that Yani's wish to see Prime Minister Satō privately was refused because the issue was so sensitive, although this too has not been confirmed by other sources.

Although most of the leading Indonesian generals had been trained after the war at the Fort Leavenworth Staff and Command School in the United States,[55] they had little overt contact with U.S. Defense Department officials after the confrontation began and the United States suspended economic and military aid. Because Japan was the only pro-Western nation who retained friendly relations with Indonesia during this period, Indonesia might have felt that it had little choice but to go to Japan for assistance. Fujiwara revealed in 1966 that he had had occasion to spend a private evening with General Nasution in 1961 and that his acquaintances in Indonesia had kept him informed of the political developments in that country.[56] There is no doubt that between 1963 and 1965 intricate dealings among various political forces took place between Tokyo and Jakarta. A former wartime military officer related to me in 1972 that he had been told by Indonesian military men in Tokyo, sometime in September 1965, that there might be armed conflict in Jakarta in early October. As these rumors were circulating, the Gestapu struck.

THE SATŌ GOVERNMENT AND THE GESTAPU

The Japanese Government's Reaction to the Gestapu

During the first three weeks of October the Japanese embassy in Jakarta and the Foreign Ministry in Tokyo struggled to analyze the Indonesian upheaval. A Japanese banker close to embassy officials told me in 1970 that the embassy had reacted passively to Colonel Untung's radio announcement on the morning of October 1 and that they were prepared to accept the emerging communist regime.[57] But when the anticommunist military crushed Untung's coup, the Japanese embassy believed that they were in control of the government. On October 2 the Foreign Ministry expressed the view that Sukarno had lost power and that the military would lead the nation under some sort of collective leadership.[58] It also stated that the military would not be likely to change Indonesia's foreign policy drastically and added that the economic relations between Japan and Indonesia would not be affected very much by the new situation in Indonesia. In short, the Foreign Ministry expected no major policy change to occur except that change in the leadership. The Foreign Ministry seemed to think that the military had already taken control and that order would soon be restored. The ministry viewed the Gestapu affair as a loss of control by Sukarno over the military and not as a conflict between the Sukarno-PKI group and the military.[59] Only after the anti-PKI demonstrations expanded, proceeding from the capital to the countryside after October 3, did the Foreign Ministry begin to consider the upheaval as a conflict between the military and the Sukarno-PKI group.

On October 9 Sukarno returned to Jakarta, and on October 13, Ambassador Saitō Shizuo visited the president at his palace.[60] This visit was made possible most likely through Dewi's assistance, and because it was not dangerous politically for the president to meet with a neutral nation's ambassador.[61] Saitō's long association with Sukarno had facilitated his diplomatic activities in Jakarta since his term began in September 1964, but at the same time this association appears to have made him misjudge the situation in Sukarno's favor. After their meeting, the Japanese Foreign Ministry ceased to take for granted the advance of the military group.[62] Although Saitō made no comment on his meeting with Sukarno, it was believed by the press that he was sympathetic toward Sukarno and his group. Kusayanagi Taizō, a political commentator, wrote that the Foreign Ministry had received a report from Ambassador Saitō that Sukarno would regain control of the situation "within three months."[63] An *Asahi Shinbun* correspondent, Hayashi Risuke, also wrote that the embassy had felt until the end of November 1965 that Sukarno would overcome the military.[64] An anti-Sukarno pamphlet written by Nakajima Sinzaburō's group in 1969 stated that Ambassador Saitō had believed Sukarno when he told him during their meeting on October 13 that he would gain control of the situation "within six months."[65]

The Japanese government had supported the Sukarno regime since the inception of diplomatic relations with Indonesia in 1958 and had committed a large amount of economic aid through the reparations funds, private capital investment, and deferred payment import credits. Japan was convinced that Sukarno was the only charismatic leader who could maintain political unity within Indonesia's large heterogeneous society. In addition, it would be very difficult for Japan to assist a group opposing the government with which it had maintained close relations. This neutral (though leaning toward Sukarno) position was maintained at least superficially until mid-January 1966.

In the autumn of 1965 Indonesia had a severe shortage of food and clothing owing to Sukarno's inadequate economic policies. Both Sukarno and the Nasution-Suharto military group realized that the resolution of this crisis was vital in order to control unrest and to gain popular support. While political and military tension continued, the two sides competed to obtain foreign aid. There was a report indicating that Indonesia needed an emergency supply of at least 250,000 to 350,000 tons of rice to assuage its food crisis.[66] As early as October 13, Malaysian Prime Minister Abdul Rahman revealed that the Indonesian army had requested foreign assistance.[67] Another report stated that the military was considering an emergency procurement of rice from Burma, Thailand, and South Korea—all under military regimes.[68]

Under these circumstances it was necessary for the Japanese government to reexamine the situation in Indonesia. Kiuchi Akitane, chief of the Southeast Asia Section of the Foreign Ministry, visited Indonesia from October 18–21, and Ambassador Saitō was summoned back to Tokyo on October 28.[69] They issued similar statements in their press conferences: civil war was not likely to occur, Indonesia's foreign policy would not change drastically, and Japan should respond favorably to Indonesia's economic aid requests. On November 1 the Foreign Ministry decided to provide food and clothing, if requested, "from a purely humanitarian standpoint."[70] A certain source suggests that these remarks and policy statement concealed the apparent severe competition for Japan's assistance taking place between the Sukarno and the military groups. Being caught between them, Japan carefully worded the response so that it would not appear partial for either group. In actuality, with Ambassador Saitō's brief return to Tokyo, the Japanese government gradually moved to favor the Suharto leadership. Yet it was difficult to have formal contacts with the military group fighting against the group with which Japan had maintained official relations. Thus in practice Japan turned out to be assisting the Sukarno group. As expected, the minister of textile industry, Brigadier General D. Ashari, went to Japan on December 4 and requested that clothing be supplied before the end of the year. This was Indonesia's first official request to Japan in the postcoup period. Japan agreed.[71] However, there are grounds on which to believe that Sukarno used these funds for his political needs. A *Mainichi Shinbun* journalist, Ōmori Minoru, wrote that Subandrio was trying to obtain $10 million in emergency credit under the guise of clothing supplies.[72] A political commentator, Kusayanagi Taizō, wrote that, assuming Sukarno would reestablish himself again soon, Japan extended $6 million in clothing aid but that Sukarno used this not to purchase clothing but to arm the Sukarno front organized on January 16, 1966.[73] The Sukarnoists also negotiated with China for rice. On January 27, 1966 Sukarno announced that Indonesia would receive 10,000 tons of rice from China.[74] Kusayanagi writes that Suharto sent a secret emissary to Japan to appeal for rice supplies. But the Japanese government was reluctant on account of Sukarno's negative reaction. According to him, "a private Japanese group" (which he does not identify) arranged for an emergency supply of rice to be sent via Hong Kong and Bangkok.[75] According to Ōmori, Suharto obtained an additional 250,000 tons of rice from Burma but refused an offer by United States Ambassador Green because it was clear that it would include a provision for the immediate ouster of Sukarno.[76]

During this period the Japanese government was extremely cautious. Except for the $6 million credit, it delayed all other humanitarian aid lest it should be interpreted as a partisan gesture. It also feared that additional credits and grants to Indonesia might harm Japan's relations with Malaysia.[77] On December 28, 1965, when Indonesia's foreign currency reserves were gone and Indonesia's overdue trade debt to Japan had mounted to some $2 million and total trade and reparations-secured loan debts to $200 million, Japan suspended government insurance for exporting to that country.[78] This halted all exports to Indonesia, including business related to the reparations-secured loans. For Indonesia this was a double blow, as it was clear that Japan would resume trade and extend large-scale aid only if political stability were achieved.

Promilitary Lobbyists and the March 11, 1966 Affair

At the beginning of 1966 there were two significant moves. First, the Japanese government began to use economic power as a lever to help achieve political stability in Indonesia. Second, promilitary lobbyists shuttled between Tokyo and Jakarta. On January 18, 1966, Minister of International Trade and Industry Miki Takeo initiated a proposal for an international consortium to refinance Indonesian trade debts to the West, amounting approximately to $1 billion.[79] Then Miki discussed the necessity of propping up Indonesia's economy.[80] This was probably the first time that a high-ranking government official had referred to Japanese economic aid as an explicit means of controlling another country's politics. The Japanese government began to take positive steps toward long-range aid. From the January 27 cabinet meeting came a proposal for a discussion of the idea of a creditors conference among Japan, Netherlands, and West Germany.[81] But on January 27 Sukarno rejected any proposal of an international consortium as it would oppose his concept of NEFOS.[82] Then Nishiyama Akira, director of the Economic Cooperation Bureau of the Foreign Ministry, visited Indonesia in late January and urged the Indonesian finance minister to draw up an economic construction program, which Japan regarded as a prerequisite to Japanese aid.[83] On January 30 Miki stated that "Japan should play a leading role in reconstructing Indonesia's economy and to do that Japan would have to make a bold political judgment."[84] Miki did not elaborate what he meant by "a bold political judgment." However in retrospect the Japanese government must have foreseen the change in Indonesia's power structure, even though Sukarno, Subandrio, and Saleh were regrouping their forces.

A study reveals that at about this time there were several individuals working behind the scenes in a private capacity to promote Suharto. Up to that point the Japanese government had agreed with Ambassador Saitō that Sukarno and Nasution would work out some kind of political compromise. An anti-Sukarno pamphlet that was published in Tokyo in late 1967 states that Yanagawa, who had been in Indonesia since 1963, had promoted a Sukarno-Nasution coalition in Indonesia through his PETA student, Sudirgo, commander of the military police.[85] Yanagawa returned to Japan in January and February 1966. The pamphlet accuses him of going back to Tokyo to lobby for the coalition, but Yanagawa denies being part of such a maneuver.[86] On the other hand, Fujiwara Iwaichi appears to have promoted Nasution as a new president, probably because Fujiwara had close contacts with the north Sumatran people, the area from which Nasution hailed, and because they had met in Japan in 1961. Fujiwara wrote that he had been informed that the Indonesian military's plan to take over power from Sukarno had been formulated on December 20, 1965.[87] He himself retired from the Self-Defense Forces in January 1966 and became an executive director of the Foreign-Ministry–subsidized People's Diplomatic Association (Kokumin Gaikō Kyōkai).[88] In February, at the height of tension between Sukarno and the Nasution-Suharto forces, Fujiwara visited Indonesia. He described later how he was received at the Hotel Indonesia by the young officers and KAMI leaders. They were desirous of a coup against Sukarno and spoke to Fujiwara of their disappointment when the military did not stage one, particularly on February 25 when student demonstrations had reached a climax.

Nakajima Shinzaburō also visited Jakarta in February 1966.[89] Nakajima told me in 1972 that he had promoted the idea of Suharto

as president and Nasution as vice-president.[90] He claims that for a long
time the United States government hoped for a Nasution regime and
that only after a member of the former Sumatra Rebellion, Jan
Walandow, visited Washington and advocated Suharto as a leader,
did Washington move behind him. Also in February 1966 Sumitro
Djojohadikusumo, another leader of the Sumatra Rebellion, secretly
visited Tokyo from his hideout in Bangkok and talked with Fukuda
Takeo, then Japan's finance minister. Nakajima's pamphlet explains
that Sumitro appealed to the Japanese government to refrain from
extending any aid to the Sukarno regime.[91] *Antara* on March 2, 1966
confirmed the former rebel's visit and reported that Sumitro attempted
actively to make contact with top Japanese figures and leaders appealing
that Japan would stop helping Indonesia as long as Sukarno led the
Indonesian Revolution.

Finally Adam Malik assisted in promoting anti-Sukarno drives.
In 1958 he had disengaged himself from the anti-Sukarno movement
and worked for Sukarno but in late 1964 had again become critical of
Sukarno. While still in Sukarno's cabinet, Malik attended, on January
20, 1966, a seminar on the Indonesian economy sponsored by the
anti-Sukarno student and scholar organizations, KAMI and KASI.[92]
It was a defiant and courageous move. A Japanese journalist close to
Nishijima Shigetada believes that through Japanese friends the future
foreign minister secretly sounded out the Japanese government as to
whether it would recognize and support a military government in
Indonesia, and that Tokyo's positive response led Malik to encourage
the Suharto group. It is highly likely that Malik had the assistance of
his old friend Nishijima, who had been back in Japan for a short visit at
the time of the Gestapu but hurried back to Jakarta to observe its
aftermath. An *Asahi Shinbun* correspondent, Hayashi Risuke, later
observed that he and his press colleagues in Jakarta had considered
Nishijima and Ambassador Saitō as the most reliable sources of private
information about the political developments.[93] Hayashi wrote that
Nishijima seemed to have had advance knowledge of the scenario
leading to the March 11, 1966 affair, enabling him to make accurate
analyses and predictions of the student demonstrations and military
moves.[94] These moves behind the scenes must have sufficiently prepared
the Japanese government for the March 11, 1966 affair. The last man
and the highest-ranking official that visited Jakarta before the March 11
affair was Ushiba Nobuhiko, deputy vice minister of the Foreign
Ministry.[95] In retrospect there are grounds to believe that he contacted
high-ranking members of the military group and discussed their future
policies, including economic development policies and China.

On March 11 Sukarno was forced to sign a decree transferring the substance of his presidential power to Suharto in exchange for his own safety. On March 12 the Japanese Foreign Ministry stated optimistically that Indonesia would take an anti-China position and adopt a non-alignment policy.[96] It added that, if Indonesia's economic development programs were pursued earnestly and if its foreign policies were based on practical considerations, political and economic relations between Japan and Indonesia would be improved. That same day Kawashima Shōjirō also expressed a more optimistic view than that of the Foreign Ministry and remarked:

> "Although the leadership of Indonesia has changed, Japan's basic policy toward Indonesia remains unaltered. It is to tie Japanese economic power and technology to Indonesia's rich natural resources in order to promote the prosperity of both countries. Indonesia will need more Japanese assistance than before to reconstruct its economy. The voice calling for the dismissal of Subandrio signifies that the military regime intends to cut off relations with China, which means that the military are not thinking of soliciting aid from China. This means increased reliance upon Japan. It would be in our national interest to respond to such a need."[97]

The Foreign Ministry was more cautious, pointing out that the army still referred to Sukarno as "the President," that his future status was not yet determined, and that it was not clear where the navy, the air force, and the police stood in reference to the March 11 affair.[98] However both the Foreign Ministry and Kawashima implied in their statements that the PKI would be banned and that Foreign Minister Subandrio would eventually be ousted. As the Japanese leaders prophesized, the PKI was banned on March 12. Before Subandrio was arrested and succeeded by Adam Malik on March 18 and before the new regime announced that it would give priority to economic policy, Japanese Foreign Minister Shiina Etsusaburō urged in the cabinet session on March 15 that Japan should consider supporting the "realistic policy" that the new Indonesian regime had seemed to adopt.[99] This statement by Shiina sounded as though his ministry had had substantial communications with the new regime. One may well speculate that Ushiba, who was in Jakarta just before the March 11 affair, was responsible for this information.

Japan was among the first countries to endorse the Suharto regime. The *Asahi Shinbun* on March 25 reported that soon after March 11, the Suharto regime made a request for large amounts of aid, through informal channels, to the Japanese embassy in Jakarta. Reportedly

Indonesia needed an emergency supply of food amounting to $125 million and clothing amounting to $100 million. With Subandrio's departure from the political scene, Japan made several new proposals to Indonesia. On March 24 Japan proposed an international consortium called the "Tokyo Club" to settle Indonesia's debt and new credit;[100] on March 29 it extended an emergency grant of food and clothing amounting to $2.5 million, including 10,000 tons of rice;[101] and in late March, Japan pressed the new Indonesian regime to reverse Sukarno's earlier stand against Indonesia's participation in the Japanese sponsored Southeast Asian Ministerial Conference on Economic Development.[102] Indonesia complied and sent the new Ambassador Rukmito Hendraningrat as an observer. On May 10 the Suharto regime chose Japan as the first country which its economic mission would visit.[103] Japan promised $30 million in credit on the condition that Indonesia would settle the confrontation with Malaysia and return to the United Nations at the earliest opportunity, as was mentioned in chapter 6. On May 30 and 31 Malik and Deputy Prime Minister of Malaysia Tun Razak met and made good progress toward a settlement.[104] In August Japan provided $30 million in credit;[105] relations between Tokyo and Jakarta seemed to have found a more solid foundation than before.

AN ASSESSMENT

Japan's relationship with the current Indonesian military leadership has had a long history. The original overtures were made during the Pacific War, and some of the Indonesian leaders had maintained contact with the Japanese officers. Some of these individuals plus other "Indonesia experts," radical nationalists, and a Self-Defense Forces officer then assisted, after about 1955, the anti-Sukarno and anti-communist elements in the military. Private Japanese support of the Sumatra Rebellion in 1958 was the forerunner of the contacts between the Japanese and the Indonesian military during the second half of the 1960s. The friendship between Sumitro and Fukuda began in 1957 and Sumitro appeared to have worked behind the scenes to link Indonesia's right-wing military to Japan's conservative government. Nakajima, who had been sympathetic toward the Sumatra rebels, served as an anti-Sukarno group coordinator during the Sukarno period. The former intelligence officer, Fujiwara, kept contact with such military figures as Nasution. When the Sumatra Rebellion leaders joined the Suharto group, Japanese sympathizers also extended their support. One may also speculate that Nishijima and Malik as well as Ambassador Saitō also helped to build a bridge between Tokyo and the new Suharto regime and paved the way for Japan's early decision to support the

Suharto regime.

These individuals became the core of the new Indonesia Lobby in Japan. The association between Sumitro and Fukuda is still discussed today, as is the contact between Nakajima and radical nationalists and that between the former rebels and the military leaders. Nakajima, Tamai Kenji, and some twenty others formed the "Indonesia Center" in mid-1966. All the rebels who had been imprisoned in Indonesia were released in August 1966. Other rebels exiled in Kuala Lumpur worked after August 1965 toward a peaceful settlement of the confrontation, as mentioned in chapter 6. Sumitro joined the Suharto Cabinet as trade minister after 1968. The Kawashima Lobby, which attempted to placate Sukarno's position on the confrontation issue, did not side with either of the political forces and played almost no part in consolidating the new regime. Being so close to Sukarno and Dewi, there was no room for Kawashima to maneuver in the post-Gestapu period.

Between the Gestapu and March 11 affairs, the Japanese government did not extent any new grant other than the $6 million release out of "Kawashima credit." It carefully avoided interfering in the domestic turmoil but from early January 1966 it began intentionally to use its economic power to exert influence over the course of Indonesian politics and toward stabilizing the situation. The emerging military regime took strong measures against Communists and emphasized economic policies. Since 1958, this was the kind of government with which Japan had wished to deal. As Kawashima stated on March 12, 1966, Indonesia's rich natural resources and potential market were the main factors that attracted Japanese capital and technology. The image of an economically viable and politically noncommunist Indonesia thus was fundamental for Japan's support of the current military regime.

NOTES

1. For the genesis of the Indonesian military, see Guy Pauker, "The Role of the Military in Indonesia," in *The Role of the Military in Underdeveloped Countries*, ed. by John J. Johnson (Princeton, N.J.: Princeton University Press, 1962), pp. 190–193.
2. Bōei Sangyō Kyōkai, ed., *Jieitai nenkan 1961* (Tokyo: Bōei Sangyō Kyōkai, 1961), p. 1041.
3. *Antara*, June 23, 1958; and *Sankei Jiji*, June 21, 1958.
4. Japan-Indonesia Association, *I-koku seifu kakushō betsu shonendo baishō haibunhyō* (mimeographed, September 1958, special data no. 2), p. 3.
5. See also Japan, Foreign Ministry, *Waga gaikō no kinkyō*, no. 8 (1964), p. 96.
6. *Asahi Shinbun*, September 1, 1960.
7. Sakata Zenzaburō, *Indoneshia: genjō to mondaiten* (Tokyo: Federation of Economic Organizations [Keidanren], 1968), p. 76.
8. When I observed the Independence Day parade on August 17, 1967, I saw that almost all the new army vehicles were Toyota jeeps and Nissan trucks. There is

also a report that the Toyota Motor Company has sold the army 30,000 jeeps and station wagons since the late 1950s. See Kikawata Sakae, *Gunkokushugi to Nihon keizai* (Tokyo: San'ichi Shobō, 1971), p. 187.

9. Unless otherwise specified, information in this section is primarily based on Nakajima Shinzaburō, private interview in Tokyo, August 11, 1972. I wish to express my deep thanks to Mr. Nakajima for his cooperation.

10. Herbert Feith, *The Decline of Constitutional Democracy in Indonesia* (Ithaca, N.Y.: Cornell University Press, 1962), pp. 442, 501–502.

11. Yanagawa Tomoshige, private interview in Jakarta, January 23, 1971.

12. Feith, pp. 503–504.

13. Warrouw had served as commander of South Sulawesi in 1949–1952 and commander of East Indonesia territory in 1952–1956 before he was assigned to Peking. His command post in East Indonesia was later assumed by Lt. Colonel Ventje Sumual.

14. Iwakuro was an army officer who in early 1942 built an intelligence organization in Bangkok to assist India's independence movement against the British. See Umemoto Sutezō, *Nihon daibōryaku senshi* (Tokyo: Keizei Ōrai Sha, 1971), pp. 124–130. Obata, a businessman at this time, had served as secretary-general of the Imperial Rule Assistance Association (Taisei Yokusankai) formed in October 1940. See *Jinji kōshinroku 19-han* (Tokyo: Jinji Kōshinjo, 1957), I, section O, p. 31. Nakata was on the advisory committee of the Society for Economic Cooperation in Asia (Ajia Kyōkai) and was the executive director of the Central Headquarters of the Popular Movement for Good Neighbors in Asia (Ajia Zenrin Kokumin Undō). See *Jinji kōshinroku 22-han* (1964), II, section Na, p. 52. Tanaka Tatsuo was the son of Tanaka Giichi, former president of the Seiyūkai party and former prime minister. Since 1953 Tanaka Tatsuo has been a Liberal Democratic party member of the Diet, belonging to the Kishi faction and later to Fukuda Takeo's faction. See Nihon Minsei Kenkyūkai, *Kokkai giin sōran 1965* (Tokyo: Hyōron Sha, 1965), p. 130.

15. Feith, pp. 505–506.

16. Prime Minister Djuanda's parliamentary statement of February 3, 1958. See *Antara*, February 3, 1958.

17. Feith, pp. 525–526.

18. For this Kuhara used Tanaka Tatsuo because Kuhara was virtually a father to Tanaka after his own father died. See *Kokkai giin sōran 1965*, p. 130.

19. *Antara*, February 15, 1958.

20. Omar Tusin, private interview in Jakarta, July 13, 1971.

21. Ishii was an influential figure in the ruling party and in 1967 became speaker of the House of Representatives. Takasugi was president of the Mitsubishi Electric Corporation in 1947–1956. In 1967 he became chairman of the Indonesia Committee of the Federation of Economic Organizations (Keidanren). For his views on Indonesian economy, see Takasugi Shin'ichi, "Attitude of Japanese Business Circles toward Economic Cooperation to Indonesia," *Keidanren Review*, no. 8 (March 1968): 7–11.

22. He was referred to as the rebels' "ambassador" in Asia. See for example James Mossman, *Rebels in Paradise* (London: Jonathan Cape, 1961), p. 192.

23. Nishijima Shigetada, private conversation in Tokyo, April 22, 1972.

24. *Antara*, February 3, 1958.

25. *Antara*, February 3, 1958.

26. *Antara*, February 3, 1958.

27. To protect the president's life, the president hired a private body guard headed by Kubo Masao of the Tōnichi Trading Company, as mentioned in chapter 5.
28. *Antara*, February 5, 1958; and *Asahi Shinbun*, February 4, 1958. The others in the mission were Captain Daan Mogot, Major J. M. J. Pantow, and Jan Walandow, and two unidentified members. All of them were from eastern Indonesia. See *Antara*, February 7, 1958.
29. *Antara*, February 7, 1958.
30. *Yomiuri Shinbun*, February 16, 1958.
31. Maludin Simbolon, private interview in Jakarta, May 24, 1971.
32. *Antara*, February 6, 1958.
33. *Antara*, February 7, 1958.
34. Mossman, p. 96.
35. Zulkifli Lubis, private interview in Jakarta, July 27, 1971.
36. Nishijima, interview.
37. See for instance, Adam Malik, "Indoneshia to Kyōsanshugi undō," *Sankei Jiji*, March 11 and 12, 1958. Malik and Nishijima were probably assisted by their wartime friend Andō Michikuni, a Dōmei staff member, who in 1958 worked for *Sankei Jiji*. Relations among the three were also mentioned in chapter 3. ·
38. As of December 1962 Indonesia obtained a commitment of the Soviet Union for $600 million in military aid and $367.5 million in economic aid. See Japan, Foreign Ministry, *Indoneshia Kyōwakoku benran* (Tokyo: Nihon Kokusai Mondai Kenkyūjo, 1964), p. 135. More recently, the United States State Department learned that during the Sukarno period Indonesia had received $1.1 billion in Soviet military aid. See *New York Times*, November 19, 1972.
39. Oku Genzō, *Indoneshia no kakumei* (Tokyo: Ushio Shuppan Sha, 1966), p. 157.
40. *Asahi Shinbun*, March 15, 1958.
41. Sumual left for Manila on February 13 with a British passport identifying him as a Chinese merchant. See *Antara*, February 13, 1958. Pantow departed on February 12 for Singapore under the name of Tanged, while Walandow went to Taipei, then Manila and New York. See *Antara*, February 15, 1958.
42. *Tokyo Shinbun*, June 10, 1959.
43. *Antara*, June 20, 1959.
44. Yanagawa, interview; and Benedict R. O. Anderson, *Java in a Time of Revolution* (Ithaca, N.Y.: Cornell University Press, 1972), pp. 22–23.
45. Yanagawa, interview.
46. Nikkan Rōdō Tsūshin Sha, *Uyoku undō yōran* (Tokyo: Nikkan Rōdō Tsūshan Sha, 1964), p. 159.
47. Ibid., p. 192.
48. Ibid., p. 192.
49. Kōan Keibi Kenkyūkai, *Uyoku zensho* (Tokyo: Kindai Keisatsu Sha, 1957), pp. 208–209.
50. Fujiwara Iwaichi, *Fujiwara Kikan* (Tokyo: Hara Shobō, 1966); and Joyce C. Lebra, *Chandora Bōsu to Nihon*, trans. by Horie Yoshitaka (Tokyo: Hara Shobō, 1968).
51. Marzuki Arifin, "Orang2 Indonesia" (2), *Harian Kami*, April 19, 1967.
52. Anonymous *Nihon Keizai Shinbun* correspondent, private conversation in Jakarta, June, 1970.
53. Anonymous, *Indoneshia gendai seijishi* (mimeographed; Tokyo: Indoneshia Sentā, 1969), p. 29.
54. For Yani's visits, see Indonesian Embassy, Tokyo, *Laporan Tahunan 1962*, p. 155; Japan, Foreign Ministry, *Waga gaikō no kinkyō*, no. 8 (1964): 96; and ibid., no. 9

(1965): 98. For Nasution's visits, see Fujiwara Iwaichi, "Kono me de mita Indo-neshia seihen no uchimaku," *Shūkan Bunshun*, April 4, 1966, p. 38; *Laporan Tahunan 1962*, section IV; and *Antara*, January 17, 1964.

55. Howard P. Jones, *Indonesia: The Possible Dream* (N.Y.: Harcourt Brace Jovanovich, 1971), p. 203.

56. Fujiwara, "Kono me de mita," p. 38.

57. Itasaka Isao, private conversation in Jakarta, June 28, 1970.

58. *Asahi Shinbun*, October 2, 1965.

59. Anonymous Japanese embassy official, private interview in Jakarta, June 1971.

60. *Asahi Shinbun*, October 14, 1965.

61. The United States Central Intelligence Agency and China were accused of interfering in the abortive coup. China, although an ally, did not take a position on Indonesia until October 20, and Ambassador Yao Chung Ming met with Sukarno on October 26. See *Asahi Shinbun*, October 27, 1965. The Associated Press reported from Singapore on November 6 that President Sukarno had revealed in a cabinet meeting on November 6 that U.S. Ambassador Marshall Green had met with him and offered aid "in a few days after the Gestapu affair." See *Asahi Shinbun*, November 8, 1968. If this were true, Green must have been the first ambassador to meet the Indonesian president after October 1, but this is not confirmed by any other sources.

62. Anonymous Japanese embassy official, interview.

63. Kusayanagi Taizō, *Shin jitsuryokusha no jōken* (Tokyo: Bungei Shunjū Sha, 1972), p. 160.

64. Hayashi Risuke, *Urotaeruna Nihon* (Tokyo: Jitsugyō no Nihon Sha, 1972), p. 76.

65. *Indoneshia gendai seijishi*, p. 55.

66. Ōmori Minoru, *Sukaruno saigo no shinsō* (Tokyo: Shinchō Sha, 1967), p. 143.

67. *Asahi Shinbun*, October 14, 1965.

68. *Asahi Shinbun*, October 15, 1965.

69. *Asahi Shinbun*, October 24 and 30, 1965.

70. *Asahi Shinbun*, December 2, 1965.

71. Ashari's visit was reported in *Asahi Shinbun*, December 4, 1965. Japan's consider-ation to offer a $6 million emergency supply of cotton textiles was reported in *Nihon Keizai Shinbun*, December 10, 1965.

72. Ōmori, p. 147.

73. Kusayanagi, p. 160. In trying the governor of the Central Bank of Indonesia, Jusuf Muda Dalam, on April 8, 1966, the special court revealed that the bank had received $6 million of textile credits from Japan in January 1966. See Indonesia, Attorney-General, *Proses Peradilan Jusuf Muda Dalam* (Jakarta: Pembimbing Masa, 1967), p. 86.

74. *Asahi Shinbun*, January 29, 1966.

75. Kusayanagi, pp. 160–161.

76. Ōmori, p. 143. *Antara* on January 7, 1966 reported that Burma offered 100,000 tons of rice to Indonesia. These figures, on the whole, are not necessarily reliable.

77. *Asahi Shinbun*, January 19, 1966.

78. *Nihon Keizai Shinbun*, December 29, 1965. Reportedly the overdue debt would increase to $15 million by December 31. The same newspaper on January 9, 1966 reported that by March 1966 the overdue debt, including reparations-secured loans, would be $200 million. The *Asahi Shinbun* on January 19, 1966 said that the trade debt alone was estimated at as $83 million.

79. According to a report by the International Monetary Fund, as of June 1966

Indonesia's total debt was estimated at as $2,353 million, of which the debt to the Communist bloc was $1,336 million. The debt to Japan was estimated here as $224 million. Quoted in Japan, Economic Cooperation Survey Mission to Indonesia, *Indoneshia Keizai Kyōryoku Chōsadan chōsa hōkoku* (Tokyo: Foreign Ministry, 1969), p. 32.

80. *Asahi Shinbun*, January 19, 1966.
81. *Asahi Shinbun*, January 28, 1966.
82. *Asahi Shinbun*, January 28, 1966.
83. *Asahi Shinbun*, January 28, 1966.
84. *Asahi Shinbun*, January 30, 1966.
85. Anonymous, *Indoneshia tsūshin* (mimeographed, Indoneshia Sentā, December 1967), p. 43.
86. Ibid., p. 43.
87. Fujiwara, "Kono me de mita Indoneshia," p. 42.
88. Zenkoku Kakushu Dantai Rengōkai, *Zenkoku kakushu dantai meikan 1972* (Tokyo: Zenkō Sha, 1971), p. 13.
89. Lubis, interview.
90. Nakajima, interview.
91. Anonymous, *Suharuto taisei no mōretsu otoko, Rikugun Shōjō Ari Murutopo* (mimeographed; Tokyo: Indoneshia Sentā, 1971), p. 31.
92. His speech was published as "Tjeramah Menteri Koordinator Pelaksanaan Ekonomi Terpimpin oleh Adam Malik," in *The Leader, The Man and the Gun*, compiled by KAMI (Jakarta: Yayasan Badan Penerbit Fakultas Ekonomi Universitas Indonesia, 1966), not paged.
93. Hayashi, pp. 75–76.
94. Ibid., pp. 76–77.
95. *Asahi Shinbun*, February 26 and March 11, 1966.
96. *Asahi Shinbun*, March 13, 1966.
97. *Asahi Shinbun*, March 13, 1966.
98. *Asahi Shinbun*, March 13, 1966.
99. *Asahi Shinbun*, March 15, 1966.
100. *Asahi Shinbun*, March 24, 1966.
101. *Asahi Shinbun*, March 29, 1966.
102. *Asahi Shinbun*, March 26, 1966.
103. *Asahi Shinbun*, May 11, 1966. As early as April 3, Rukmito arrived in Japan and announced that Indonesia would send an important economic mission to Japan in late April. See *Asahi Shinbun*, April 4, 1966.
104. *Asahi Shunbun*, June 1, 1966.
105. *Asahi Shinbun*, August 9, 1966.

Chapter 9
The Japanese and Sukarno's Indonesia: Summary and Conclusions

This monograph has attempted to analyze the interactions between Japan and Indonesia from 1951–1966, with particular attention given to both governmental and nongovernment levels of interactions. Among the major issues covered were the negotiations over the terms of Japan's war reparations, the allocation of its funds, the Sumatra Rebellion, the West Irian campaign, the confrontation, and the Gestapu affair. In each instance not only intergovernmental communications were discussed but also the roles of private citizens and organizations were examined. Those private citizens included former Japanese military officers, occupation personnel, traders, industrialists, and the wives of President Sukarno, whereas the organizations were the Liberal Democratic party, the Japan Socialist party, the Japan Communist party, the Japan-Indonesia Association, the Indonesian military forces, the Indonesian Nationalist party, the Indonesian Communist party, the Indonesia-Japan Friendship Society, and the Indonesian Students Association (PPI in Tokyo). The individuals were treated primarily as the lobbyists, or informal diplomats, who constituted the Peace Lobby (1951–1957), the reparations lobbies (1958–1966), the Kawashima Lobby (1964–1965), and the anti-Sukarnoist lobby (1955–1966), whereas the organizations were seen as interest groups. The interlocking relations among these individuals, organizations, and governmental ministries demonstrate the importance of the study of nongovernmental contacts. The fifteen-year period of contact between Japan and Indonesia bears witness to the persistent legacy of the Japanese occupation during the Pacific War, particularly in the form of personal bonds between the two peoples and their functions in settling binational conflicts and promoting binational interests.

This period also testifies to the greater dependence of Indonesia upon Japan than of Japan upon Indonesia. Chapter 1 examined this relationship through the statistics of trade, flow of people, and frequency of visits by high-ranking officials. The remaining chapters also substantiate this unbalanced interdependency; the Japanese became involved in the major Indonesian issues such as the Sumatra Rebellion, the West Irian campaign, the confrontation, the Gestapu affair, as well as the reparations issue and the 1945 Proclamation of Independence. But few Indonesians concerned themselves with Japan's domestic political issues. Japan's overwhelming presence in Indonesia in 1972 was symbolically visible in Jakarta's new main street along which were built the 14-story Sarinah Department Store, the 30-story Wisma Nusantara office building,[1] the 14-story Hotel Indonesia, and the 10-story building shared by the Japanese embassy, major Japanese trading companies, the Bank of Tokyo, and Japan Air Lines. All of them were built with Japanese capital, reparations, and otherwise.

Japan and Indonesia have many and various differences that it is difficult to understand their mutual attraction. Climatic conditions, ethnic heterogeneity, religion, colonial experience, and degree of economic development are a few of the factors that differ. The countries' political systems are different: Japan has never had a political party resembling Indonesia's Communist party of three million members, nor such a charismatic leader as Sukarno, and their respective positions in international politics are very different. In evaluating their close relationship, one must weigh the complementary interests of the two countries and the similarity of some values in their political culture.

Japan's interest in an economically viable and politically noncommunist Indonesia was owing to a desire to explore the latter's natural resources, to expand its potentially large market, and to secure a safe oil route through the Strait of Malacca. Four official Japanese positions can best be observed in the light of these interests: (1) Japan's concessions in the reparations negotiations (the inclusion of capital goods as an item of payment and cancellation of Indonesia's trade debt to Japan); (2) the Japanese government's efforts to strengthen Sukarno's domestic position by means of the reparations fund, yielding to Indonesia's protests in the *Karel Doorman* incident and the KLM incident; (3) its attempts to mediate in the confrontation; and (4) Japan's readiness to support the Indonesian military in March 1966. These are not just postwar interests but rather are a continuation of Japan's prewar policy to advance into the south seas when its development of Manchuria became deadlocked. Even after the war many Japanese businessmen and entrepreneurs still thought of Indonesia as a sort of second Manchuria.[2]

Indonesia's postwar interest in Japan began in an atmosphere of indifference and hostility. Its anticolonialist policy considered Japan as an old imperialist nation and also as a defeated nation. However, with the recovery of the Japanese economy and the stagnation of its own in 1957, Indonesia began to view Japan's industrial capability and capital in a different light. It was at this point that the two countries found their national interests complementary. Thus Indonesia reduced its reparations demand from $17.5 billion to $223 million, viewing the payment more as foreign aid than as a war debt. Sukarno took advantage of the reparations fund to promote his "prestige projects" and his doctorines, and Suharto has continued this practice. Despite Indonesia's "active independent policy" swinging from left to right after the abortive coup in 1965, Japanese economic power has always been vital to its economy.

Japanese-Indonesian relations from 1958 to 1965 have often been termed "special," because the two countries have maintained a close relationship despite opposing political positions. Yet this same sort of relationship was established between Peking and Tokyo in September 1972.

Values common to both Japanese and Indonesian political culture have formed another bond. There is, generally, little cultural and ethnic common ground between the two peoples. A study shows that Switzerland and the United States lead those countries favored by the Japanese; all Asian countries appear farther down the list.[3] The Japanese and the Indonesians speak different languages and have different religions. If there is any affinity at all between them, it is the Indonesians' one-sided attraction to the Japanese and their culture. The Indonesians have been more widely exposed to things Japanese than the Japanese have been to things Indonesian. This began soon after the Pacific War broke out, when the Indonesians were forced to encounter the Japanese en masse.[4] Most of them must have felt hostility toward Japan's military conduct, although at this outset of the invasion the army was welcomed because it ousted the colonial power.[5] Later, however, some did develop respect for Japanese discipline and esprit de corps. Kemal Idris, who had gone through tough military training in 1944 under the Japanese officer Yanagawa, related later that he had learned much of the values of sincerity, honesty, and, above all, fighting spirit (*semangat perjuangan*) from this experience.[6] The Indonesians also were taught to like the Japanese through indoctrination by the Japanese military. Twenty years after the end of the Pacific War many Indonesians still talk about what they were forced to learn during the war: "The

Japanese and the Indonesians are 'saudara-saudara' (brothers). The Japanese are older brothers, the Indonesians are younger brothers. We are the same people." Today old Indonesians discuss this partly with cynicism but mostly with nostalgia, while younger Indonesians speak of this relationship mostly with cynicism but also with affection. For all Indonesians, young or old, Japanese commodities are synonymous with high-quality goods. Popular Japanese songs are often hummed and sometimes translated into Indonesian. Japanese movies attract local audiences. One aspect of Indonesian affection toward the Japanese is typified by Sukarno's meetings with former officers during his frequent visits to Tokyo,[7] and another by the popularity among Indonesian men of marrying Japanese women, with Sukarno's marriage to Dewi as the supreme example.[8]

Although most Japanese have little knowledge of and interest in Indonesia, the few who have had contact with Indonesia and the Indonesians have tended to develop a strong affection for the country and its people. Pan-Asianists who visited the Dutch East Indies in the 1930s and 1940s and those Japanese who were moved by their zeal for independence built "comradely friendships" with the Indonesian people.[9] The Japanese soldiers and occupation personnel who were stationed in Indonesia came to like the country, because they were not obliged to fight the Indonesians except in minor, sporadic anti-Japanese incidents occurring toward the end of the Pacific War.[10] They were impressed with the country because strange as it may sound, the country looked richer and more economically advanced than did Japan's rural areas from which most of the soldiers hailed.[11] To these military and civilians Batavia, Bandung, and Surabaya of Java were "little Amster-dams" with hotel and sports facilities for the colonialists, and their well-planned streets and intercity road systems throughout Java must have looked much more sophisticated than their hometowns. Besides, the Japanese were masters over the Indonesians, who procured whatever they wished. Furthermore, when they demobilized and returned home after the war, they found in Japan a bitter contrast to their peaceful life in wartime Indonesia. They suffered from lack of food, housing, and jobs. Senior military officers were affected further by the directive of January 1946 issued by the Supreme Commander for the Allied Powers (SCAP) prohibiting those Japanese responsible for the war from assuming any public office. Their despair must have constantly been intensified by memories of the "good old days" in Indonesia.

It is against this background that many Japanese emerged as "Indonesia experts" and in the postwar period went into the trading business, either privately or with large companies.[12] The reparations lobbies of 1958–1966 are typical of this. This background plus the comradely friendships explain the emergence of binational lobbies such as the Peace Lobby and the anti-Sukarno lobby. Some of the Japanese lobbyists raised funds for their Indonesian counterparts to come to Japan to conduct lobbying activities: Nishijima invited Subardjo and Adam Malik to Tokyo, and Kuhara, Nakajima, and Fukuda maintained contact with Sumitro and the Sumatra Rebellion leaders. The web of personal contacts at the governmental level is exemplified by the cases of Sudjono and Subardjo and of Ambassador Saitō, Shirahata, Kai, and Malik. Both the Japanese and Indonesian cultures value total personal commitment such as that between these lobbyists. The governments of both countries tried to take advantage of this in settling the reparations, allocating funds, mediating the confrontation, and appointing government representatives, particularly ambassadors.

Another cultural similarity between Japan and Indonesia is the practice of personal favoritism and of gratuity or commission. While these are not confined to Japan and Indonesia, they are particularly favored there. As a general social practice Japanese and Indonesians make extensive use of gifts and souvenirs (*omiyage* in Japanese and *oleh-oleh* in Indonesian). When this practice is applied to business transactions, it takes the form of monetary commissions (*orei* or *tesūryō* in Japanese and *komisi* in Indonesian) and personal favoritism. Commissions from business transactions, appointments to important government positions, the biased selection of young men for the reparations fellowships and introductions to influential figures all can be seen in this context. The anticipation of commission seemed to have been a great attraction to the lobbyists for reparations. While the Peace Lobbyists and anti-Sukarno lobbyists were bound by unselfish comradeship, the reparations lobbyists were bound more by selfish contractual relations.

By definition, lobbyists base their activities on their personal ties. However, Asian and Western lobbying practices differ. For the American lobbyist gratuity and favoritism are not only illegal but in many cases are ineffective in the long run for successful lobbying.[13] But for many Japanese and Indonesians they are not only socially acceptable (if illegal) but also often effective. In Japanese and Indonesian societies commissions function as an unofficial way of redistributing wealth and reallocating profits and are a major source of political funds as well. Consequently, while favoritism and payoffs were strong elements joining the two countries during the Sukarno period, they were not unique to this period. As long as there is a cultural base supporting such practices, lobbies such as the reparations lobbies will prevail in the two countries.

Conversely, when a group tried to gain only ideological support without appealing to personal ties, it will not become a lobby but rather an interest group. This was the case with the Sukarnoist group, which was internally disparate with regard to ideological and monetary interests, but whose members clung together for political and business expedience as well as for their shared interest in the Indonesian Revolution and promoting Sukarnoist doctrines. As a result the PPI, the embassy, the PKI, and the Japan Communist party functioned more as interest groups than as lobbies. It will be interesting to see if some of the members of these interest groups, particularly the PPI students, will act as future lobbyists, utilizing the personal ties that they must have developed while in the interest group.

Indonesia's dependence upon Japan economically and culturally brings into question the extent of Japan's responsibility for postwar political developments in Indonesia. In retrospect one may speculate that the Japanese reparations funds that the Kishi government used to prop up the Sukarno regime after early 1958 might have encouraged Sukarno to issue the presidential decree of July 5, 1959, restoring the 1945 constitution and initiating the Guided Democracy period. One may also speculate that the reparations lobbies, including the Kinoshita and Tōnichi trading companies and Dewi, that reportedly gave commissions and gratuities to obtain reparations programs, were partially responsible for the alleged, extensive corruption in the Sukarno government. Japan should be held accountable partly for the failure of reparations projects, many of which were unfinished or inoperable, for it could have offered more technical advice on the feasibility of these projects than was actually given. Further, Japanese Prime Minister Ikeda and the Kawashima Lobby might have contributed to Sukarno's leftist leanings because, although they thought they were wooing Sukarno with a series of credits in competition with China's courting, they actually might have encouraged Sukarno to lean farther toward China since, the closer Indonesia drew to China, the more promises of economic aid it received from Japan. Finally, the popular suspicion of misuse of the reparations funds and Japanese aid, and the popular displeasure over Sukarno's relations with women, including Dewi, added to the anti-Sukarno sentiment, which was accentuated by the 1965 political upheaval. One may argue that, in this sense too, Japan was partly to blame for Sukarno's political downfall. These are only speculations but they remain a focal point of criticism regarding binational relations during the Sukarno period.

In the period from 1951 to late 1960s Japan carried out its diplomatic policy toward Indonesia through moderate means. A close observation of it reveals an important change in quality, occurring about 1962 or 1963, from a moralistic bent to a remunerative one. This change involved both Japan's increased economic dominance over Indonesia and a more confident self-image. Until the early 1960s, the Japanese government suffered from an "atonement complex" caused by Japanese wartime atrocities and the people pictured their country as a lesser power. A short war story entitled *Harp of Burma*, written by Takeyama Michio in 1947, typifies the Japanese feeling of shame for their conduct during the war.[14] *Harp of Burma* is about a Japanese soldier who fought in Burma and decided to become a Buddhist monk there. While all of his colleagues were happily returning home after the war, the monk gathered up the dead bodies of Japanese and other soldiers, cremated them, and put their ashes into urns. The fact that this short story, originally written for primary school children, became a best seller and was made into a film is evidence of the prevailing feeling of regret among the Japanese for their wartime conduct in Asia. Coinciding with this sentiment was the popular image of Japan as a small, weak nation. The *Asahi Shinbun* on September 27, 1948, discussed the role of Japan as a small nation with respect to world peace in an editorial. Then as Japan's economic recovery accelerated, the same newspaper of October 11, 1960 editorialized about Japan's role in the world as "a medium-sized power."[15] This moderate or reserved self-image changed to that of "a big-power Japan" after about 1962. It was Prime Minister Ikeda Hayato, among others, who convinced the Japanese people that Japan was economically a big power.[16] In this period both Japanese and foreign observers began to talk about the resurgence of Japanese nationalism. Using the lure of trade credits, Ikeda, Kawashima, and Satō made positive efforts in mediating in Indonesia's confrontation policy against Malaysia. This promise of remuneration symbolized the change from the tactic of moralistic persuasion used prior to the early 1960s.

Indonesia's diplomatic policy toward Japan for the same period was more drastic. This can be seen in Jakarta's first reparations demand of $17.5 billion in 1951–1955, and its threat to restrict Japan's trading activities and the entry of Japanese nationals into Indonesia in 1956 during the reparations negotiations. It can also be seen in similar threatening moves to boycott Japanese goods and to break off economic relations with Japan over the *Karel Doorman*'s planned visit to a Japanese port in 1960 and the KLM flights to Tokyo in 1962. Indonesia's un-yielding diplomatic attitude became more conspicious after 1963 in its confrontation policy against Malaysia, the government-sponsored demonstrations against the American and British embassy buildings, seizure of their estates, and the withdrawal from the UN.

Sukarno's uncompromising posture on foreign issues toward the end of his tenure stemmed largely from his strong self-pride and, more basically, his small-nation complex. This complex may continue to manifest itself in future relations between Indonesia and other countries; and so far as Japanese-Indonesian relations are concerned, Japan's increasing dominance over the Indonesian economy may aggravate Indonesia's subordinate-nation complex. The use of the Strait of Malacca for Japan's oil imports from the Middle East, fishing concessions in the Java seas, lumber concessions in Kalimantan and Sumatra, oil concessions in Sumatra and off the coasts of Java and Kalimantan, textile and paper mills, as well as the wide use of Japanese consumer goods might make Japan Indonesia's scapegoat if the latter's economy fails to improve in the future.[17] Yet if the two peoples find their national interests complementary and their cultural values mutually acceptable, and if Indonesia's economic development efforts prove rewarding, the unbalanced interdependency between the two countries may lead to a healthier phase in Tokyo-Jakarta interactions.

NOTES

1. It originally began as a 29-story building under the reparations program. When the unfinished project was resumed in 1971, it added another floor on the top of the previous structure, thus making it a 30-story building.

2. Ishihara Hiroichirō is known to have wished to lease oil-rich central Sumatra in exchange of his responsible development of the whole area for city planning as well as mine-exploring. In the 1920s the Japanese began to develop cotton estates in West New Guinea. In 1930 there were 1,299 Japanese settlers. However, the Dutch East Indies became sensitive about the growing Japanese migration to the islands and began after 1932 to restrict their number. As a result the number of Japanese settlers in 1938 decreased to 608. The possibility of Japanese lease of West New Guinea was deliberated in the Imperial Diet in February 1937. See Taniguchi Gorō, *Nishi Irian* (Asahi Shinbun Research Office report for internal use no. 99; mimeographed, July 1962), pp. 8–9. It was reported in 1954 that business groups in Osaka proposed that the Japanese government buy the whole of New Guinea for $3 billion from the Netherlands and Australia. See Indonesia, Foreign Ministry, *Pewarta Kemulu* 1 (1955): 190. When President Suharto visited Japan in May 1972, a rumor grew that the Japanese Federation of Economic Organizations proposed that Japan would lease West Irian for $15 billion as partial means of reducing Japan's foreign reserve surplus and assisting Indonesia's economic development. Shimonaka Yasaburō entertained the idea of moving the Indonesian capital from the heat-ridden Jakarta to a cool mountainous area in Kalimantan and of spurring large-scale development of Kalimantan, which, he suggested, Japanese migrants could assist. See Shimonaka Yasaburō Memoirs Committee, ed., *Shimonaka Yasaburō jiten* (Tokyo: Heibon Sha, 1965), p. 21.

3. Hayashi Chikio, et al., *Zusetsu Nihonjin no kokuminsei* (Tokyo: Shiseidō, 1965), p. 158.

4. The Sixteenth Army landed 55,000 troops in Java in March 1942. See Masuda Atō, *Indoneshia gendaishi* (Tokyo: Chūō Kōron Sha, 1971), p. 148.

5. Koentjaraningrat, "Indonesian Images of Japan," *International House of Japan Bulletin*, no. 24 (October 1969): 1–23.

6. Benedict R. O. Anderson, *Java in a Time of Revolution* (Ithaca, N.Y.: Cornell University Press, 1972), pp. 22–23.

7. During his first visit to Japan in 1958 Sukarno had a reunion with Vice-admiral Maeda Tadashi, head of the navy's Jakarta Liaison Office. See *Asahi Shinbun*, February 15, 1958. During his 1961 visit Sukarno met with Yamamoto Moichirō, chief of staff of the Sixteenth Army, Imamura Hitoshi, commander of the same army, and Maeda. See *Antara*, June 27 and 29, 1961.

8. Many of the students and youths who had come to study in Japan under the reparations fellowship returned with Japanese wives. Many of the wives joined the Nadeshiko Club.

9. Masuda, pp. 115–147.

10. One such incident is the so-called Blitar incident of February 14, 1945 when the PETA officers revolted against their Japanese officers. See Nugroho Notosusanto, *Pemberontakan Tentara PETA Blitar Melawan Djepang* (Jakarta: Department of Defense and Security, 1968).

11. See, for instance, Kuroda Hidetoshi, *Gunsei* (Tokyo: Gakufū Shoin, 1952), pp. 80–83; and Machida Keiji, *Tatakau bunka butai* (Tokyo: Hara Shobō, 1967), pp. 113–254.

12. Most of the trading companies that they formed by themselves were small in size and obscure and failed before too long. Those who entered large firms such as Mitsui and Mitsubishi tended to have a more stable life, but many of them served as public relations men rather than businessmen.

13. Lester W. Milbrath, "Lobbying," in *International Encyclopedia of the Social Sciences*, ed. by David L. Sills (27 vols.; N.Y.: Macmillan Co. and The Free Press, 1968), 9, p. 445.

14. The story originally appeared in a series in a children's magazine *Akatonbo* from 1946 to 1947. Several publishers reprinted it in book form since 1948. It won several prizes and was used in a textbook too. Shinchō Sha published it in 1959 and by 1967 it achieved its 25th printing. It was translated into English in 1966 as *Harp of Burma* (Rutland, Vt.; C. E. Tuttle Co., 1966).

15. Japan's Welfare Ministry issued a 1957 white paper in which it evaluated Japan's welfare conditions and rated Japan as a "half-advanced nation." See its *Kōsei hakusho 1957* (Tokyo: Ōkurashō Insatsukyoku, 1958), p. 18.

16. *Asahi Shinbun* of November 15, 1963 warned of Ikeda's boast of Japan as a big power. It maintained that Japan might well remain as a small power but that its people should be a great people.

17. "Yellow Yankees" and "ugly Japanese" are in increasing use. See for instance Tokuoka Takao, *Ierō Yankī* (Tokyo: Ēru Sha, 1970).

Bibliography

BOOKS

Aidit, D. N. *Atarashii Indoneshia* [The new Indonesia]. Translated by the Japan Communist party. Tokyo: Shin Nihon Shuppan Sha, 1958.

Anderson, Benedict R. O. *Java in a Time of Revolution*. Ithaca, N.Y.: Cornell University Press, 1972.

——. *Some Aspects of Indonesian Politics under the Japanese Occupation: 1944– 1945*. Ithaca, N.Y.: Modern Indonesia Project, Cornell University, 1961.

Asian-African People's Solidarity Organization. Japan Committee. *Indoneshia kakumei:chi no kyōkun* [The Indonesian revolution: a lesson by blood]. Tokyo: Tōhō Shoten, 1967.

Bahri, Saiful. *Skandal sex Sukarno* [Sukarno's sex scandals]. Kuala Lumpur: Perchetakan Wah Liau, 1968.

Bartlett, Anderson G., III. *Pertamina, Indonesian National Oil*. Jakarta: Amerasian Ltd., 1972.

Benda, Harry, Jr. *The Crescent and the Rising Sun*. The Hague: van Hoeve, 1958.

Boyce, Peter, ed. *Malaysia and Singapore in International Diplomacy: Documents and Commentaries*. Sydney: Sydney University Press, 1968.

Brackman, Arnold C. *The Communist Collapse in Indonesia*. New York: W. W. Norton & Co., 1969.

Conde, David. *Indoneshia no henbō* [Indonesia's invisible coup]. Translated by Kasahara Yoshio. Tokyo: Kōbundō, 1966.

Daiyamondo Sha. *Nippon Kōei* [Nippon Kōei company]. Tokyo: Daiyamondo Sha, 1971.

Douglas, Stephen A. *Political Socialization and Student Activitism in Indonesia*. Urbana, Ill: University of Illinois Press, 1970.

Feith, Herbert. *The Decline of Constitutional Democracy in Indonesia*. Ithaca, N.Y.: Cornell University Press, 1962.

Fujiwara Hirotatsu, et al. *Hadaka no Devi fujin* [Madame Dewi unmasked]. Tokyo: Yagumoi Shoin, 1970.

Fujiwara Iwaichi. *F Kikan* [The F(ujiwara Intelligence) Agency]. Tokyo: Hara Shobō, 1966. Reprinted as *Fujiwara Kikan* (Tokyo: Hara Shobō, 1970), and as *Daihon'ei no misshi* [A secret emissary from the Imperial General Headquarters] (Tokyo: Banchō Shobō, 1972).

Gullick, J.M. *Malaysia and Its Neighbours*. New York: Barnes & Noble, 1967.

Hatakeyama Seikō. *Hiroku Rikugun Nakano Gakkō* [A secret account of the Army Nakano (Intelligence) School]. Tokyo: Banchō Shobō, 1971.

Hayashi Chikio, et al. *Zusetsu: Nihonjin no kokuminsei* [An illustrated report: the national character of the Japanese]. Tokyo: Shiseidō, 1965.

Hayashi Risuke. *Urotaeruna Nihon* [Keep calm, Japan!]. Tokyo: Jitsugyō no Nihon Sha, 1972.

220   *The Japanese and Sukarno's Indonesia*

Hindley, Donald. *The Communist Party of Indonesia, 1956–1963.* Berkeley: University of California Press, 1964.

Hughes, John. *Indonesian Upheaval.* New York: McKay, 1967.

Ide Anak Agung Gde Agung. *Twenty Years Indonesian Foreign Policy, 1945–1965.* The Hague: Mouton, 1974.

Indoneshia gendai seijishi [Contemporary political history of Indonesia]. Tokyo: Indoneshia Sentā, 1969. (Mimeographed.)

Indonesian Communist Party. *Yakushinsuru hyaku-gojū-man no Kyōsantō* [The 1,500,000-member Communist party on the march]. Translated by the Japan Communist party. Tokyo: Nihon Kyōsantō, 1960.

Itagaki Yoichi. *Ajia to no taiwa* [A dialogue with Asia]. Tokyo: Shin Kigen Sha, 1968.

Itō Masaya. *Ikeda Yahato, sono sei to shi* [Ikeda Hayato, his life and death]. Tokyo: Shiseidō, 1966.

Jones, Howard P. *Indonesia: The Possible Dream.* New York: Harcourt Brace Jovanovich, Inc., 1971.

Kahin, George McT. *The Asia-African Conference, Bandung, Indonesia, April 1955.* Ithaca, N.Y.: Cornell University Press, 1956.

Kajima Morinosuke. *Nihon no gaikō, kako to genzai* [Japanese diplomacy, past and present]. Tokyo: Kajima Kenkyūjo Shuppankai, 1967.

Kajiyama Toshiyuki. *Ikenie* [A living tribute (to Sukarno)]. Tokyo: Tokuma Shoten, 1967.

Kawashima Shōjirō Memoirs Publishing Committee. *Kawashima Shōjirō.* Tokyo: Kōyū Kurabu, 1972.

Kikawata Sakei. *Gunkokushugi to Nihon keizai* [Militarism and Japan's economy]. Tokyo: San'ichi Shobō, 1971.

Kinoshita Hanji. *Uyoku tero* [Right-wing terrorism]. Kyoto: Hōritsu Bunka Sha, 1960.

Kishi Kōichi, et al. *Indonesia ni okeru Nihon gunsei no kenkyū* [A study of the Japanese military administration in Indonesia]. Tokyo: Kinokuniya Shoten, 1959.

Kitagawa Mamoru. *Tokyo, onna supai* [Tokyo, female spies]. Tokyo: Sankei Shinbun Sha, 1970.

Kobayashi Kazuhiko. *Ajia o kakeru otoko* [A man (Iwata Yoshio) hustling around Asia]. Tokyo: Kokusai Kaihatsu Jānaru Sha, 1972.

Kunitō Yoshimasa. *Seishō makari tōru* [political brokers' swagger]. Tokyo: Akita Shoten, 1966.

Kurahara Korehito. *Indoneshia kikō* [An account of (my) Indonesian trip]. Tokyo: Shin Nihon Shuppan Sha, 1964.

Kuroda Hidetoshi. *Gunsei* [The military administration]. Tokyo: Gakufū Shoin, 1952.

Kusayanagi Taizō. *Shin: jitsuryokusha no jōken* [Criteria for men of power: a new version]. Tokyo: Bungei Shunjū Sha, 1972.

Lebra, Joyce C. *Chandora Bōsu to Nihon* ["The jungle alliance"]. Translated by Horie Yoshitaka. Tokyo: Hara Shobō, 1968.

Lev, Daniel. *Transition to Guided Democracy.* Ithaca, N.Y.: Modern Indonesia

Project, Cornell University, 1966.

Machida Keiji. *Tatakau bunka butai* [Cultural troops (i.e., propaganda teams) in the battlefield]. Tokyo: Hara Shobō, 1967.

Mackie, J. A. C. *Confrontation; The Indonesia-Malaysia Dispute.* Oxford: Oxford University Press, 1973

Malik, Adam. *Riwajat dan Perdjuangan Sekitar Proklamasi Kemerdekaan Indonesia, 17 Augustus 1945* [The story and the struggle of Indonesia's Proclamation of Independence, August 17, 1945]. Jakarta: Widjaya, 1970.

Matsunaga Monzaemon Memoirs Publishing Committee. *Matsunaga Monzaemon ō no omoide.* 3 vols. Tokyo: Chūō Kenkyūjo, 1963.

Masuda Atō. *Indoneshia gendaishi* [Contemporary history of Indonesia]. Tokyo: Chūō Kōron Sha, 1971.

McVey, Ruth and Anderson, Benedict R.O. *A Preliminary Analysis of the October 1, 1965, Coup in Indonesia.* Ithaca, N.Y.: Modern Indonesia Project, Cornell University, 1971.

Mossman, James. *Rebels in Paradise.* London: Jonathan Cape, 1961.

Murofushi Tetsurō. *Oshoku no susume* [An argument in favor of corruption]. Tokyo: Kōbundō, 1963.

Nagatsuka Toshikazu. *Kubota Yutaka 1966* [Kubota Yutaka 1966]. Tokyo: Denki Jōhō Sha, 1966.

Nakazono Eisuke. *Missho* [Secret documents]. Tokyo: Kōbun Sha, 1964.

Nihon Keizai Shinbun Sha, ed. *Wakakushi no rirekisho* [My personal history]. 36 vols. Tokyo: Nihon Keizai Shinbun Sha, 1957–1969.

Nugroho Notosusanto. *Pemberontakan Tentara PETA Blitar Melawan Djepang* [The revolt of the Blitar PETA forces against Japan]. Jakarta: Department of Defense and Security, 1968.

——— and Saleh, Ismail. *The Coup Attempt of the "September 30 Movement" in Indonesia.* Jakarta: Pembimbing Masa, 1968.

Obata Shin'ichi. *Seikai issun saki wa yami* [The political world one inch ahead is dark]. Tokyo: Kōho Sha, 1972.

Oku Genzō. *Indoneshia no kakumei* [The revolution in Indonesia]. Tokyo: Ushio Shuppan Sha, 1966.

Olson, Lawrence. *Japan in Postwar Asia.* London: Pall Mall Press for the Council on Foreign Relations, 1970.

Ōmori Minoru. *Sekai no seijika enmachō* [Evaluations of world leaders]. Tokyo: Bungei Shunjū Sha, 1967.

———. *Sukaruno saigo no shinsō* [The truth behind Sukarno's downfall]. Tokyo: Shinchō Sha, 1967.

Reparations Problems Study Group [Baishō Mondai Kenkyūkai]. *Nihon no baishō 1963* [Japan's reparations 1963]. Tokyo: Sekai Jānaru Sha, 1963.

Sakata Zenzaburō. *Indoneshia: genjō to mondaiten* [Indonesia: present conditions and problems]. Tokyo: Federation of Economic Organizations (Keidanren), 1968.

Shimonaka Yasaburō Biography Publishing Committee. *Shimonaka Yasaburō jiten* [A (biographical) dictionary of Shimonaka Yasaburō]. Tokyo: Heibon Sha, 1965.

Simon, Sheldon W. *The Broken Triangle: Peking, Jakarta, and the PKI*. Baltimore, Md.: The Johns Hopkins University Press, 1969.

Social Problems Study Group [Shakai Mondai Kenkyūkai]. *Uyoku jiten* [A dictionary of the right-wing (groups)]. Tokyo: Futaba Sha, 1971.

Suharuto taisei no mōretsu otoko: Rikugun Shōjō Ari Murutopo [A hard-working man in the Suharto regime: Army Major General Ali Murtopo]. Tokyo: Indoneshia Sentā, 1971. (Mimeographed.)

Sugimori Hisahide. *Arabiya Tarō* ["Arabian" (Yamashita) Tarō]. Tokyo: Bungei Shunjū Sha, 1960.

Sukarno. *Sukarno: An Autobiography as Told to Cindy Adams*. Indianapolis, Ind.: The Bobbs-Merrill Co., 1965.

———. *Waga kakumei no saihakken* [My rediscovery of revolution]. Translated by Okakura Koshirō. Tokyo: Riron Sha, 1962.

Suryadharma, Mahabrata. *Sukarno di-tengah2 Wanita* [Sukarno among women]. Kuala Lumpur: Penerbitan Pustaka Sari, 1967.

Takeda Shigesaburō, ed. *Jagatara kanwa* [Remniscences of Java]. Nagasaki: By the editor, 1968.

Takeyama Michio. *Biruma no tategoto* [Harp of Burma]. Tokyo: Shinchō Sha, 1959.

———. *Harp of Burma*. Translated by Howard Hibbet. Rutland, Vt.: C. E. Tuttle Co., 1966.

Tokuoka Takao. *Ierō Yankī* [Yellow Yankees]. Tokyo: Ēru Sha, 1970.

Tsūshō Sangyō Chōsakai [International Trade and Industry Research Council]. *Sengo Nihon no bōeki nijūnenshi* [A history of twenty years of postwar Japanese trade]. Tokyo: Tsūshō Sangyō Chōsakai, 1967.

Umemoto Sutezō. *Nihon daibōryaku senshi* [A history of Japan's great wartime intelligence activities]. Tokyo: Keizai Ōrai Sha, 1971.

Weinstein, Frank B. *Indonesia Abandons Confrontation*. Ithaca, N.Y.: Modern Indonesia Project, Cornell University, 1969.

Yanagawa Tomoshige. *Rikugun chōhōin Yanagawa Chūi* [Lieutenant Yanagawa: army intelligence officer]. Tokyo: Sankei Shinbun Sha, 1967.

ARTICLES

"A-A shokoku jinmin to no rentai kyōka no tame ni" [In favor of strengthening solidarity with the Afro-Asian peoples]. *Gekkan Shakaitō* (July, 1965): 36–43.

Abdulgani, Roeslan. "Indonesia's National Council, The First Year." *Far Eastern Survey* 27 (July 1958): 97–104.

Arifin, Marzuki. "Orang2 Indonesia di Djepang" [Indonesians in Japan]. *Harian Kami* (April 18 and 19, 1967).

"BAMUNAS Alat Manipulasi Sukarno" [BAMUNAS as a tool for Sukarno's manipulation]. *Harian Kami* (February 28, 1967).

"Devi fujin no kage no otoko 'Kirishima Masaya' no tōjō" [The rise of the man behind Madame Dewi: 'Kirishima Masaya']. *Shūkan Shinchō* (January 6, 1968): 36–38.

Dewi, Ratna Sari. "Daitōryō fujin e no ketsubetsu" [A farewell to being the First Lady]. *Shūkan Gendai*, December 11, 1969, pp. 44–49; December 25, pp. 118–122; January 1, 1970, pp. 84–89; January 8/15, pp. 80–85; and January 22, pp. 64–69. A major portion this six-part series article was translated into Indonesian in *Indonesia Raya* (January 24–March 18, 1970).

———. "Tjatatan Nj. Dewi Sukarno: Sekitar Insiden 30 Sept '65" [Notes by Madame Dewi Sukarno: about the incident of September 30, 1965]. *Harian Kami* (October 12–14, 1966).

———. "Tjatatan Pribadi Dewi" [Personal notes by Dewi]. *Indonesia Raya* (March 12, 1970).

Fujishima Udai. "Kishi Nobusuke shi ni okeru 'sensō hanzai' no kenkyū" [A study of 'war criminal' as applied to Mr. Kishi Nobusuke's case]. *Ushio* (July 1972): 318–325.

Fujiwara Iwaichi. "Kono me de mita Indoneshia seihen no uchimaku" [The inside story of Indonesia's political changes as I saw them]. *Shūkan Bunshun* (April 4, 1966): 38–42.

Gordon, Bernard K. "The Potential for Indonesian Expansionism." *Pacific Affairs* 36 (Winter 1963–1964): 378–393.

Hindley, Donald. "Indonesia's Confrontation with Malaysia: Search for Motives." *Asian Survey* 4 (June 1964): 904–913.

Honda Masaharu. "Kajima Morinosuke ikka" [The Kajima Morinosuke family]. *Bungei Shunjū* (August 1972): 248–262.

Ide Jun'ichirō. "Indoneshia Kyōsantō no tō kensetsu ni manabu" [Emulating the construction of the Indonesian Communist party]. *Zen'ei*, no. 200 (August 1962): 54–62.

"Indoneshia no Kokuren dattai" [Indonesian's withdrawal from the United Nations]. *Zen'ei*, no. 233 (March 1965): 131–137.

Ishii Isamu. "Ajia no Nihonjin wa minikui ka" [Are the Japanese in Asia ugly?]. *Bungei Shunjū* (August 1970): 236–244.

"Iwayuru 'baishō oshoku' no arasuji" [A synopsis of the so-called 'reparations corruption'], *Ekonomisuto* (February 14, 1959): 24–25.

Kahin, George McT. "Malaysia and Indonesia." *Pacific Affairs* 37 (Fall 1964): 253–270.

Kajiyama Toshiyuki. "Shūbun ni irodorareta Devi fujin hiroku" [A secret and scandalous account of Madame Dewi]. *Yangu Redi* (March 31, 1966): 146–153.

Kakijima Yoshitaka. "Indoneshia no '9:30 jiken' wa Nihon Kyōsantō ni donoyōna eikyō o motarasu de arō ka" [What kind of influence will Indonesia's 'September 30 incident' exert upon the Japan Communist party?]. *Kōan Jōhō*, no. 148 (January 1966): 18–31.

"Kita Sumatora sekiyu o gyūjiru otoko" [The man (Nishijima Shigetada) who controls North Sumatra's oil]. *Jitsugyō no Sekai* (April 1965): 96–101.

Kiyama Kazuo (Nishijima Shigetada). "Ajia rōninden: Yoshizumi Tomegorō" [The masterless Asian samurai: Yoshizumi Tomegorō]. *Shisō no Kagaku* (September 1954): 59–68.

Koentjaraningrat. "Indonesian Images of Japan." *International House of Japan Bulletin*, no. 24 (October 1969): 1–23.

Kurahara Korehito. "Indoneshia Kyōsantō taikai no bunken kara nani o manabu ka" [What is to be learned from the literature from the Indonesian Communist party congress?]. *Akahata* (July 6, 1962).

————. "Indoneshia no minzoku tōitsu sensen" [Indonesia's united national front]. *Zen'ei*, no. 200 (August 1962): 47–53.

Lie Tek-tjeng. "An Indonesian Perspective: Japanese-Indonesian Relations in the Seventies." *International House of Japan Bulletin*, no. 28 (October 1971): 23–46.

Lubis, Mochtar. " 'Indonesia Lobby' di Tokyo" ['The Indonesia Lobby' in Tokyo]. *Indonesia Raya* (March 31, April 1, and April 2, 1970).

Malik, Adam. "Tjeramah Menteri Koordinator Pelaksanaan Ekonomi Terpimpin oleh Adam Malik" [A presentation by the Coordinating Minister for the Implementation of Guided Economy by Adam Malik]. *The Leader, The Man and The Gun*. Compiled by KAMI and University of Indonesia Faculty of Economics. Jakarta: Yayasan Badan Penerbit Fakultas Ekonomi Universitas Indonesia, 1966. (Mimeographed.)

Maruyama Kunio. "Kajima Morinosuke: butsuyoku, meiyoyoku, kenseiyoku no sankan ō" [Kajima Morinosuke: the king with three-pointed crown of desires for possessions, fame, and power]. *Gendai no Me* (May 1965): 164–168.

Masuda Atō. "Ajia no shōrai to Nihon" [Asia's future and Japan]. *Ajia Nōgyō 2*, no. 2 (1968): 24–30.

Matsunaga Yasuzaemon. "Isai, Ayukawa san" [A great talent: Mr. Ayukawa]. *Ayukawa Gisuke sensei tsuisōroku* [Recollections of Mr. Ayukawa Gisuke]. Compiled by the Ayukawa Memoirs Publishing Committee. Tokyo: Ayukawa Memoirs Publishing Committee, 1968.

"Mengapa Ibnu Sutowo Turunkan Harga Minjak ke Djepang?" [Why did Ibnu Sutowo lower the price of oil for Japan?] *Indonesia Raya* (December 26, 1969).

Milbrath, Lester W. "Lobbying." *International Encyclopedia of the Social Sciences*. Edited by David L. Sills. Vol. IX. N.Y.: Macmillan Co. and The Free Press, 1968, pp. 441–445.

Miyoshi Shunkichirō, "Jawa senryō gunsei kaikoroku" [Recollections of the military administration in Java]. *Kokusai Mondai* (April 1965–January 1967).

Mogi Masa. "Tōnan Ajia no munazoko" [The inner heart of Southeast Asia]. *Asahi Jānaru* (April 4, 1965): 12–19.

Nakamura Kōji. "The Samurai Spirit." *Far Eastern Economic Review* (October 16, 1971): 22–25.

Nakatani Yoshio. "Ko Sukaruno Daitōryō to watakushi" [The late President Sukarno and I]. *Indoneshia Bungaku*, no. 3 (1972): 61–68.

"Neagari machigai nashi no Devi fujin no 'Kawashima Shōjirō kaisōroku' " [The guaranteed sale of a 'Remniscences of Kawashima Shōjirō' by Madame Dewi]. *Shūkan Posuto* (November 27, 1970): 48–50.

"Nihon no gaikō, minkan no hitobito: Nishijima Shigetada shi" [Japanese diplomacy (carried out by), nongovernmental people: Mr. Nishijima Shigetada]. *Sankei Jiji* (April 8, 1958).

Ōda Takio. "Kokoro no atatakai shin no ningen—Sukaruno shi o itamu" [Mourning a truely warm-hearted man: Mr. Sukarno]. *Nihon Keizai Shinbun* (June 22, 1970).

Oka Masayoshi. "Miyamoto Mōtakutō kaidan no uchimaku" [The inside story of the Miyamoto-Mao Tse-tung conference]. *Nihon Kyōsantō honbu: kokode nani ga okonawarete iruka* [The Japan Communist party headquarters: What is taking place here?]. Edited by the Institute of Ideological Movement Studies [Shisō Undō Kenkyūjo]. Tokyo: Zenbō Sha, 1967.

Pauker, Guy. "The Role of the Military in Indonesia." *The Role of the Military in Underdeveloped Countries*. Edited by John J. Johnson. Princeton, N. J. Princeton University Press, 1962.

"Permina Beli Kapal Selalu Lewat 'Broker'—Tunas Ltd. dan Kinoshita Beli Lagi dari Orang Lain" [PERMINA always buys ships through the 'brokers' Tunas Ltd. and Kinoshita who have bought (them) from somebody else]. *Indonesia Raya* (December 31, 1969).

Rosihan Anwar. "Some Observations on the Promotion of Japanese-Indonesian Cultural Relations." *International House of Japan Bulletin*, no. 28 (October 1971): 47–59.

Saga Sen. "Kuromaku Kodama Yoshio" [The man behind the scene: Kodama Yoshio]. *Hōseki* (February. 1966): 252–271.

"Seishō tōjō" [The rise of political brokers]. *Asahi Shinbun* (March 10, 1959).

Soewarso, J. M. Anton. "Politik Bebas Aktif" [Active, independent policy]. *Research Publikasi* 1, no. 1 (1969): 12–14.

Subardjo, Ahmad. "Indonesia's Contribution to World Peace." *Indonesian Review* 1, no. 5 (1951): 359–362.

"Sugao no Indoneshia" [Indonesia as it is (as told by Nishijima Shigetada)]. *Mainichi Shinbun* (November 16, 18, 19, 20, 21, 22, 23, 26, and 27, 1969).

"Sukaruno o megutta Nihonjin" [The Japanese who knew Sukarno]. *Shūkan Shinchō* (April 2, 1966): 36–40.

"Sumatora e no kyōshū" [Nostalgia for Sumatra]. *Mainichi Shinbun* (July 31, 1959).

Sutter, John O. "Two Faces of *Konfrontasi*: 'Crush Malaysia' and the *Gestapu*." *Asian Survey* 6 (October 1966): 523–546.

Takagi Hiroichi. "Indoneshia to Nihon no keizai kyōryoku" [Economic cooperation between Indonesia and Japan]. *Kokusai Jihyō*, no. 79 (November 1971): 48–49.

Takasaki Tatsunosuke. "Ajia no han'ei to Nihon no unmei" [Asia's prosperity and Japan's destiny]. *Chūō Kōron* (January 1958): 105–109.

Takasugi Shin'ichi. "Attitude of Japanese Business Circles toward Economic Cooperation to Indonesia." *Keidanren Review*, no. 8 (March 1968): 7–11.

Togawa Sachio. "Showa kaijintan, shishi Yoshizumi Tomegorō" [The story of a brilliant man in the Shōwa Period: The loyalist Yoshizumi Tomegorō]. *Bessatsu Bungei Shunjū* (September 1963): 192–210.

"Yanagawa, Bapak PETA" [Yanagawa (Tomoshige), father of PETA]. *Berita Yudha* (October 13, 14, and 15, 1970).

PUBLIC DOCUMENTS, REPORTS, REFERENCES, UNPUBLISHED
WORKS, ETC.

Antara. *Antara Ichtisar* [A summary of Antara (news)]. Jakarta. 1963–1968.
Asahi Shinbun Sha. *Asahi nenkan* [Asahi almanac]. Tokyo. 1950–1972.
Australia. Ministry of External Affairs. *Current Notes on International Affairs*.
   Canberra. 1953–1970.
Bōei Sangyō Kyōkai [Defense Industry Association], ed. *Jieitai nenkan* [Self-
   Defense Forces' almanac]. Tokyo: Bōei Sangyō Kyōkai. 1961–1971.
Indoneshia tsūshin [Indonesian news]. Tokyo: Indoneshia Sentā, 1967. (Mimeo-
   graphed.)
Indonesia. Army. Information Center. *Fakta2 Persoalan Sekitar "Gerakan 30
   September"* [Facts of the problems concerning the "September 30 Move-
   ment"]. Jakarta: The Army, n.d.
———. Justice Education Office. *G-30-S dihadapan Mahmillub di Djakarta
   (Perkara Dr. Subandrio)* [The September 30 Movement tried before the
   Special Military Tribunal in Djakarta (the case of Dr. Subandrio)]. 2 vols.
   Jakarta: Pembimbing Masa, 1967.
———. Attorney General. *Proses Peradilan Jusuf Muda Dalam* [The court process
   in Jusuf Muda Dalam's case]. Jakarta: Pembimbing Masa, 1967.
———. Bank of Indonesia. *Indonesian Financial Statistics, December 1970*.
———. *Report for the Years 1955–1956*.
———. *Report for the Years 1959–1960*.
———. *Report for the Years 1960–1965*.
———. Central Bureau of Statistics. *Statistical Pocketbook of Indonesia 1968–1969*.
———. *Almanak Indonesia 1968* [Indonesian almanac 1968].
Indonesia. Department of Foreign Affairs. *Asia-Africa Speaks from Bandung*.
   Jakarta: n.p. 1955 [?].
———. *Dua Puluh Lima Tahun Departemen Luar Negeri 1945–1970* [Twenty-five
   years of the Department of Foreign Affairs, 1945–1970]. Jakarta: Yayasan
   Kesejahteraan Karyawan Deplu, 1971.
———. *Kumpulan Bahan2 Mengenai Masalah "Malaysia"* [Collected materials on
   the "Malaysia" issue]. 24 vols. 1963–1966. (Mimeographed.)
———. *Pewarta Kemlu* [Bulletin of the Ministry of Foreign Affairs]. 1954–1960.
———. *RUU Persetudjuan Perdjandjian Perdamaian dan Persetudjuan Pampasan
   antara Republik Indonesia dan Djepang* [Bills for the agreement of the peace
   treaty and reparations between the Republic of Indonesia and Japan].
   December 18, 1957.
———. Research Bureau. *Hubungan Indonesia dengan Negara-Negara 1963* [Indo-
   nesia's relations with (foreign) countries, 1963]. 1964 (?). (Mimeographed.)
———. *Research Publikasi* [Research reports]. 1969–1971.
———. Department of Information. *Gelora Konfrontasi Mengganjang "Malaysia"*
   [The storm of confrontation against "Malaysia"]. Jakarta: Department
   of Information, 1964.
———. *Kami Perkenalkan...!* [We introduce...]. Jakarta: Department of
   Information, 1954.

————. *Susunan Kabinet 1945–1970* [The composition of the cabinets, 1945–1970]. Jakarta: Pradnja Paramita, 1970.

————. *The Treaty of Peace and the Reparations Agreement concluded between Indonesia and Japan.* Special Release no. 2, 1958.

————. Embassy, Tokyo. *Laporan Tahunan* [Annual report]. Tokyo. 1957–1969. (Mimeographed.)

Indonesia. House of Representatives (DPR). *Risalah Sementara* [Provisional compilation (of parliamentary proceedings)]. 1958.

Japan. Bank of Japan. *Hundred-Year Statistics of the Japanese Economy.* Tokyo: Bank of Japan, 1966.

————. Economic Cooperation Survey Mission to Indonesia. *Indoneshia Keizai Kyōryoku Chōsadan chōsa hōkoku* [A survey report of the Economic Cooperation Survey Mission to Indonesia]. Tokyo: Economic Cooperation Bureau, Ministry of Foreign Affairs, 1969.

————. Economic Planning Agency. *Keizai yōran* [Economic survey]. Tokyo: Ōkurashō Insatsukyoku. 1966–1972.

————. Economic Stabilization Board. *Indoneshia sangyō shinkō taisaku* [Policies to promote Indonesian industries]. Tokyo: Economic Stabilization Board, 1951.

————. Ministry of Finance Printing Office. *Shokuinroku* [Japanese official roster]. Tokyo: Ōkurashō Insatsukyoku. 1952–1970.

————. Ministry of Foreign Affairs, ed. *Gaimushō no hyakunen* [One hundred years of the Ministry of Foreign Affairs]. 2 vols. Tokyo: Hara Shobō, 1969.

————. *Gaimushō shokuinroku 1940* [Foreign Affairs Ministry roster, 1940].

————. *Gaimushō shokuinroku 1941.*

————. *Waga gaikō no kinkyō* [The recent state of our (Japan's) diplomacy]. 1957–1971.

————. Asian Affairs Bureau. *Indoneshia Kyōwakoku benran* [A handbook on the Republic of Indonesia]. Tokyo: Nihon Kokusai Mondai Kenkyūjo, 1960, 1964.

————. Economic Affairs Bureau, ed. *Indoneshia* [Indonesia]. Tokyo: Nihon Kokusai Mondai Kenkyūjo, 1972.

————. Economic Cooperation Bureau. *Baishō nado jisshi jōkyō, 1971-nen 7–9 gatsu* [The state of the implementation of reparations, etc., July–September 1971]. Economic Cooperation II [71] 138. October 1, 1971. (Mimeographed.)

————. Public Information Bureau. *Collection of Official Foreign Statements on Japanese Peace Treaty.* 3 vols. no date.

————. *Gaimusho Press Releases 1963.*

————. Ministry of International Trade and Industry. *Sōgō enerugī tōkei* [Comprehensive statistics on energy]. Tokyo: Ministry of International Trade and Industry. 1968–1971.

————. *Tsūshō hakusho* [White paper on (Japan's) foreign trade]. Tokyo: Tsūshō Sangyō Chōsakai, 1959–1971.

————. Trade Promotion Bureau. *En shakkan, baishō nado shihon kyōryoku jisshi jōkyō, 1968* [The stage of implementation of capital cooperation such as yen credits, reparations, etc.]. April 1968. (Mimeographed.)

———. *Keizai kyōryoku no genjō to mondaiten, 1970* [Present conditions and problems of economic cooperation, 1970]. 1971.

———. Ministry of Justice. *Shutsunyūgoku kanri tōkei nenpō* [Annual statistical report on immigration]. Tokyo: Ministry of Justice. 1964–1971.

———. Ministry of Welfare. *Kōsei hakusho 1957* [White paper on welfare, 1957]. Tokyo: Ōkurashō Insatsukyoku, 1958.

———. National Diet. House of Representatives. Budget Committee. *Dai 31-kai Kokkai Shūgiin Yosan Iinkai gijiroku* [The proceedings of the Budget Committee of the House of Representatives of the 31st National Diet]. No. 10 (February 13, 1959) and No. 11 (February 14, 1959).

———. Overseas Technical Cooperation Agency. *Gijutsu kyōryoku nenpō* [Annual report of (Japan's overseas) technical cooperation]. 1964–1969.

Japan. Overseas Technical Cooperation Agency. *Kaigai keizai kyōryoku benran 1971* [A handbook on (Japan's) overseas economic cooperation]. Tokyo: Kokusai Kaihatsu Jānaru Sha, 1971.

———. Prime Minister's Office. Bureau of Statistics *Nihon tōkei nenkan* [Japan statistical yearbook]. Tokyo: Nihon Tōkei Kyōkai and Mainichi Shinbun Sha. 1949–1971.

Japan-Indonesia Association. "I-koku seifu kakushō betsu shonendo baishō haibunhyō" [The table of the reparations funds' allocations for the first year by the Indonesian ministries]. Special report no. 2, 1958. (Mimeographed.)

———. *Jigyō narabini kaikei hōkokusho* [A report on the (association's) activities and finances]. 1958–1972. (Mimeographed.)

Japan Petroleum Federation. *Naigai sekiyū shiryō* [Data on foreign and domestic oil]. Tokyo. 1965–1970.

Jiji Tsūshin Sha. *Jiji nenkan* [Jiji almanac]. Tokyo: Jiji Tsūshin Sha. 1952–1971.

Jinji Kōshinjo. *Jinji kōshinroku 19-han* [Who's who, 19th edition]. Tokyo: Jinji Kōshinjo, 1957.

———. *Jinji kōshinroku 22-han*. 1964.

———. *Nihon shokuinroku* [Japanese who's who]. 10th edition. Tokyo: Jinji Kōshinjo, 1964.

Kōan Keibi Kenkyūkai [Public Security Study Group]. *Uyoku zensho* [A survey of the right-wing (groups)]. Tokyo: Kindai Keisatsu Sha, 1957.

Nihon Minsei Kenkyūkai [Japanese Democratic Studies Group]. *Kokkai giin sōran 1965* [Who's who of the members of the National Diet, 1965]. Tokyo: Hyōron Sha, 1965.

Nikkan Rōdō Tsūshin Sha. *Uyoku undō yōran* [A handbook on the right-wing movement]. Tokyo: Nikkan Rōdō Tsūshin Sha, 1964.

Nishijima Shigetada. "Subarujo gaishō [sic] kikokugo seizaikai yōjin e no yōbōsho" [(My) requests to prominent political and business figures subsequent to Foreign Minister Subardjo's return (to Indonesia)]. No date. (Typed.)

Nishijima Shigetada, et al. "Tai Indoneshia baishō mondai kaiketsu sokushin no tame ni" [In favor of an early solution to the problem of Indonesia's reparations]. 1951. (Typed.)

Malaysia. Ministry of External Affairs. *Indonesian Aggression against Malaysia.* 2 vols. Kuala Lumpur: Government Printer, 1964.

————. Ministry of Internal Security. *Indonesian Intentions towards Malaysia.* Kuala Lumpur: Government Printer, 1964.

Miyoshi Shunkichirō. "Indoneshia ni taisuru baishō mondai" [Reparations problems in Indonesia]. Tokyo: Japan-Indonesia Association, no date. (Mimeographed.)

Roeder, O. G. *Who's Who in Indonesia.* Jakarta: Gunung Agung, 1971.

Taniguchi Gorō. *Nishi Irian* [West Irian]. Asahi Shinbun Research Office report for internal use no. 99. Tokyo. 1962. (Mimeographed.)

United States. Department of State. Office of Public Affairs. *Conference for the Conclusion and Signature of the Treaty of Peace with Japan, San Francisco, California, September 4–8, 1951; Record of Proceedings.* Department of State Publication no. 4392, 1951.

Zenkoku Kakushu Dantai Rengōkai [National Association of Various Organizations]. *Zenkoku kakushu dantai meikan 1972* [A national directory of various organizations, 1972]. Tokyo: Zenkō Sha, 1971.

SELECTED NEWSPAPERS AND PERIODICALS

Akahata. Daily. Tokyo. 1962–1966.

Antara. Daily English edition. Jakarta. 1957, 1958, 1960, 1965, and 1966.

Asahi Shinbun. Daily. Tokyo. 1952–1970.

Berita Yudha. Daily. Jakarta. 1970.

Bungei Shunjū. Monthly. Tokyo. 1960–1972.

Ekonomisuto. Weekly. Tokyo. 1959.

Chūō Kōron. Monthly. Tokyo. 1958–1970.

Gekkan Indoneshia. Monthly. Tokyo. 1970–1971.

Gendai no Me. Monthly. Tokyo. 1965–1967.

Harian Kami. Daily. Jakarta. 1966–1967.

Indonesia Raya. Daily. Jakarta. 1969–1970.

Indonesian Observer. Daily. Jakarta. October–December 1957.

International House of Japan Bulletin. Biannual. Tokyo. 1969–1971.

Kōan Jōhō. Monthly. Tokyo. 1965–1967.

Kokusai Jihyō. Monthly. Tokyo. 1966–1970.

Kokusai Mondai. Monthly. Tokyo. 1965–1970.

Mainichi Shinbun. Daily. Tokyo. May 1952, September 1957. July 1959, and November 1969.

Merdeka. Daily. Jakarta. 1967.

Nihon Keizai Shinbun. Daily. Tokyo. December 1965–March 1966, and June 1970.

Sankei Shinbun. Daily. Tokyo. 1958–1959.

Shūkan Bunshun. Weekly. Tokyo. 1964–1970.

Shūkan Gendai. Weekly. Tokyo. 1964–1970.

Shūkan Posuto. Weekly. Tokyo. 1964–1970.

Shūkan Shinchō. Weekly. Tokyo. 1964–1970.

Tokyo Shinbun. Daily. Tokyo. June 1959–January 1960.

Yangu Redi. Weekly. Tokyo. 1964–1970.

Yomiuri Shinbun. Daily. Tokyo. February–September 1958, and April–August 1966.

Zen'ei. Monthly. Tokyo. 1960–1966.

Index

Reparations Division, Foreign
Ministry (Japan), 45, 99–100, 110
Reparations fellowship, 86–87,
94–95, 96n, 156, 182n, 218n
Reparations fund, 80–81, 88, 90, 122,
215
  by categories, 84–86
  payment formula of, 98
  political distribution of, 100
  used to support Sukarno, 57, 198
Reparations Implementation
Committee (Indonesia), 99–100
Reparations Implementation
Coordinating Committee (Japan),
99, 111
Reparations, Japanese positions on,
40–41, 44–45, 47
Reparations Mission, Indonesian
(MISPRI) (Tokyo), 86, 99–100,
102, 106, 110, 155–156
Reparations negotiations, 118, 211,
216
  formal negotiators, 35–57
  informal negotiators, 61–76
  San Francisco conference, 36–38
  Djuanda Mission (1951), 38–39
  Sudarsono Mission (1952), 40
  A-A conference (1955) used for,
    42
  delayed by general elections, 42
  hampered by ideological
    differences, 55
  Suez Conference (1956) used for,
    43
  Kobayashi proposal, 47–48
  Kishi and Sukarno meet for
    (1957), 50
  Kishi-Djuanda communique
    (1957), 51
  Kobayashi-Djuanda
    Memorandum (1957), 52
  settled at $223 million, 53
  assessed, 54–56
Reparations payment, 80–83
  bidding system, 99
  overpricing, 102
Reparations programs, *or* projects
  kinds of, 86, 92–94, 96n
  priorities of, 86, 93
  effects on Indonesian economy,
    87–91
  regional distributions of, 101
  and Japanese firms, 104–105
  mismanaged, 95, 215
  assessed, 87–91
  Japan held responsible for, 215
Reparations scandal. *See* Kinoshita,
Shigeru; Kinoshita Trading
Company
Reparations-secured loans (projects),
81, 87, 104, 200, 208n
  by categories, 84–85
  by regions, 101
Revolutionary Council, 167–169
Revolutionary Government of the
Republic of Indonesia (PRRI), 53,
149n, 195. *See also* Sumatra
Rebellion
Revolution Fund (Dana Revolusi)
(1964), 153, 181n
Riam Kanan (*or* Kanan River)
project, 92, 96n, 104
Right-wing nationalists, Japanese, 196
Rōmusha (involuntary workers), 62
Royal Dutch Petroleum, 118
Rubber, 18
Rukmito Hendraningrat, 142, 172,
204, 209n
Rusk, Dean, 37

Sabur (Palace Guard commander),
174, 176, 180
Saitō jōhō (Saitō's information), 138
Saitō, Shizuo, 64, 73, 139–140, 155,
198–199, 202, 204, 214
  and Kawashima Lobby, 137, 155
  and Dewi, 137, 198
  and Sukarno, 64, 198
Saleh, Chairul, 64, 73, 152–153, 155,
163, 175, 177–178, 201
  and Nishijima, 120, 138
  and reparations fund, 101, 155
Saleh, Ismail, 173–174
"Saleh men" in Tokyo, 155
Salim, Emil, 173
Sambas Atmadinata, 112
San Francisco Peace Conference
(1951), 9, 35–37, 45, 54
San Francisco Peace Treaty (1951),
1, 35, 38, 54